PHILOSOPHY
OF NURSING

PHILOSOPHY OF NURSING

A New Vision for Health Care

JANICE M. BRENCICK
and
GLENN A. WEBSTER

State University
of New York
Press

Published by
State University of New York Press, Albany

© 2000 State University of New York

Production by Susan Geraghty
Marketing by Anne Valentine

Printed in the United States of America

For information, address State University of New York
Press, State University Plaza, Albany, N.Y., 12246

Library of Congress Cataloging-in-Publication Data

Brencick, Janice M.
    Philosophy of nursing : a new vision for health care / by Janice
M. Brencick, Glenn A. Webster.
        p.   cm.
    Includes bibliographical references and index.
    ISBN 0-7914-4379-5 hc : alk. paper. — ISBN 0-7914-4380-9 pb :
alk. paper
        1. Nursing—Philosophy. I. Webster, Glenn A. II. Title.
RT84.5.B74 1999
610.73'01—dc21   99-11409
                                                                        CIP

10 9 8 7 6 5 4 3 2 1

To Tony Puopolo II
who has the training of a physician
and the heart of a nurse

CONTENTS

ACKNOWLEDGMENTS

Janice Brencick acknowledges the dedication and assistance of her original dissertation committee whose encouragement and support helped to make this book possible: Francelyn Reeder, Jean Watson, Sally Phillips, Denise Webster, and Mark Tanzer.

CHAPTER 1

Introduction

DESCRIPTION OF THE PROBLEM

Nursing makes use of knowledge from science and technology for healing the individual patient. Nursing is concerned with the relationship between universals, known through the sciences, and unique individuals, known by direct acquaintance. The problem for nursing is how to increase and apply its repertory of universals, while at the same time respecting the unique individuality of the patient and the unique individuality of each nursing occasion. Nursing gathers its generalizable knowledge from experience with unique individuals, from the sciences, and from other sources such as everyday nonscientific knowledge, yet nursing always returns to the individual for the application of its knowledge. Hence, nursing continually travels in a circle between universals and irreducibly unique individuals.

Extant nursing theories, largely derived from fields other than nursing practice, such as physics, anthropology, or cybernetics, are only partially successful in developing an adequate concept of nursing. There are at least two reasons for this.

First, because fields other than nursing practice are often tilted in the direction of universals. They are theoretical sciences interested in the generalizable. Consequently, they do not address the tension between the aspects of universality and singularity which are combined in every individual. This is because the sciences are not interested in singularity. Singularity, if it is addressed at all, is regarded as noise, spoiling the perfect replicability of experiments.

On the other hand, nursing practice is richer than the fields from which it draws some of its knowledge. Nursing practice embraces the totality of human experience from before birth through death in a most human and intimate manner. Because of the intimate relationship of nurse and patient, nurses are closely involved in the unique moments of human tragedy and human triumph. It is nurses at the patient's bedside who attend the patient at a time when the patient is most vulnerable, when the patient's needs are critical for survival. It is the nurse who attends the patient's needs in a manner that preserves the patient's dignity as an experiencing unique individual. The nurse remains at the patient's bedside when other members of the health care team have finished for the day. It is this personal care of the patient that is the heart of nursing. The intimacy of this experience is not adequately knowable by individuals in fields other than nursing practice itself. As a consequence more adequate concepts for understanding nursing can be derived from nursing practice than from fields outside nursing.

The second reason for the relative inadequacy of extant nursing theories to elucidate nursing practice is that extant nursing theories have been unable to successfully connect nursing practice with other areas of nursing—education, administration, and to some extent, theory itself. Without a fuller understanding of nursing practice, it is impossible to relate one nursing theory to another, or to understand which theories apply to which times and aspects in the practice of nursing. And without a more adequate understanding of nursing practice, the other components of nursing remain independent islands in themselves, driven primarily by such external factors as market demands, institutional profits, institutional prestige, fads, slogans, and so forth, rather than by nursing practice itself.

Since extant nursing theories less than fully elucidate nursing practice, a theory of theories, a metatheory of present theories, will only result in moving further away from an understanding of nursing practice. What is needed is a philosophy of nursing focused on nursing practice itself. Granted that all philosophy is in process and any particular stage in the development of a philosophy is less than fully adequate (Collingwood 1933). Similarly, but in a different sense, nursing is in process, and will hopefully be more adequate in the future than it has been in the past. It is hoped that a philosophy of nursing, such as the one attempted in this work, will help improve nursing itself. This will be done by making what has been invisible, visible, by illuminating the nature of nursing. The goal of this work as a philosophy of nursing is to illuminate the nature of nursing.

But what more specifically is a philosophy, and how does it differ from a theory, a metatheory, or a treatise?

Calling this a treatise would not be merely so helpful or accurate; for a treatise according to Merriam Webster is "a systematic exposition or argument in writing including a methodical discussion of the facts and principles involved and conclusions reached."[1] In a general sense, all works in philosophy are treatises. But philosophy differs from treatises in general in philosophy's lack of new facts and in philosophy's deepening of understanding of the key concepts involved in what is already known. It is more appropriate to call a lengthy written argument on such a topic as the place of nursing within the hospital system of the

United States in the 1990s, a treatise. But a lengthy exposition of concepts already "understood" (for example, *person*) is not usually called a treatise. A philosophical inquiry will examine at length exactly those concepts that a treatise brushes over as already understood. For example, the treatise just mentioned would be concerned with salaries, or with the number of nurses in each type of hospital system. This data might be used for an argument for a change in regulations. But such a treatise is unlikely to examine the concept of nursing, or the concept of system.

In his *Idea of History*, the early-twentieth-century Oxford professor of philosophy R. G. Collingwood defines philosophy as reflective thinking, or thought about thought in relation to its objects (Collingwood 1946, p. 1). In his earlier *Essay on Philosophical Method* he tells us that philosophy does not inform us about new things, it does not add to our knowledge quantitatively. Rather, philosophy enables us to know what is already known, but in a new and better way. Philosophy deepens understanding of what is already known (Collingwood 1933). It is in this sense that this is a philosophy of nursing and not a theory about nursing. For the goal of most theories is to add new knowledge. But the goal of the present book is not to know something new about nursing, but to know what is already known about nursing in a new and better way—better in the sense that understanding of the nature of nursing is deepened. The goal of our philosophy of nursing is an illumination of nursing using the lens of universality and singularity. At the same time it is an illumination of the nature of individuals and universals using the lens of nursing. Hence it is a cocreative synthesis of philosophy and nursing that deepens and strengthens both perspectives.

With respect to Collingwood's definition of philosophy, nursing and perhaps even phenomenology might appreciate a slight modification, and one that is relevant to the philosophy that is done is this book: Rather than call philosophy "thought about thought in relation to its objects," we prefer a different emphasis in which philosophy is defined as "thought about experience in relation to its (experience's) objects." Philosophy is reflection on experience and the relationship between experience and its objects; philosophy is not simply "reflective thinking," as Collingwood worded his definition. Collingwood's original definition in his *Idea of History* might be said to be too "intellectualistic." The suggested modification helps in understanding such philosophies as that of Hegel and Husserl, as well as the philosophy that is developed in this book.

Philosophy expounds or develops basic concepts, concepts that apply to all of reality. The basic concepts underlying our philosophy of nursing are universality and singularity. Nursing is not unique as a domain to which these concepts are applicable, for they are applicable to all of reality, to any thing or event that is actual. But nursing is special in the degree to which it allows for the development of these concepts. A research scientist can ignore singularity as noise, but a practicing nurse cannot. A healer can ignore the universals of interest to science, but a practicing nurse cannot.

This philosophy of nursing includes a few specific theories about nursing, such as the theory above that nursing practice is an especially fertile ground for understanding the difference and interconnectedness between universality and singularity in that which is actual. The nurse patient relationship is better for this purpose than the use to which many teachers of philosophy put cups in their classroom (we use the coffee cup to illustrate the difference between *this* unique individual cup here and now and the characteristic of cupness that is shared by all cups). But the exigencies of nursing practice are better for calling attention to the importance of the distinction that most students simply fail to see when confronted with individual cups and talk about cupness. It is hard to see a cup as a unique individual. It is lifeless and misleadingly enduring. Whereas experiences in the lives of individuals, especially in health crisis situations, underscore the difference between repeatable universals and the unique individuals. For example, in Meleis' chapter, "Theory Development and Domain Concepts," it is very difficult not to see universality and singularity in almost every item on the list (Moccia 1986, 5–7).

"Theory" is at least as controversial a word as "philosophy" (Chinn and Jacobs 1991, pp. 57–77). But in general theories are about limited domains of reality, and are intended to increase our knowledge, practical or theoretical, about these domains. Also, empirical theories are grounded in particular sense experiences in ways that philosophies are not. Theories use basic concepts, but do not develop them. One of the tasks of a philosophy of nursing is to extend the development of the basic concepts used by nursing, such as the concept of a person.

Metatheory is theory about the nature of theory (Chinn and Jacobs 1991, p. 123). Grand theory covers broad areas of concern within a discipline (Chinn and Jacobs 1991, p. 123). The present work is neither a metatheory nor a grand theory because it is not a theory about theories, but because it is concerned with basic concepts that apply to all of actuality with special attention to their application to nursing. However, just as some specific theories are spun off from the present philosophy of nursing—for example, that persons are communities of experiencing entities—so is some material in this work of a metatheoretical nature. Walker and Avant (1988, p. 5) say that "proposing the criteria most suited for evaluating theory in nursing" is part of metatheory. We shall be doing some of this in the last chapter, but this is not the focus of this work.

Nor is our work best described as a hermeneutics of nursing, for nursing is not merely a text to be interpreted. Nor is our philosophy just a hermeneutical philosophy, because again hermeneutics presupposes existing texts to be interpreted, and focuses narrowly on questions of meaning. Even when hermeneutical philosophy is construed broadly, it is concerned with language in a manner different from this present work. Hermeneutics focuses on language and meaning. And when hermeneutics is used to uncover the meaning of experience it is done by interpreting the words spoken or written by an individual. Our concern is about basic aspects of reality and only incidentally are we concerned with the best language for discussing these aspects. Questions of meaning arise in this philosophy of nursing, but for the most part it is not words or text that is the occasion of the questioning, but the fundamental aspects of reality, and the relation of these fundamental aspects to nursing. The central problem of the philosophy of nursing is to produce a new text that will facilitate understanding nursing more adequately and in a different and better way. This is philosophy in the broad or general sense.

Philosophy of nursing is needed to provide key unifying concepts to unite nursing practice with its other components. Such a philosophy of nursing will provide an exposition and development of concepts above the level of nursing theories, of concepts that will be applicable to all of nursing.

While any nursing experience can reveal the complexity of the interrelatedness of universality and singularity, our philosophy of nursing begins with a narrative derived from and descriptive of an actual nursing experience.[2] The narrative reveals the tension in nursing practice between the uniqueness of individuals and their situations, and the generalizations of science that the nurse applies to the individual. Later, the narrative becomes a means for the analysis of the interrelatedness between universals and individuals within nursing practice. It is the exposition of the interrelatedness of universality and singularity that forms the general basis for our philosophy of nursing.

The problem of the tension between universality and singularity is not peculiar to nursing. Contemporary philosophy is grappling with a similar problem. In fact every discipline, including medicine is troubled by this distinction (Downie and Charlton 1992, pp. 91–102). But the concepts may not be labeled universality and singularity. Different language may be used to refer to the same insights or ideas. For example, Downie and Charlton distinguish what is *typical* of patients in general from what is *unique* to an individual patient (Downie and Charlton 1992, p. 90).

While nursing illustrates the problem more concretely, philosophy grapples with it on a more abstract level: the relationship between universality and singularity within each unique individual person or experience. Hence nursing practice can enrich philosophy by providing a fertile ground of concrete experiences in which the philosophical concepts and the tensions between universality and singularity can be identified and refined. At the same time the several thousand years philosophy has spent refining and elucidating the problem of universals and individuals is of help to nursing. Nursing can make use of the arguments and distinctions already developed by philosophy while at the same time making its own contribution to these arguments and distinctions.

Universals and individuals have been called several different things during the history of philosophy. Plato referred to them as Forms or Ideas and sensible particulars (Plato, *Republic* bk VI). Aristotle called them form (*morphe*) and substance (*ousia*), with the ground of the uniqueness of individuals, singularity, being called matter (*hyle*).[3] The medieval philosophers, such as Aquinas, called them universals and particulars. Contemporary philosophy has also been wrestling with the problem.[4] Unique singularity and the difficulty of expressing singularity with words is a concern of contemporary philosophy, since words themselves are general formula.[5]

Nursing is in a privileged position to understand the contrast between universals and individuals. Nursing is too closely involved with individual persons and events to overlook the unique. Yet nursing must also apply scientific principles, ethical standards, protocols, and generalizable procedures to the treatment of the individual. Fields of study that value science first and the individual second have a harder time recognizing, let alone articulating, the tension and interrelatedness between the two poles of universal form and unique individuality grounded in singularity. Science is interested in the repeatable and hence must distance itself from the individual. Empathy and personal involvement on the part of the researcher are impediments to pure research, yet are essential to good nursing practice. Consequently, science alone cannot elucidate the full range of nursing practice.

The fertile ground of nursing practice will be used to deepen understanding of the tension and interrelatedness between unique individuals and universals. And since there are no experiences in nursing that do not have the elements of universality and singularity, an understanding of these concepts will allow for the development of a philosophy of nursing. We anticipate that this philosophy of nursing will help remove the present gap between nursing theory and nursing practice. Such a philosophy of nursing will provide a clearer understanding for making the many connections that are needed between nursing practice and the other components of nursing.

ASSUMPTIONS ABOUT NURSING

- Nursing practice is the individual nurse[6] providing care to the individual patient.[7,8]
- Nursing practice drives sound nursing theory.
- Nursing practice defines nursing administration.
- Nursing practice constitutes nursing education.
- From the above assumptions it follows that nursing education, nursing administration, nursing research, and nursing theory are nursing in a secondary sense.
- There is tension between nursing practice and nursing in its secondary senses.
- All forms of nursing in the secondary sense—administration, research, theory, and education—are nursing only because they support nursing in the primary sense, nursing practice.
- The existence of nursing practice is the necessary condition for the existence of nursing education, administration, theory, and research—without nursing practice, none of the latter would exist. Hence nursing practice is said to be nursing in the primary sense, and nursing's other components are said to be nursing in secondary senses.
- The health of nursing practice determines the health of the other components of nursing.
- The tensions that exist between nursing practice and the other components of nursing can be explained in part by the lack of a unifying philosophy of nursing.
- The insights gained from examining the relationship between universals and individuals, or universality and singularity, will provide the basis for a philosophy of nursing, one that explains nursing practice and the relationship between nursing practice and the other components of nursing.
- An adequate philosophy of nursing will be able to unify the various perspectives of nursing theories, allowing the practicing nurse to make use of the valuable aspects of each theory.
- Universality and singularity are impossible to separate as entities from one another. They are aspects of actuality, rather than separately actual in themselves. But for the purposes of a philosophy of nursing, the concepts of universality and singularity will initially be examined separately.

- A nursing theory, if it is to be a complete nursing theory must address both elements, universality and singularity, and explain the relationship between the two.   .

- Nursing is a relational practicing profession that uses scientific principles together with the personal experiences of the practicing nurse and the experiences of the patient in the care of the sick and the promotion of health in the well.

- Nursing practice cannot be separated from its own history. The history of nursing is the history of the individual nurse and the individual patient involved in the nursing experience.

- Philosophy of nursing provides a new vision for health care.

PRELIMINARY EXPOSITION OF UNIVERSALITY AND SINGULARITY

No one set of terms is adequate for expressing the contrast and tension between two fundamental aspects of reality—universality and singularity. Still more difficult is the task of expounding the nature of these contrasted aspects of reality. On the one side, individuals are ever flowing or changing, and are irreducibly unique. The individual is uncopiable. Each person, and each experience or event, is unique. Singularity is that aspect of reality that guarantees the irreducible uniqueness of the individual.[9]

On the other side reality consists of universals. And though individuals are unique, they share universals with other individuals. Universals are possibilities for definiteness that can be actualized or instantiated without any effect on them as possibilities. Universals do not change as a result of their actualization in individuals. That a particular shade of blue characterizes part of the sky on one day in no way effects it as a possibility for the color of the sky on other days. This pole of reality is general or universal, and is permanent or eternal. It is not effected by the flow of time.

Nursing experience involves universals. Medical and biological sciences and technology inform nursing by providing research data and theories that form the basis of many nursing interventions and the instruments of their application. Experience involves individuals—nurse, patient, and the caring experience. Yet nursing experience is more complex than any simple contrast between universals and individuals. Consider a nurse interacting with a family. The nurse is uniquely individual. The family is uniquely individual. In addition, each person in the family is uniquely individual, as is each experience of each person, both the nurse and the members of the family. Further, these individuals are ever flowing, ever changing. And if this were not complicated enough, nursing experience includes local and global communities and an ever changing environment. Yet in the face of all of this unique individuality there are shared universals or generalities. For example, all members of the family, as well as the nurse, are persons. And all of these persons at the time of the nursing experience are alive and conscious. But personhood, life, and consciousness are universals.

Among other things, what will be explored in this book are the grounds of singularity. The exposition of singularity will include an understanding of singularity itself that includes the presence in the present of a unique past, and an anticipation of what will be a unique future. An exposition of singularity through the use of language, however, is problematic. Since language consists of the general, that is, of that which can be spoken or written more than once and still be of the same, language biases us toward universals. Language tempts us to regard fluency and uniqueness as illusions and permanence and the general as reality. Even the word "individual" fails to adequately express unique individuality.[10] Hence a major task of this philosophy of nursing is to understand the nature of the singularity that grounds the irreducible uniqueness of the individual.

To better understand the distinction and interrelatedness between universality and singularity, we have chosen to use a thought experiment in chapters 3 and 4. In this thought experiment a nurse is involved in imaginary discussions with selected philosophers in an imaginary setting, St. Francelyn's Hospital. The intent in the use of this thought experiment in chapters 3 and 4 is to simplify and render enjoyable material that in itself is very complicated and nearly inaccessible, but at the same time is essential to the philosophy of nursing. In presenting the philosophers as ordinary human beings interested in helping a nurse with her confusions about universality and singularity as they apply to nursing, we are able to use the philosophers as a foil for elucidating universality and singularity, while at the same time avoiding scholastic wrangling over various interpretations of the works of these philosophers. For this book is not about the philosophers per se, but about universality and singularity in nursing practice.[11]

The philosophers used are no longer living and none to our knowledge addressed the nature of nursing. Some have not even addressed the problem of universals and individuals as it is addressed in this philosophy of nursing. But all of them have grappled with related problems, so that we are able to extrapolate from what they actually said to what they might say about universality and singularity in our own language and our own time. We caution the reader that though every attempt has been made to be historically accurate, the present work is not a history of philosophy, but a use of philosophy for elucidating nursing. Hence, we leave out much thought to be important by the historians of philosophy and we focus on insights from the philosophers often ignored by traditional history of philosophy. Further, the imaginary conversations allow us to bring the great philosophers from all ages into the beginning of the twenty-first century, and to ask them questions that they were not able to understand or answer in their original historical setting, but might be expected to understand and answer at the beginning of the twenty-first century.

After the imaginary discussions with the philosophers, the theory of caring of Jean Watson is addressed in chapter 5. Watson's theory was chosen because it is a theory that illustrates the tension and interrelatedness between unique individuals and universals in nursing. In addition we find her major concept of the caring occasion to be a basic concept in nursing. As such, it is a fertile ground for the elucidation and development of our philosophy of nursing. It is this concept, caring, which expresses the human intimacy of the nurse/patient relationship. Yet in the same manner, Watson's caring versus curing premise is fertile ground for further analysis. Last but not least, Watson was chosen because her work was especially inspiring to the nurse co-author. It was her personal preference.

Chapter 6 is the capstone chapter in the development of our philosophy of nursing. That chapter builds upon the distinctions and insights that are introduced and developed in the earlier chapters—2 through 5. We do not encourage that it be read without the preceding chapters— for it was not intended to be understandable without the foundations provided by the earlier chapters. We have taken care to introduce only the topics that are needed for construction of the philosophy of nursing in chapter 6. Chapter 6 is not intended to stand alone; it internalizes the preceding chapters.

We will explore the implications of universality and singularity within the context of nursing practice. Implications will be drawn from the analyses in this book as they relate to nursing education, nursing administration, and nursing research.

We pay particular attention to the philosophies of Plato, Aristotle, Whitehead, and Kierkegaard because their writings are the basis for the distinction between universals and unique individuals. But we also visit the philosophies of Hildegaard of Bingen, Hume, Kant, Hegel, Dewey and Heidegger, as they relate to this problem.

CHAPTER 2

Narrative

THE NARRATIVE

Golden ribbons of the late afternoon's light fell softly and brilliantly on the large clock hanging on the wall of the hospital room. For a brief time each autumn this spheric understudy steals center stage from all the significant activities below it. And this was its special day. This was the day that nature's own spotlight illuminated its face in radiant splendor. And so the exalted timepiece silently but distinctly announced "Four O'clock" to all who would care to look at it. But to the patient lying on the bed beneath it, the clock's conscientious message would remain unobserved and unnoticed.

The second hand marched in a one-step tempo around its orbit passing proudly in review each of its numbers as it went. Ten seconds. Twenty. Thirty. And still the patient gave it none of his attention. If the clock were conscious, perhaps it would be thinking, "But why does he pay me no mind? Look how brilliantly I display the time today! Also am I not the most accurate clock in the hospital? Have I not always served you well?"

But what the clock could not have known was that its master no longer had any use for such a splendid timekeeper as he. In fact its young master no longer had use for time at all. It would no longer matter to him if his clock kept time properly or if it lost a second or two each year. And neither would he notice how quietly the sunlight filled his room on this particular day, nor how splendidly it would transform the stark hospital white into soft autumnal hues of magenta and gold. He would not feel the sun's warmth. Nor would he witness the last glow of this amazing sunset. The patient would feel nothing. He would attend to nothing. He could see or hear or touch nothing. He had been pronounced dead two hours earlier.

Yet even as all these events were unfolding, the young man still lay there in his bed, the same in which he had lain since his admission two weeks earlier. His bed! With its steel rails up, this bed had been his cradle. It had protected him from falls and had buffeted him from jostles. Its air mattress had been a worthy sentinel. It was always at the ready to protect him against nasty pressure points on his increasingly bony and thin-skinned areas. These nasty pressure points could lead to even nastier bedsores. The swelling and then deflating in alternate waves beneath him repeated rhythmically the same pattern over and over again—inflate, hold steady, deflate. In his deep semiconscious states he had taken small notice of it and yet had accustomed himself to the gentle tidal pattern. He had accustomed himself as well to its strange almost breathing-like sounds as it moved its air about, first this way, then that.

And all those other machines! He had also accustomed himself to the sounds of those other machines enveloping his bed. The mechanical trees with limbs of steel, vines of plastic, and leaves of labels so tightly interlocking each other that it made it seem as though his small area of the planet was confined to a dense artificial forest, a forest emitting a cacophony of strange sounds and hisses. Yet on occasion, but only rarely, he could hear the soft faint resonance of a human voice. At those times he would strain to hear its familiar sound becoming more clear and more clear. He would hear it reaching its crescendo and then fade away again slowly, slowly until it was once more devoured within the endlessness of the din.

This bed was his world, and though he had no choice in the matter, it was his home for two weeks. It was his tiny private island in the midst of a vast uncharted ocean of hospital clamor and odors sweet and pungent. He had been its tenant since his admission to the Intensive Care unit. And what had once served him as his cradle and his protector was now to serve him as his funeral bier.

Pictures and mementos decorated the walls and adorned his bedside tables. Bright colorful get-well cards nestled among them. There were so many greetings that they had long ago spilled across the boundaries of the small bulletin board meant for their display. The photos and cards comprised a strange collage of the patient's past life. It seemed to the nurse that the scene spread out before her just now was starkly surreal. Immediately in her view was her patient lying still and motionless without feeling or expression. Around him were the photos of smiling faces and of happier times. Spirited times. Exuberantly vital times! And yet here he is, in the here and now, lying quietly beneath the pictorial witnesses of how he once had been.

The scene was a dialectic of life within death and death within life, of a past finally overtaking the present. It was one great drama played out on the stage of this tiny room. Past and present were embracing in an odd and disharmonious dance, with the life of the silent form on the bed as their choreographer. How could it be that the charming football hero teasing his friends and smiling with his family in those pictures was indeed the same individual the nurse was seeing now lying here before her? How could it be that the lifeless form resting beneath the clock and under the sheet had once been that energetic stranger in those photos? It seemed scarcely possible.

His family kept their bedside vigil as they had done since his accident. The nurse was his primary care provider since his admission. She now stood waiting beside his grieving family. Oddly, nurse and family had been strangers just two short weeks before. But for an odd and tragic twist of events, they might have remained unknown to one another. Now they were here in this room together, beside the young man's bed, grieving. Countrymen and family in a community of sorrow.

The nurse puzzled over the events she had experienced these past two weeks and about the feelings she was having now. In just two weeks she had become so attached to this young man and his family. How could she have allowed her feelings to become so intense? Why was she grieving for someone she hardly knew?

She had never known this young man in any of the ways the pictures on the walls suggested that he had been. To her, he was now as he had always been, unconscious and expressionless. He never showed any recognition of her. He never smiled at her, nor indicated to her that he was in pain. He had not responded to her gentle touch in any conceivable way. He had never once turned to hear the sound of her voice as she gave him care each day. How could her feelings be so strong for him just now? How could she be grieving so intensely? His family's grief was understandable. They were losing someone they had known and loved all his life. And if the photos were any indication, he loved them too. But how could she explain her own grief?

The sounds of the respirator interrupted her thoughts. Click-ha, click-ha, click-ha. The patient was still breathing. Then, bleep, bleep, bleep. The cardiac monitor proclaimed that his heart was still beating.

The bewildered family heard the sounds too. Sounds of life. They gazed at their son scrutinizing him as he lay there, then turned to look up at the nurse. The family spoke no words. Their expressions alone were enough to give away their secret doubts. In silent language they asked what the nurse could not answer.

Their son was still breathing. His heart was still beating. How could he lie there so peacefully, as though in some dreamless sleep, and yet still be called dead? Dead people don't breathe, do they? Their hearts don't keep on beating. They're supposed to look cold, stiff, pale.

Now look at our son. One look at him and anyone can see that he does not fit this description of death. Even now as he lies there in his peaceful slumber, he is so much like he always was on Saturdays after the end of football season. On those Saturdays when he could sleep in, he couldn't be roused til noon. Do you see him now? This is how he always looked. He hibernated until only an empty stomach could awaken him! Perhaps that is what he is doing now!

He lies here before you. Sleeping. Peaceful. Had the pronouncement of his death been premature? Would he awaken any moment, just like on any of those Saturdays before his accident, and open his eyes? Would he then clutch his stomach in a feigned "Big Mac attack" and demand to be taken home immediately pausing only for an emergency visit beneath the Golden Arches?

But no. We have been told that he will never awaken from this last sleep. We accept that. But what about those sounds? His breathing? Those machines? What is this mystery called death that it can deceive the living so skillfully with the sounds of life? How cruelly it tortures the soul of the living with sweet rememberances of a nevermore. How brutally it tortures the mind with the reality of a will-never-be!

They waited together in that small confined room, nurse and family, for the arrival of the "organ harvesters." The harvesters had telephoned the nurse just an hour before apologizing for the delay in picking up "the corpse." They had instructed the nurse to "keep those organs nourished," and to "keep the fluids running in." Further they wanted to "make sure the IV bags don't run dry, and (to) keep the ventilator on." They would be delayed until around 6. The nurse was to give their apologies to the family as well as their condolences. But the nurse required no instructions from the harvesters. She had experienced occasions of this kind before. The instructions from the harvesters were only pro forma, more for the benefit of the harvesters than to inform the nurse.

But what was taking them so long? It seemed to her as though time had suspended itself. How painful it was to sit with this family just now. How easy it would be to find some busy work to suppress the weeping and churning in the pit of her own stomach. Engaging in tasks and giving instructions were ways of shielding feelings. Nurses are always busy. The family would think nothing of it if she were to do other things just now. Legitimate tasks. Tasks that needed doing.

Again no. She would stay with this family until they themselves dismissed her. They had entrusted her completely with the care of their son, the dearest person to them in all of life. They had observed how professionally competent she was. They were impressed by her skillful technological know-how. Her knowledge and her skill comforted them in these past two weeks. With the uncertainty of their son's condition they needed someone to take care of him properly and competently.

And they also needed something for themselves. They needed her to explain in simple terms what all that medical jargon meant. They needed her to help them make sense of the reasoning behind the treatments.

They trusted her and needed her. In that chaotic time, care meant competence. They were confident that she would guide them through the maze of treatment protocols, hospital regulations, and required forms. They were educated and competent in their own world, yet kindergartners in this environment. They had been convinced that the nurse would do everything possible to help their son get better. The rest they would have to leave up to God.

The nurse comforted herself in her grief with the thought that someone else would benefit from this family's loss. Others would have a chance to live because the family had donated their son's organs for transplant. Perhaps her patient would remain alive in some way after all. She reflected on this idea for several moments. How ironic. The young man who lay before her seems alive and yet he is dead. But his heart, his lungs, his liver, his kidneys, and his eyes remain alive. She found herself wondering how many different body parts would have to remain alive before we can say that the person himself is still alive? And could it be said that the person was still alive if his body parts are scattered over the world living in many different people? And further, would this young man's eyes remember the visual interests of the former person of which they were part? For instance, would they automatically turn to watch football even though the new person they have joined finds more pleasure in reading?

She wondered if the people whose lives were about to be renewed through the donation of this young man's organs were as worthy as the life of the person whose life had been taken. But she quickly brushed this thought from her mind. That kind of thinking was playing God. How could the value of one life be measured against the value of another? A long lengthy sigh of relief issued from her. She was glad she was not on the hospital's ethics committee. The members of this committee would have to make those kinds of decisions. Could the decision makers make their decisions if they had taken care of each of those persons so intimately as she had cared for this young man and his family?

Perhaps it is easier, and maybe even necessary, if the decision makers are detached from the persons they must make decisions about. The task is more difficult the closer one is to them. She became a nurse because she wanted to be close to her patients. And nursing was like no other field in the intensity and breadth of its relationships in the care of one human being for another. How could she determine now that one life is more valuable than another?

All of her patients are valuable to her. Being with them, giving them care, gives her a sense of purpose in her own life. She knows she makes a difference to many people. And she herself grows as a person through her intimate relationships with her patients and their families. She makes better choices about her own life as a result of her intimate involvement with the lives of other persons. Nursing others helps her rethink and adjust her own values. The nursing relationship allows both her patient and herself to learn from each other.

Her thoughts quickly returned to the young man lying before her and to his grieving family. They were the focus of her immediate concern now. She consoled herself with the thought that she had done all that she could for him. And that his family was as aware of this truth as much as she was. And though the waiting just now for the harvesters was almost unbearable, she would remain with this family keeping watch with them in their grief. The loud hollow grunting and clicking of the machines that only a little more than two hours ago reassured her that her patient was breathing and still alive, now seemed to mock that earlier confidence and of all that was once hopeful and alive.

The nurse knew that the organs needed to be preserved by keeping the patient on the machines. But that little piece of scientific knowledge was hardly comforting to her just now. She could not detach herself from her feelings as she sat with this family in pain. She could not bring herself to explain to them with any kind of cold scientific detachment that their son was indeed dead. And that what they interpret as sounds of life are simply machines keeping his organs fresh for use by someone else.

Yet oddly and perhaps ironically, the detachment of science can also be comforting. She wondered if her personal feelings at this moment would be overwhelming without some degree of detachment from them. It was her job to make sure the machines were running smoothly and that all the tubes were patent. She had no feeling for the machinery while she manipulated and adjusted their gauges and dials. The impersonal manner by which she acted upon the machines and their equally impersonal reactions to her, were a kind of safety valve protecting her from her own feelings, which just now weighed heavily on her. She reflected on this situation a moment longer and extended her imagination to a "what if."

What if she were to break down now, how could she care for this family? And without her dauntless vigilance, the machines would soon stop working. The organs would die. The transplants would not take place. Those awaiting their own chances for survival would have to wait longer. Perhaps they might even die before their next opportunity would present itself.

No. She could not let herself break down now. Perhaps she would allow herself to break down later. On the way home maybe. Maybe she could take the longer route home so she could leave this day and its sorrows behind her as she had done repeatedly before. She always tried not bring feelings from work home with her. Sometimes she even succeeded. She took a deep breath. There'll be time for her to think more about that later. But just now, she had to complete the care of her patient. She would stay as long as necessary, until the tasks were complete. It would be her personal requiem to him and to his family. It would be her final closure with them.

The harvesters were apologetic when they finally arrived. They did not like to keep the family waiting. What's more they knew that intensive care beds were at a premium. They had not wanted to keep the bed occupied longer than necessary. They were sensitive to the inconvenience they had caused the nursing staff. They wished to make restitution for their delay. Six o'clock. Supper time! They called the local pizza parlor and ordered large pepperoni pizzas to be delivered ASAP. In a few minutes, the harvesters, the patient, and his family were all gone.

The nurse sat at the desk in the nurses' station. The pizzas were cold and untouched. She completed her paperwork. She returned to the room where the young man had lain. The once commanding clock was now in darkness. Though it continued to measure time, time no longer seemed significant. She completed tending the now vacant room. And finally when all the details were taken care of and everything was in its place, the nurse took herself to the ladies' room behind the nurses' station, locked the door, sat herself down on the toilet seat, and wept.

ANALYSIS OF THE NARRATIVE

What follows is only a preliminary analysis. Analysis of the narrative will take place thoughout this book from various perspectives, especially our own philosophy of nursing. This preliminary analysis raises questions about universality and singularity that are addressed at much greater length in the discussions with the philosophers. The narrative describes a paradigmatic nursing event that provides the focus for the imaginary discussions with the philosophers.

There are many individuals in the narrative—the patient who died, the nurse, each member of the patient's family, the organ harvesters. In the background are the physician or physicians who made the determination of death. These are individuals because they are unique and non-repeatable. Yet on the other hand the terms "patient," "nurse," "organ harvester," designate universals, because the terms refer to something that is repeatable or shareable. More than one person can be a nurse or a patient.

And then easily overlooked are the events, each of them uniquely individual as well, such as the death of the patient, the grieving of the relatives, the phone call of the organ harvesters, the final closure with the patient and his family on the part of the nurse, and the pizza delivery. But the most striking event, implicit in the temporal background of the narrative, is the death of the patient.

Death is another and more mysterious universal. Strictly speaking a "person" cannot be dead, for death marks the cessation of the existence of a "person," at least in this world and in this time. If a person is dead, he simply is not, regardless of hope of resumption of life in some other world or future time. But in the narrative, the organs that were parts of what was once a person continue to live. Death of the person is not death of his parts. And yet death of one part in particular, the brain, is part of what determines death of the person as we understand it. Here the tension between science and nonscientific knowledge[1] might be commented on: the family is troubled by the fact that their son is still breathing though he has been pronounced dead under the protocols derived from science.

Birth and death are unique individual events marking the beginning and the ending of the lives of unique individuals. And yet, in another sense, they are shareable or repeatable. The terms "birth" and "death" are used to refer to universals, that is, the coming to be or ceasing to be of individual persons. Yet there is fuzziness in both notions. We are not certain that an individual begins to be at birth, nor are we certain that they cease to be because they have experienced death as determined by science (the flat EEG waves). This tension between the scientific determination of death and the actual death of the young man is part of what the family and nurse were puzzled about in the narrative.

There is an element of singularity that makes each of these individuals unique, both individual persons and the individual events. Already in the narrative the history of each person or their unique past is part of the ground of the singularity making the individuals unique. Although not mentioned in the narrative, the nurse will have compiled an individual history of her patient in order to know the idiosyncrasies of that unique individual. This is helpful in adjusting general protocols to the needs of the individual patient. But if the questions the nurse asks in the taking of the patient's history are molded by prescriptive protocols, such as in a standard questionnaire form, she may dismiss what is truly unique in the life of the individual patient in favor of expected kinds of "uniqueness." Such expected kinds of "uniqueness," which are really disguised universals, might include allergies to medications or favorable responses to past treatments. But the truly unique is not what is shareable or expected, nor is it what can be successfully anticipated in a standard set of questions.

Another example of the tension between universals and individuals illuminated by the narrative is the instance of the clock on wall. Though the hands on the clock pass by the same numbers again and again, each time the hands pass a particular number it is a later and different time than the time before. Time is bound up with singularity in some special way. It is the unique time when an event occurs that guarantees the non-repeatability of the event. Later events may be like it, can even share many universals with it, but the individual event cannot be repeated because its time (and place) cannot be repeated. That the patient in the narrative had been living in a coma several days earlier, but was now clinically dead, made this later time a very different time than the earlier time.

In addition to the formal uniqueness provided by time (and space) there is an added significance that makes such events as birth and death especially unique. This additional ground of singularity is beyond the formal one of the nonduplicatability of spatial-temporal location. The content of what actually happens at a unique time and place adds to the significance of the event. Hence, we celebrate or mourn the anniversaries of births and deaths in our conventional cycle of time, that is during an interval of a year, noting the actual time on the day of the original event. But the events surrounding the birth or death or other significant events are more clearly remembered than events of our lives that are not significant and not associated with such significant events.

Hence, a third ground of singularity is the context of the individual event. To the family in the narrative, and to a lesser extent to the nurse, the death of the young man colored the meaning of all of the surrounding events in a special way. The family will long remember the details of what they were doing in that crucial hour. But since the nurse's experience with the patient was brief, albeit intense, she will most likely later remember only that the event occurred. As time passes, the significance of this one event will merge with the significance of similar events in her nursing career. Consequently, unlike the patient's family, she will be less likely to remember the details of what she was doing at this individual time.

The patient in the narrative is distinguishable from other patients by being the football hero who suffered an accident two weeks before the dramatic setting of this story. The presence of his past in the present is symbolized by the memorabilia and pictures in the patient's room. This presence of the past in the present is one important ground of singularity. Each individual has a unique past. The uniqueness of the past is important in constituting the uniqueness of the present individual. But the element of *significance* of the past event for the present event plays a more important role as a ground for the singularity of the present event than the mere presence of just any past event in the present event.

Hence singularity is grounded partially in fact, but seems to be much more extensively grounded in value—the value that each individual places on their unique past and the future.

We cannot know which particular individuals the patient's organs will be implanted in, if they are implanted at all. But again the ground of the uniqueness of these individuals must be sought. The unique history of each individual, with special emphasis on those events that are deemed important by each individual, is a fertile starting place for discovering the secret of singularity.

Space and time will play a role in distinguishing the history of one person from all other persons. The clock on the wall in the patient's room vaguely but definitely symbolizes one of the most important grounds of singularity, space-time. Not only is it four o'clock but it is four o'clock in that room on a unique day never again to be repeated. Though the hands of the clock pass the same numbers at least twice a day in the case of the hour hands, each time that they do so is a later and uniquely different time. Our means of measuring time may mislead us into thinking that time is a universal because times are said to be to be "shared" or "repeated." For example, friends may meet at the same time for high tea at the Ritz Carlton in Boston every week. The tea time, 4 pm, comes every day. This is what makes time seem to be repeatable, a universal.[2] But each "time" is actually uniquely individual. Time as a whole is an individual that contains all of the individual "times."[3] This totality of time is devoid of content in itself.[4] It awaits "occurrences" to provide the content. And furthermore, it is persons and other entities that give the content of time its meaning.[5] It would be hard to imagine time without reference to individual events. And it would also be hard to make sense of the past without the reference events that are of special importance.

In the example above, "shared" and "repeated" are enclosed in shudder quotes, because there is only the illusion of being shared or repeated. When space is combined with time in order to provide a more complete and accurate picture it is discovered that the spatial temporal addresses are each unique and different from all others. Four o'clock in the afternoon on the 23rd of December is not the same as 4 pm on the 22nd of December, nor is 4 pm on the same day the same as one moves from one spatial location to another. The people sharing the afternoon tea at 4 pm are sitting in different chairs. Hence, though the time is shared, space is not. No two events can share the same space-time address.

The people sitting together in the patient's room in a state of grief illustrate the tension between universals and individuals. Though there is a universal, grieving, shared by all of these individuals, the grieving of each individual is made unique from the grieving of any one else. The way each person grieves reflects their individual history and uniqueness. Hence, each person combines universality and singularity.

Returning to the narrative, universality is encountered at every turn. To be a member of a family or a patient or nurse is to be determinate in a manner that is shareable or repeatable. There have been more than one patient and there are apt to be many patients in the years to come. Similarly there have been many nurses and many families. In fact, being an organ is another possibility for definiteness indicating the presence in unique individuals of shareable universals. The consciousness that the patient enjoyed before his accident is another universal, one shared with all other living persons, past and present, and with all persons who might come to be in the future.

The self-reflection of the nurse indicates singularity. On the one hand, shareable knowledge from science has contributed to her self-confidence and to her competence in technological mastery. Yet that which is shared cannot account for her compassion. Neither can it account for her feeling of affection toward the young man and his family. That she could recognize the person within the patient meant that there was something beyond scientific explanation in order to account for this.

Though science is helpful in determining how to care for a patient, it is not helpful in understanding how to care about a person. Reflection in itself is a significant event in a unique time and place, and it is about earlier significant events in the nurse's life and in the life of the patient. That the nurse's direct awareness of the person within the unconscious patient was part of her experience was an indication of a kind of non-scientific knowledge unaccountable for by the scientific notion of sense perception.

The noises of the life-support machines are noticed in terms of the embodiment of universals in unique individual events. The uniqueness of the events is scarcely noticed. Similarly the implicit determination of death on the part of some physician or physicians must have been made in terms of the absence of criteriological universals in the readouts from the instruments monitoring the patient. Hopefully the physician was wise and took a long hard look at the patient after noticing that the lines on the EEG indicating cerebral activity had been straight lines for several days. Death itself is a possibility for definiteness on the part of living individual persons. But it is a more fundamental kind of change in that the actualization of this universal ends the existence of the individual. In the present world, the person no longer exists—only a remnant, a corpse continues to exist. A grieving moment, though unique, is similar to other grieving moments through the universal of grieving. The list of universals present in the uniquely individual events recounted in the narrative is literally without limit, infinite. The narrative only sampled a small finite set of these universals.

The initial conclusion to be drawn from examination of the narrative is that the individual is a synthesis of universality and singularity. There is no individual which is not determinate in a large number, probably even an infinite number, of different ways. And yet there is no individual that is not unique because of elements of singularity that distinguish each individual from all other individuals. The conclusion from the initial analysis of the narrative is that singularity is grounded in time and space, in the presence of the actual past in the actual present, in the judgments of importance that present events pass on past events, both the events themselves and events in their context, and on creativity in the present events themselves. We anticipate that this list of the grounds of singularity is not exhaustive, that an additional ground or grounds may be discovered.

What made the patient a unique individual was in part the individual past activities depicted in the mementos and pictures on the walls and tables in his room. What made the pizza event unique was the time and place and circumstances under which it happened.

But there is more to the ground of singularity than just space and time. Decision making is noticeable in this narrative. The physician decided after two days of no activity in the higher cortex that the patient was clinically dead, though the life-support systems kept him breathing and his heart beating. This decision could have been postponed a day or two. But it was not. Consequently, decision making entered into the uniqueness of the events on the day recounted by the nurse. In turn she could have given in to her feelings, rather than tough it out in order to support the family. Her decision to tough it out was an additional ground of the uniqueness of the events of that day. And of course, there are the organ harvesters and their rather macabre decision to bring pizza. Bringing pizza on almost any other day would have been unremarkable. But in the context of the immediate past death of the patient, and the anticipation of the immediate future harvesting of his organs, the bringing of the pizza had a special negative significance.

The ongoing moment by moment decisions made by living persons deepen the uniqueness of themselves, their actions, and the events in which they participate. This is in spite of the fact that the description of these events seems to involve nothing but universals. For example, being determinate in being the bringing of a pizza is a universal—it is a possibility for definiteness that can be repeated or shared among individual events. Further, it is possible that other organ harvesters on other occasions of this kind will make the same macabre decision.[6] Perhaps it is the fact that there is a lack of sufficient reason for their decision at this particular time and place that adds to singularity. Here, the metaphysical water is deep. But it seems that in addition to the individuality of space and time, which is empty or formal, the determination of individual persons to create events that would not otherwise be, and that are neither causally nor logically determined, adds to the uniqueness of the particular chain of events that actually occurs. The decisions of persons provides content that enhances the uniqueness of the formal individuality of space and time. Here uniqueness builds on uniqueness.

The patient need not have suffered the accident. The accident need not have resulted in the brain injury. The injury did not have to be diagnosed and treated in the particular way that it was. The treatment might have worked, though it did not. Improbability piles on top of improbability seemingly without limit, and in such a manner that the actual at any particular moment was completely unthinkable, unimaginable, a few days or weeks earlier. Is this part of the ground of the singularity that guarantees the uniqueness of each individual, both person and event?

Science needs the general, universals that are not only repeatable, but that can be counted on to be repeated. An example in the narrative that is troubling to ethics committees is the nonscientific conviction or knowledge that a person needs a functioning or living cerebral cortex to awaken, to resume consciousness. Science knows nothing about consciousness. At best it allows us to "know" that flat electroencephlograph lines indicate lack of cerebral activity, and that past experience provides assurance that if there is no activity for more than two days, it is highly unlikely to ever resume. In addition consciousness is always correlated with cerebral activity, with identifiable patterns on the electroencephlograph. No one with a flat EEG has been conscious, unless the electrodes were improperly attached to his skull, or the machine was malfunctioning. The leap that is taken in current definitions of death is that it is supposed that one ceases to be a person when it becomes most improbable that consciousness will ever return. The patient in the narrative was judged to be dead because of the high improbability that he would ever awaken.

The concepts that have been discussed so far are only preliminary. There are many more to be discussed in the subsequent chapters. Each nursing event has within it the conceptual grounds for a philosophy of nursing. Our choice of the above event was arbitrary, any number of other events would have sufficed. Since the philosophy of nursing is concerned with basic concepts that are present in all or most nursing events, the richness of any one event suffices as a source for unveiling and developing the basic concepts.

CHAPTER 3

Universality and Singularity in Nursing Practice as Illuminated by Imaginary Discussions with Greek, Medieval, and Early Modern Philosophers

Earlier we introduced the reader to a list of our assumptions about nursing (chapter 1). In this and the following chapter we will examine and develop the philosophical distinction between universality and singularity. Universality is that which makes universals shareable. Singularity is that which makes individuals unique. It is easy to assume that science is interested in the universals, the shareables, rather than in individuals.[1] At the same time it is tempting to suppose that individuals, patients and nurses, are unique individuals. But the reader will discover that there is a dialectical tension and interrelatedness between universality and singularity and that this tension exists in that which we call universals as well as in that which we call individuals. Patients and nurses combine universality and singularity within themselves, and universals can only be expressed through the individuals that combine the universal with singularity and other universals than the one that is "expressed."

The key assumption pertinent to this chapter is that nursing uses knowledge from science and experience to promote the healing and the health of individual patients by individual nurses. The term "nursing" in the previous sentence is a universal or has as its meaning a universal. The knowledge referred to is an organized system of universals. Though healing and health are universals, their meaning varies with the individual. And though the words or concepts, "patient" and "nurse," are universals, individual patients or individual nurses are unique. The point of this chapter is to deepen understanding of the difference between universals and individuals and of their interrelatedness.

To achieve these goals, we use a thought experiment in the form of a series of imaginary discussions with selected individual philosophers.

This thought experiment is conducted in a fictional universe called St. Francelyn's Hospital, which is a single hospital with indeterminate temporal and spatial relations to the real universe. This indeterminacy allows individual philosophers from very different times and places to be present in the imaginary discussions. In order to elucidate the distinction between universality and singularity as it applies to nursing, we invite Plato, Aristotle, and mystics such as Hildegaard of Bingen, more recent philosophers such as Descartes, Hume, Kant, Hegel, Whitehead, Heidegger, and Dewey, among others, to answer questions and contribute insights. We have limited the imaginary conversations to philosophers who are no longer living. Since the roots of the discussion of universality and singularity go back thousands of years, and many related basic concepts essential to philosophy of nursing are uncovered in the process of expounding universality and singularity, we thought it was more appropriate to challenge living philosophers to make their own contributions to the philosophy of nursing rather than include them in the following discussions.

The key question is how to relate the elements of shareability and uniqueness in everything that is actual in the experience of nursing—living persons, events, the universe as a whole, and even God or the One. What roles do the aspects of universality and singularity play in science, in knowledge, and in theories of reality, and what is their importance to nursing? What sense can we make of the nature of persons and nursing occasions given these two intertwined though opposite aspects of reality?[2]

PLATO: THE THEORY OF FORMS

I (the nurse) first ask the advice of Plato about universality and singularity, and their role in the nature of persons and occasions within the temporal world. Plato considers my request at some length, and gives me the following advice:[3]

Why be concerned with the temporal world? The temporal world and the individuals in the temporal world are not that important. However the individuals in the temporal world are useful because of their *recollection of a perfect world in which what ought to be is. What is important are the Forms*[4] and what the individuals have to say about the Forms. When you converse with individuals, it is for the purpose of recalling that previous existence. But conversing with individuals is not a simple matter. The difficulty lies in language. The only way to recollect the Forms is through language. Unfortunately, no one uses language adequately for this purpose.

But I suggest to Plato that we might attempt to overcome the deficiencies of language by asking many people, by finding points of agreement. Plato disagrees. He says that he had already tried that, but it only heightened confusion. Many individuals lack the language skills and education needed for clearly recalling the Forms. Hence, it is better to engage in a one-on-one dialogue with another individual—one who is as wise and intelligent as possible. *Truth is not to be obtained by a vote*, or survey taking, but by deep, clear, and sustained thinking on the part of an individual.[5] We must transcend the limitations of language in the attempt to say something about that which cannot be verbally described.

Here I am a bit confused about whether an individual alone through deep, clear, sustained dialectical thinking can succeed in recalling the Forms, or if it is necessary to have dialogue with another person in order to recall the Forms. If dialogue is necessary, how can I be certain that what is being recalled are the Forms themselves, or merely an artifact of the dialogue? Plato assures me that I already know the Forms, and hence will be able to recognize them when reminded by the dialogue with another individual, or possibly in a process of dialectical thinking with myself which forces language to transcend itself, to become more adequate (Plato, *Republic* 531d–535a).

The trick if one chooses dialogue is to find those individuals who are wise and intelligent enough to engage in dialectical discussion. Plato has no way of helping me with this problem of identifying suitable individuals, of even distinguishing one individual from another. Plato is content that he is able to find such individuals often enough for his purposes. When he engages an individual in conversation, he can quickly determine whether the person is suitable. Suitable individuals he labels *"philosophers"* (cf. *Republic* 520a–e). When pressed about how he is able to distinguish one individual from another, or the same individual more than once for that matter, Plato admits that he cannot do this with certainty, because he must rely on the senses. But the senses, as well as the objects of the senses, are in perpetual flux. Knowledge of individuals would be possible only through the senses; but according to Plato, *the senses can only ground opinion, never knowledge* (*Republic* 508e–511e).

But if my questions are concerned with St. Francelyn's, and individuals within St. Francelyn's, how would learning about a transcendent world of Forms help me say something meaningful about the imaginary world of St. Francelyn or the actual temporal world, and individuals in either world? According to Plato, what I could learn from the philosophers is about a world that transcends the temporal world, a perfect eternal world. For Plato, *knowledge or certainty is possible only about Forms; whereas only uncertain opinion is possible about individuals*. Individuals are useful only as conduits to the Forms (*Republic* 508e–511e).

Yet Plato himself is an individual. Perhaps Plato as an individual is revealing something about himself and his times in view of the semireality of the sensible world in contrast to the full reality of the Forms. Plato had witnessed much change during his lifetime including rapid social, economic, and political changes. In his expressed nostalgia, perhaps Plato longs for a return to a state in which the soul had full knowledge of the Forms. This world of eternal Forms is a world in which there is no chaos, no uncertainty, no change. This is the realm of Beauty itself, Goodness itself, Truth itself, Unity itself, Being itself, Wisdom itself, Temperance itself, Piety itself, and Justice itself—among other perfect Forms. Such a world of eternal Forms offers the attraction of respite and security to those who have despaired of being able to do anything to improve the temporal world, as Plato experienced.

Is the world of Forms real apart from the imagination or conception of human beings? Or do persons create the Forms because of psychological and conceptual needs at particular times? Do we *create* the Forms or do we merely *recognize* the Forms? Are the Forms fully real only in a transcendent world, or are they present in this world? It would be difficult to deny that discoveries in science and medicine turn our attention at least momentarily from world transcendent to world imminent. Yet these same discoveries reawaken awareness of the beauty and order of a universe that transcends human capabilities.

The Forms are *alluring* to the (just) soul, the core of the individual. But the Forms do not *act on* the soul (*psyche*, in Plato's terms). Because the soul is attracted to the Forms, and not acted upon by the Forms, the Forms are final causes, not efficient causes. A final cause in Platonic/Aristotelian terms attracts but does not act. It is passive rather than active. In the sense that they attract, final causes are goals rather than agents of change. Efficient causes act to produce change. Hence, since the higher Forms lure, but do not act, they are final rather than efficient causes. I find it significant that Plato finds dialogue with other individuals helpful in order to gain access to these higher Forms, that this is a task he finds difficult to accomplish alone. If so then Plato is implying that individuals are important. Dialogue between persons (individuals) is so useful and nearly necessary that knowing the Forms at all adequately may be practically impossible without dialogue. Each person benefits by the dialogue.

In the process of remembering the Forms (recollection), facilitated by dialogue with others, Plato notices that certain Forms have higher value than others. *He places the highest value on the Form of the Good. All other forms derive their value and emanate from the Form of the Good.*[6] But by separating[7] and reifying the Forms, Plato has turned the

Forms into individuals in conflict with their original status as universals. Can something be both individual and universal at the same time? Or is this contradictory? And how does this help me understand the difference between universals and individuals, and between universality and singularity—aspects of reality that are inextricably intertwined in every nursing event, and in every person, both nurse and patient?

I am surprised to realize that I agree with Plato's placement of the Form of the Good above all other Forms. I "know" that Goodness Itself is the highest Form without knowing how I know it. Yet how can this be? Plato assures me that this is because *I already know the Forms. I am merely recalling being in the presence of the Forms (anamnesis); I am merely recalling what I already know (episteme) (Meno, Phaedrus).*

If the contemplation of the Forms is a source of peace, then their direct presence would be ecstasy. This suggests to me that perhaps anything in the temporal world that produces pleasure or ecstasy stirs recollection of the kind of experience the soul enjoyed in the direct presence of the Forms. And could it be that the neurological receptors that produce the experience of pleasure mounting to ecstasy exist because they were a more perfect "lock and key fit" for our prehuman ancestors who were able to more directly intuit the Forms?[8] Could it be that there was loss of an earlier more blissful kind of experience like that recounted in the story of Adam and Eve? And further, could it be that in the process of becoming civilized the perfect "lock and key fit" was lost? Perhaps the quest for science interfered with the ability to have religious experience or direct awareness of the Forms, as perhaps Adam and Eve had before their quest for knowledge? Could it be that this is the reason for the basic incompatibility between civilization and human nature that Freud writes about in his *Civilization and Its Discontents* (1938)? Perhaps the emphasis of civilization on objectivity and generality interferes with our ability to have direct awareness of the Form of the Good, of the One, of God? Could it be that present earthly experiences of pleasure are diminished reminders of the earlier experience, and that we need genuine dialogue with others in order to restore the deeper values in human experience? Could the longing for this previous blissful experience explain the allure of the Forms, and our desire to retreat to them? And further, it would make sense that without the presence of the Forms any enjoyment in this life is doomed to be ephemeral, hollow, and unsatisfying. This would help to explain why pleasure that is produced artificially through the use of chemical substances is hollow and ephemeral. If ecstasy is produced artificially through use of substances, then the chemical substances become the direct efficient cause of the emotion. The emotion is a counterfeit of what it should be, because it lacks the presence of the Form of the Good.

But in contrast to the counterfeit emotion produced by chemicals, the pleasure that results from helping others, such as that which results from nursing actions, is the result of a more direct presence of the Form of the Good. It is the shadowy presence of the Form of the Good that gives pleasure to the caregiver, though the actions are not aimed at either the pleasure or the Form of the Good. The gratifying experience that accompanies helping others is the result of the Form of the Good as ultimate final cause. In this experience of gratification, the soul[9] is the efficient cause of its own emotion. Further, the soul is judged to be morally worthy in proportion to its ability to recognize and love the presence of the Form of the Good. This is illuminating because it helps to explain several phenomena in nursing. First, independently of external rewards for caring actions, caring actions are directly gratifying to the nurse because of the individual nurse's love of the Form of the Good and the presence of the Form of the Good in the caring action. But it is not the Form of the Good that causes the gratification; it is the nurse's love of the Form of the Good. Second, the presence of the Form of the Good in the action of giving care explains why the nurse can give care to a person without regard to the earthly usefulness or worth of the person who is the recipient of the care. The direct gratification of care giving is independent of the worth, thankfulness, or gratitude, of the person to whom care is given.

Yet any nurse who has experienced the pleasure that results from giving direct care to another person is aware that the care receiver must also in some way be an active participant in the caregiving process. If not, both caregiver and care receiver are denied the pleasure of the caring experience. Conversely, if the caregiving nurse is not also an active care receiver, both patient and nurse are denied a higher participation in the Form of the Good. But what kind of care can the nurse receive from the patient that is in keeping with the Form of the Good? Plato has already established that material things are distractions; they have "disvalue" rather than value. If so, what can the patient give the nurse?

What lies within each direct caring experience between patient and nurse is an opportunity for the nurse to reach a deeper level of understanding of self through the experiences of the patient. The vulnerability of the patient in the caring experience allows deeper levels to be reached in both nurse and patient than in normal circumstances. In normal circumstances universals in the form of expected roles are used by both patient and nurse to expedite communication and transactions of daily life. Though these universals are expeditious and necessary, they hide the deeper singularity of individuals. The value of the caring experience lies in its temporary removal of much of this screening. When the screening is removed, both nurse and patient are able to enter into an authentic dialogue, individual to individual. They gain insights about each other that lead to a richer understanding of what it means to be human. From the insights gained from one another a kind of self dialogue becomes possible—a self-dialogue that allows both the nurse and patient to reflect on the nature of self and value.

Through authentic dialogue, in the context of the vulnerability of the patient, the nurse can compare her own life and values with those of the patient. She can ask herself, if I were as vulnerable as this patient is now, would I have this patient's strengths? Would I make the same kind of decisions, be able to overcome similar adversity? Or the opposite? Would I be in as much despair as this patient? Would I cling to life at all costs? When would I allow myself to succumb to a peaceful death? And what about an afterlife? Deeper questions also can be asked: How do I, myself, want to be? What are the elements of a good life? Of the most valuable life? What meaning has death within a good life? How is the self related to the community of selves? The concrete actuality of the caring experience grounds answers to these questions, answers only suggested by theory in books. It is the opportunity to have such meaningful experiences that is the invaluable "gift" of the patient to the nurse, it is the opportunity for a dialogue with self, for a deconstruction of self.

Third, if the character of the soul is not morally good, then the soul is incapable of loving the good. Such souls are repelled by the good. Knowing that some souls are repelled by the good helps to understand why not all recipients of nursing care are able to accept care gracefully and indeed are repelled by it in proportion to the degree to which the caring action is good. For example, persons with a soul corrupted by love of worldly things are incapable of understanding why any nurse should care for them except for such earthly considerations as power, money, doctor's orders, fear of litigation, desire for a good reputation, and so on. Such souls remain unconvinced that there is such a thing as the Good, and that anyone could be motivated by love of It. Furthermore, they are annoyed by anyone who appears to be motivated by love of the Good. It is only when they shift attention back to the Forms that such souls can begin to appreciate the presence of the Form of the Good.

Fourth, it occurs to me that the problem with patients' failing to accept preset patient goals as good for themselves may lie in the textbook manner in which the nurse presents the goals. The missing piece in many textbook presentations is beauty. When there is no beauty there is no allure; it is beauty which makes the Good alluring, which assures that the Good will function as a final cause. In Plato's theory, Beauty and the Good are so interconnected that one cannot have one without the other. If the patient should comply with the preset patient goals regardless of the patient's inability to perceive value in them, the compliance will likely be because of the authority of the nurse or the authority of the health care team. Authority is an efficient rather than a final cause.

Thinking further, perhaps what nurses forget in developing most goals for a patient is that *there is a necessary connection between the Good and Beauty.*[10] Consequently nurses may not present the goal in such a way as to display its beauty, to make it alluring to the individual patient. But if the patients were able to recognize the beauty in the goal, the patient would also be likely to see the good in the goal. If so, it would be unnecessary to use authority to get patient to comply. But what is seen as beautiful and good varies with the individual patient. Patients have widely different backgrounds, cultures, and interests. The wise and learned nurse will be well versed in the arts, the humanities, the sciences, and the many dimensions of human interests and will be very sensitive to cultural diversity and individual differences. The nurse must be creative in presenting the goal to the individual patient in such a manner as to make Beauty and the Good manifest to the individual patient.

The caregiving action, as in the nurse/patient relationship, may not initially be recognized by Plato as a dialogue in his sense, yet it may be as effective a means of recalling the good and the beautiful as the philosophical dialogues he acknowledged to be useful in recalling knowledge of the Forms. In the action of caregiving, it could be argued that, the action itself *is* the dialogue. The pleasure for the caregiver comes from doing good. For the care receiver the pleasure comes from recognizing goodness in others. Each finds the action of the other helpful in recalling the Form of the Good.

Justice (dikaisyne), *another of Plato's Forms, is essentially connected to the Form of the Good and to Beauty.*[11] The just act is the beautiful act, the action that produces harmony within self and between self and self. The just act needs no other justification. But in the experience of nurses justice is not always possible. If the caregiving and care-receiving actions of the nurse with the patient are diverted by stern bureaucratic impositions, this will create a conflict between the nurse's and the patient's ' sense of justice, goodness, and beauty and the actions that are imposed upon the nurse by the authoritarian structure. The dialogue between nurse and patient is interrupted. Both nurse and patient are prevented from recalling the Forms. What should have been good, becomes ugly. What could have been shared, becomes egocentric. What should have been harmonious is dissonant. The result is the frustrated nurse and the demanding patient, the nurse and patient in alienation from each other. The nurse is alienated from self and from nursing. And the patient, who might have viewed his illness as an avenue toward the Good and the Beautiful, is alienated from himself and his illness.

But before I can apply the high value Forms to the nursing of individuals more adequately, I must be able to identify individuals in St. Francelyn's. I must address the problem of singularity. I must have some way of distinguishing one individual from another, of identifying the same individual from day to day. Plato is not much interested in this problem. He says that what I am looking for is a science of individuals.[12] But no such science is possible, since individuals are inconsistent and only semireal. He advises me to stick with the Forms and ignore the individuals. After all, isn't Beauty itself much truer and more real than beauty in an individual?[13] But for Plato as a philosopher it is permissible to contemplate Forms while ignoring individuals. But nursing cannot ignore individuals. It is the individual nurse and the individual patient in their individual relationships that are the breath of life in nursing. Despite Plato's advice and the lure of the perfection of transcendent Forms, as a nurse I remain convinced that the individual is fully real and just as important as the Forms. If I were to ignore the individual, I would have to turn away from opportunities in the caring for individuals that are rich with potential insight concerning the nature both of individuals and of the Forms. Yet Plato's suggestion that there might be such a thing as Beauty itself leaves me wondering what perfect Beauty might be like.

ARISTOTLE: FORM AND MATTER

I return to the problem of being able to say something meaningful about the individuals in St. Francelyn and about the universe of St. Francelyn itself. Perhaps an organized system for making statements about individuals might be helpful. I turn to Aristotle for help with this project, because Aristotle was also dissatisfied with Plato's dismissal of the problem of identifying individuals. Aristotle, contrary to Plato, views the physical world as fully real. The significance of this belief is that the Forms that Plato talks about as in another world are fully present in this world according to Aristotle.

Aristotle accepts the senses as a means for distinguishing one individual from another (De Anima). He rejects Plato's notion that the senses are flawed,[14] *and he also rejects Plato's view that sensible individuals are less than fully real.*[15] But Aristotle agrees with Plato that *a science of the individual is impossible,* though Aristotle's reasons are different.[16] For Aristotle science (*episteme*) is systematic knowledge of the *general,* "what is always or for the most part."[17] What distinguishes the general from the universal, is that the *universal* is only that which is potentially shareable, while the *general* is that which is actually shared. The problem of science is to determine which universals are general. Hence, science cannot begin its inquiry without an understanding of the nature of universals. In this respect, the focus on the universal, my quest and the quest of science are similar. Aristotle also differs from Plato in accepting the senses as a means for knowing many of the forms. I notice that capitalization of the word "form" is inappropriate for Aristotle, because *they are not transcendent and otherworldly as are Plato's Forms.*[18]

Aristotle tells me that he is using the word "form" in different senses than Plato used this word. Aristotle says the meaning of the word "form" is partially a question of language. Part of the problem is with the translation into English of two or three different words in Greek. *Idea* and *morphe* are the two principal words used by both Plato and myself, says Aristotle, that have been translated into the word "form" in English. Plato prefers the word *idea* (idea) because it suggests the otherworldliness he is interested in, whereas I prefer the word *morphe* (shape) because I am interested in this world. However, we also differ in our understanding of *morphe* (shape), partially because of our backgrounds. I am a biologist. My father was a physician. So you can understand my interest in objects in this world. Further, my former student Alexander (the Great) has sent me specimens of different plants and animals from all over the world. I need a concept of form that allows me to classify these specimens, to distinguish one species from another. I cannot find what I need in Plato's transcendent Forms. I need forms that will allow me to classify things in this world.

But in all fairness Plato is a theoretical mathematician. Even when he tries to separate the higher value forms, such as the Good, from the lower forms, the mathematicals, I still find his notion of forms unhelpful. The infinitesimal points that Plato needs for his work are not only too small to be sensed, but they are unimaginable. Can you imagine a perfect triangle? Such an entity, if one could imagine it, would be an example of Plato's concept of *morphe*. I cannot imagine such, and neither can anyone else, including Plato himself. This makes a big difference in our outlook on forms. *For me, morphe (shapes) are fully present in the world.*[19] They need to be. The senses suffice to provide me with knowledge of many of the forms. For the theoretical mathematician, like Plato, nothing in this world fully embodies a perfect geometrical form. Only reason can provide knowledge of the mathematical forms. In fact, for Plato, things in the physical world merely imitate or participate in his Forms. A triangularly shaped object in the world of sensible objects, for example, is never a perfect triangle. For Plato, the perfect geometrical shapes are in another world reachable only through reason or dialectic. For Plato, the Forms do nothing, they do not act to produce change, that is, they do not act as efficient causes. It is the attempt of things in the world to be like the Forms that is responsible for change and order in the world.[20]

But as for me, Aristotle, morphe means not just shape in the literal sense, but any aspect of things that can be shared or repeated. Morphe is anything that can be true of more than one thing at more than one time, not just shapes.[21] Hence *morphe* is a metaphor through which I intend to notice and talk about those characteristics of unique individuals that are universal, that is, repeatable or shareable,[22] those aspects of things that can reoccur. The forms understood as universals occur in different kinds. The basic kinds, which I call "suchness," are essential to the actuality of any individual. That is, no individual can be an individual without belonging to a basic kind or "suchness."

At this point I interrupt Aristotle, and ask him whether the universal comes before the individual. He answers my question with another question. Can you identify a unique individual without automatically putting him into a basic kind, without identifying his *suchness*? As I am formulating a response, an individual, Mary Jones, comes to mind. I tell Aristotle that Mary Jones is a woman who is a patient in St. Francelyn's. I can remember her red hair, blue eyes, and dazzling smile. I can also remember her optimism and good naturedness despite her struggle with breast cancer. Aristotle asks me to notice that I have failed to single out Mary Jones without the use of a number of universals. Aristotle points out that Mary Jones cannot be noticed to be a woman without being noticed to be human. Humanity is the *suchness* (the basic kind) to which Mary Jones belongs. The other universals, the accidents, are useful for the practical purpose of distinguishing Mary Jones from other humans. Mary Jones is the breast cancer patient with blue eyes, red hair, and a dazzling smile. A long string of universals are used to narrow down the class of humans to smaller and smaller classes until you have singled out Mary Jones.

Any identifiable individual must belong to a basic kind. I prefer Socrates as my example, while you prefer Mary Jones.[23] But both Socrates and Mary Jones must be human. They belong to the *suchness* called humanity. Yet they are also unique individuals. As unique they are "thises." For me, Aristotle, every individual substance is both a "this" and a "such," and hence is a "this such." Believe me, this makes more sense in my classical Greek than in your twentieth-century English. What I mean by my theory of the "this suches" is that anything fully actual, anything that I would call substance (*ousia*) is a combination of universals and singularity. Separate universals are impossible and mere singularity is equally impossible. Perhaps you have noticed that Plato and I disagree about the separability of universals?[24] *I object to his separation of the Forms. Remember that for me forms are fully present in the world.*[25]

For me, Aristotle, there are two kinds of forms, substance forms and nonsubstance forms.[26] The forms that allow the "such" in a "this such" I call substance forms. They are universals, since more than one individual can share the same form. For example, more than one individual can be an oak tree or a human. These substance forms are difficult to define satisfactorily. Though they are fully present in the world, they are not knowable through any single sense. *They are the efficient causes of the growth of an acorn into an oak tree, or a human embryo into a child, and eventually an adult. They are not knowable satisfactorily through individual senses.* For example, I recognize an individual oak tree or an individual human being, because I am aware that there are such substance forms as oak and human. In fact, my ability to identify or recognize individuals is partly dependent on my ability to recognize their substance forms. However, my sense of sight does not give me full access to these substance forms, oak and human.

There is an additional puzzle. As the efficient causes of the growth of an individual acorn into an individual oak tree or an individual embryo into an individual child the substance forms have to be individual, for only the individual can operate as an efficient cause. As an efficient cause the substance form is a "this." Yet the substance forms are the "such" of the "this suches," and as such must be universals. *Hence, the substance forms would be both thises and suches at the same time, both individual and universal. But how can something be both individual and universal at the same time?*[27]

The same puzzle occurs with your contemporary theories about the DNA molecule. In your theories DNA molecules are the efficient causes of growth and replication, of the growth of an acorn into an oak tree, or a human embryo into an adult human being. But it is the pattern of bases in the DNA that is responsible for one being human, and then for one having blue eyes, instead of brown, and so on. Unless this pattern is embodied in individual molecules, it cannot act as efficient cause. The disembodied pattern is impotent, but it is a universal. The pattern of DNA is a universal. It is the "such" in the "this such." It is only the embodied pattern that is capable of action. This is similar to my theory. Unless the substance form is embodied, unless it is present in a unique individual, it cannot act. But when so embodied, it *can* act. Hence, it is the "this such" that acts, not just the "such." The embodiment of the form results in an individual rather than a universal. It is only as a pattern capable of different embodiments that it is a universal.

Returning to my question about how it can be both universal and individual at the same time, the DNA as a pattern that could be embodied in different molecules is a universal, but as embodied in unique individual molecules, it is individual. The disembodied pattern is impotent; only the embodied pattern is potent.

I think for a moment about what Aristotle has just said. And I have a further question. Suppose the pattern of DNA of an individual is replicated so that the same pattern is embodied in another human being. I am referring here to the twentieth-century discovery of cloning. The DNA pattern is a universal, it is a "such," a substance form. But how can I say that it is individual since the same "this such" is in two different individuals? If the same "this such" is embodied in two individuals, then what makes each individual unique?

Aristotle objects. *He says that the matter (hyle) in the one individual is different from the matter in the other individual.*[28] *Consequently, it is not true that the same "this such" is present in two different individuals.* Though two DNA molecules may have identical patterns, the same form, the matter of the one is always different from the matter of the other. I ask Aristotle to explain what it is that makes the matter of one DNA molecule different from the matter of the other, when the two molecules have the same form. He is not able to satisfy me. The best he can do is suggest that the two molecules have had different histories, that they have been individuated by having different accidents through time. Thus, the DNA is both universal and individual. DNA is universal insofar as it is a pattern that can be embodied in different molecules. DNA is individual insofar as the matter of one molecule is different from the matter of any other molecule. I resolve to ask later philosophers to shed some light on the nature of singularity, which guarantees the uniqueness of each individual even when the same significant form is present.

Aristotle continues. Nonsubstance forms, such as being in the marketplace or being sunburned, or being a patient in St. Francelyn's, are also universals, because they are shareable or repeatable. But non substance forms are a different kind of universal. *I call these nonsubstance forms "accidents."* Accidents are mere possibilities for definiteness on the part of substances ("this suches"). They are ways of being determinate or definite that are shareable or repeatable, but presuppose substances that can be actual in these particular ways. Can you imagine being in the marketplace, being sunburned, or being a patient without also imagining at the same time an individual having these attributes? For these attributes cannot exist except in individuals. Thus, the accidents or non substance forms presuppose "this suches." Without "this suches" they are unthinkable. Accidents are possibilities for definiteness on the part of individuals such as Socrates or Mary Jones.

Some of these possibilities can be actualized in the same individual at the same time. For example, Mary Jones can be a sunburned patient in the marketplace. Other possibilities are contraries. For example, Mary Jones cannot be both in the marketplace and in her room at St.

Francelyn's at the same time. This is because the actualization of any one possibility in such a set makes the actualization of other members of the set impossible (within the same substance, at the same time, and without qualifications). Consequently, when I say something about a substance, I am often implicitly denying many other things at the same time. For example, the particular shade of green that the leaves of olive trees have when they are mature is the contrary of all of the other shades of color that the leaves might have had instead. If I say that Mary Jones has a normal 98.6° temperature, I am implicitly denying that she has all of the other possible temperatures.

So for me, Aristotle, the forms are fully present in the world and are reachable, at least in part, through the senses. Here you can see that Plato and I are in direct disagreement about the value of the senses as well as the nature of the forms themselves. My choice of the phrase "this such" is not intended to give any priority to either the "this" (singularity) or the "such" (universality). I debated this question at length in books Zeta and Eta of my *Metaphysics:* which has priority? On balance, my tentative conclusion was that singularity and universality were equally fundamental, with each presupposing the other. I call the element of singularity matter (*hyle*) and the element of universality form (*morphe*). Nothing can be a substance without both elements, form and matter, universality and singularity.

Perhaps Aristotle's confidence in the reality of St. Francelyn's and the individuals within it reflects his world at the time, just as Plato's philosophy reflected his somewhat different circumstances. As tutor and friend of Alexander the Great, the most powerful individual in his world, Aristotle was not as pessimistic about individuals and what individuals could do. Whereas Plato had been unable to stop the execution of Socrates, and suffered repeated failures to institute his republic at Syracuse. Aristotle spent much of his life developing a system for saying something meaningful about unique individuals, classes of individuals, and the universe as a whole. Aristotle is happy to share his method with me. He calls this method "logic."

For this system to work, Aristotle warns me that I will need to distinguish objects of discourse from the things that are said about them. The objects of discourse are called subjects (*hypeikomena*).[29] What is said about them are called predicates. But to complicate matters further, Aristotle points out that there are two kinds of terms for subjects, proper nouns and common nouns. Proper nouns are names which refer to unique individuals within St. Francelyn's, for example, "Mary Jones." Other nouns are common in the sense that their meaning is a quality or property which can be shared by more than one individual, for example, "patient" or "nurse."

I notice that common nouns refer to universals that vary from the most general to the most specific. The most general universals are shared by almost every individual. The most specific seem to belong to only unique individuals. I ask Aristotle whether it might be appropriate to call the latter "particular"—particular in the sense that though they are intended to pick out a single individual, they are still universal and *could* be shared by more than one individual, however unlikely this might be. In other words, if I were to identify Mary Jones by a string of more than a million properties such that the likelihood that another individual could have the same string is nearly impossible, would I be able to identify Mary Jones in her uniqueness with this string? The problem is that though it is highly unlikely that any other individual shares this same string, yet "unlikely" does not mean "impossible." But that two or more individuals in the entire world *could* share this long string of properties indicates that I have still have not defined the individual I know as Mary Jones. Yet the "exclusive club" of individuals to whom this string belongs is apt to be so small that it has only one member. Hence, one seems to have something that is universal, because it is potentially shareable, but particular because it is apt to apply to only one individual. But because the particular in this sense is still potentially shareable, it is universal rather than individual—the individual cannot be gotten to through the particular alone. Hence the particular cannot be the unique individual.[30]

But, continues Aristotle, you have to admit that particularity in your sense is useful in identifying Mary Jones among all of the other individuals in St. Francelyn's. Yet your sense of the word "particular" is different from what I had in mind when I classified the three different kinds of propositions in my logic. Your sense of the word "particular" is close to what I had in mind by the "essence" (the what it is to be) of an individual. Essence and individual are not the same. What I meant by the essence of an individual was a verbal string or formula so long and complex that it would be practically impossible to be true of any other individual. "Practically" is the key word here. Practically implies that the essence or particular is good enough to pick out the individual, but the particular is not the same as the individual herself. The former is a mere possibility; the latter is an actuality.[31]

And if we are not clear about the distinction between an individual essence (a particular) and a unique individual, someone may confuse the two and think particular and unique individual are the same thing. I thought the distinction between the two was sufficiently clear so that I could tell a joke about Socrates and his essence in my *Metaphysics*. There I said that Socrates and his essence *were* the same, that Socrates was the sum of all of the predicates that were true of him. Since the predicates refer to mere possibilities, but the individual himself is actual, to say that Socrates and his essence are the same thing is to say that Socrates is actual and merely possible at the same time. I thought this was a good joke. Who could seriously think I meant this literally?[32]

Yet my students and subsequent generations of scholars thought that I meant to say something that was literally true, when it was actually contradictory. How frustrating! Well, to put it another way, how many philosophers does it take to spoil a good joke? The answer is 3,000. One to originate the joke, and 2,999 to miss the point! Oh well, it just goes to show you, my mother was right. She said I had better be a philosopher because I would starve as a stand-up comic.

I challenge Aristotle one step further. If I can't get to that which makes Mary Jones an individual by her string of predicates, is it possible to know the unique individual Mary Jones if I were to find that Mary Jones has no universals, that is, if she shares absolutely nothing in common with any other individual? Can there be an individual with absolutely nothing shareable or repeatable with anyone else? Is such a thing even thinkable?

This is what I meant by the problem of "prime matter," Aristotle is quick to remind me. *Prime matter would be pure individuality devoid of all universals. But universals are possibilities for definiteness. Without definiteness, Mary Jones would be metaphorically a blob devoid of shape, characteristics, life, or any other shareable forms. Pure matter would be pure potentiality devoid of actuality, which is impossible.* As soon as any form is actualized in Mary Jones, she ceases to be pure matter and possesses something that is shareable with other individuals. That is why I denied the possibility of prime matter.[33]

Thus it is impossible for Mary Jones to be a singular individual without being determinate in a very large number of ways. Each way in which she is determinate is a form or universal shareable with other individuals. But Mary Jones has never been before, nor ever will be again. As an individual she is unique, because she is not a universal. She is not repeatable, she is not shareable.

Aristotle's last comment prompted me to think about whether or not Mary Jones could be repeated. What about in an afterlife? Plato is positing an afterlife when he talks about a soul returning to the presence of the Forms. In my nursing experience I have encountered the importance to a patient of spirituality and of the hope for an afterlife. Nursing endorses the importance of spirituality in both the patient and in the nurse without providing much help in determining what spirituality might be. What is spirituality and how does it relate to an afterlife? How does spirituality and an afterlife fit into my problem with understanding universals and individuals in nursing?

Aristotle takes a breath, and tells me I have really fallen into deep water. I, Aristotle, will try to throw you a life preserver. First of all, Aristotle continues, I am not sure what you mean by "spirituality." Could you mean the contemplative life? I recommend this as the highest activity a human can engage in, because it is most godlike.[34] *Unlike Plato, I believe it is possible to contemplate the eternal, now, in this life; and insofar as one does this one is eternal. This type of contemplation brings peace. It makes a person one with the Unmoved Mover (God).*[35]

I interrupt Aristotle for a moment. Could that explain why so many of my patients have a sense of peace when they are contemplative? The experience is a healing experience. It is as if through contemplation the finite temporal person transcends time and finitude and such worldly problems as disease, and even impending death, becoming one, so to speak, with the eternal.

I think I understand your concern, Aristotle continues. I talk about the problems of aging, illness, and the relationship between active and passive intellect in my book *On the Soul (De Anima)*. But there I may be a bit misleading in my use of the words "active" and "passive." *The active intellect doesn't do anything, and the passive intellect does an individual's thinking.* To make this simpler, approach it in terms of actuality and potentiality. *The active intellect is fully actual. There are no potential thoughts for it to think that it is not thinking. It is thinking all possible thoughts at once. The passive intellect on the other hand goes from one thought to another, and is in a state of potentiality with respect to what it could think, but is not thinking, most of the time.*[36]

Aristotle's notion of an active intellect interests me as a nurse. I have known patients who have described to me the experience of having many thoughts at the same time. The experience is described as troubling. The medical term is "psychotic." When the patient is unable to focus on any one thought because of interference from other thoughts, the personal safety of the patient can be compromised. Sequencing of thoughts is important in providing basic necessities for survival, like finding water and food or protection from the elements. Yet, I have noticed that such patients, clearly preoccupied by intrusive thoughts can and do protect themselves at times when necessary, such as evacuating a building when its fire alarm is sounding. I ask Aristotle how his Active Intellect (Unmoved Mover) avoids being psychotic, that is, preoccupied by thoughts. How does the Unmoved Mover avoid the problems faced by my patients?[37]

Aristotle finds my remarks quite humorous. I guess it takes you nurses to keep us philosophers sane. Nursing's experience with individuals and universals is very useful to us philosophers. First, I want to congratulate you for noticing what I thought I had hidden quite well, the connection between the Unmoved Mover and the Active Intellect. Yes, the two terms refer to the same thing. If I were to have made this connection more explicit, I was afraid I would be accused of being a mystic. But now that you have forced my hand I guess I had better be clear about what I mean. Unlike your patient who is psychotic, the Unmoved Mover does nothing and never has a second thought. The Unmoved Mover has no daily necessities that must be satisfied in order for him to continue to live. Your patient has too many thoughts coming and going. This is not the same thing. The Unmoved Mover thinks all possible thoughts in a *nunc stans* (a stationary now, the "now" of eternity).

The passive intellect thinks sequentially, one thought at a time. One thought may lead to many potential avenues of thought. The intellect has potential to select the avenue it will next pursue. The way in which the intellect actualizes and selects the avenue to pursue is a cocreative process with the Unmoved Mover who is the One Active Intellect possessed by all passive intellects. This union of the one Active and many Passive Intellects is what I mean when I say "The One in the Many." But if the Unmoved Mover is psychotic, as your patient was, this might explain the craziness in the world. Aristotle chuckles and then changes to a more serious composure. The Unmoved Mover is common to all, as my predecessor, Heraclitus, believed was the case with what he called the Logos.[38] *But while his Logos was an efficient cause of order in the world, my Unmoved Mover functions merely as a final cause.*[39] But Heraclitus and I are both thinking of the One as involving thoughts or words (*logos* means "word").

I have another question for you, Aristotle. What did you mean by the term "mystic"? Does it have anything to do with belief in an afterlife? And, is your theory of the Unmoved Mover mystical?

The word "mystic" is one that I borrowed from your own time. In my time I was worried about being confused with the mystery religion people, with the Orphics, who used substances to achieve artificial ecstasy. But there are more fundamental differences between myself and later mystics. Heraclitus and I are thinking in terms of thought or language. Language is a system for symbolizing and communicating thoughts. The mystics want to "rise above" language and thought. They believe that Being is simply One, with a simplicity inconsistent with a multiplicity of words or ideas. Their One is not just an eternal system of all possible thoughts, but has a unity inconsistent with the very notion of thought.[40] Hence, when I am accused of being a mystic, my interpreters are misunderstanding either me or the mystics.

About your question concerning my belief in the possibility of an afterlife for the individual, I do not believe that such will occur.[41] But I have some problems with consistency in the manner in which I am trying to use the concepts of soul and form. Earlier I described my theory of forms. If you recall I talked about forms being in the world. But what I left out is that souls are substance forms individualized by the matter and experiences of the individual.[42] By this I mean that essentially an individual is a soul. *Though the species form was a universal, it ceased to be universal when it became the soul of a unique individual. By ceasing to be a universal it surrendered the eternality that formed the basis of Plato's arguments for the immortality of the soul. Forms can't change; but souls can. This is why just actions make a just soul and unjust actions an unjust soul—the soul is continually being reshaped by the actions and experiences of the living person. Hence, I, Aristotle, am doubtful that the soul will survive the death of the individual. I believe that death ends both the individual and the soul at the same instant.*[43] But if you ask me whether I know this, I must admit that I do not. There are too many unresolved puzzles for a knowledge claim on this subject.

Aristotle continues. When I identify the individual Mary Jones as a patient, I notice that saying something about Mary Jones already identifies Mary Jones with a kind or class, that is, a patient. Mary Jones is a "this such." Hence, the predicate terms turn out to be like the second kind of subject term, the common nouns. In other words, "Mary Jones, the patient, (common noun modifying subject) _____" means the same as "Mary Jones is a patient (predicate)." From the distinction between proper nouns and common nouns comes the distinction between "forms" and "individuals." Proper nouns, or names, are intended to point to individuals who are singular, that is, absolutely unique. Common nouns and other types of predicates refer to shareable or repeatable forms, ways in which more than one individual at more than one time might be definite. Over the history of St. Francelyn Hospital many individuals have been born, lived, and died. Many have been patients. Thus "patient" has as its meaning a repeatable form; while "Mary Jones" has as its meaning the unique individual who was born in Room 163 in St. Francelyn Hospital, at 9:05 am, July 23rd, 1963, and was reared in Room 318, but subsequently lived in Room 473.

I reflect on Aristotle's statements. I notice that as I am describing Mary Jones, the unique individual, the "this" of the "this such," it is almost impossible to identify or know her in her uniqueness because the "suches" are always present. Is it possible to know an individual separately from the forms? Is it possible to identify an individual without the forms? Can an individual be an individual without the forms?

But while I am referring to Mary Jones, using qualifiers such as where she was born, where she spent part of her life, and where she lived another part of her life, I am also contrasting her with everything that is not her. For example, by assigning places and dates to episodes in her life, I am distinguishing her from other individuals named "Mary Jones" who were born at different times and in different places than the unique Mary Jones I have in mind. But what is interesting to note is that the unique individual who is Mary Jones still remains elusive. The more qualifiers or disqualifiers I place on Mary Jones, the better are my chances for identifying and reidentifying her. Yet at the same time the singularity or uniqueness of Mary Jones is hidden behind a screen of universals. The name "Mary Jones" is a universal in the sense that it can be spoken or written more than once, and also can be used by more than one person. It is impossible to say anything about Mary Jones without using common nouns or forms. In order to recognize Mary Jones as a unique singular individual must I take a giant leap into the unknown?

Aristotle notices my perplexity. He says had been bothered by the same problem. The individual senses, such as sight, and hearing, provide only some of the forms associated with Mary Jones. No one of these senses individually provides knowledge of the unity of Mary Jones. But we must be experiencing Mary Jones in her unity, otherwise we would not know that sight, hearing, and touch, are giving us information about the same individual. He suggests that there is something in addition to the five senses that he labels "general sensibility." This is not a sense in addition to the five senses, but some other direct or intuitive mode of experience that provides knowledge of the oneness of a substance such as Mary Jones.[44]

As a nurse I am interested in the individual person, Mary Jones, in her singularity or uniqueness. I agree with Aristotle that there must be something that helps me notice a unique individual and to recognize the unity of that individual. If it were only sense data that helped me recognize Mary Jones, then I would be unable to distinguish Mary Jones from her clone or identical twin. Yet I do succeed in knowing Mary Jones in her uniqueness. If I have some faculty that allows me to organize the data from the different senses, and provides me with additional data, as data about the same individual, but a faculty that is not a sense, where did it come from and what is it?

I think a moment about the dawning of the ideas of singularity and universality in the experience of each human being. From infancy human beings notice objects (things and events) in their world. At first these objects are individual phenomena. At some point the infant notices similarities between individual phenomena. In addition some phenomena occur with repeatability first and then predictability. At the same time when the infant recognizes similarities in phenomena, he has begun to recognize what is not part of the phenomena. Is this perhaps what Aristotle had in mind when he talked about contraries? What is included and what is excluded is no longer capricious or completely open. When similarities are recognized, the infant's openness to novelty is truncated. When the infant begins to anticipate universals, the universal takes on the power to direct the perception of the infant.

REFLECTIONS OF THE NURSE
CO-AUTHOR ON THE BIRTHING EVENT

I continue to reflect on Aristotle's notion of universals (forms) and unique individuals (this suches) and wonder when the earliest dawning of the distinction between the two aspects of reality occurs. My thoughts take me back to the moment of conception, and the consequent development of the fertilized egg into the fetus that will become a human being. While the embryo is developing into the fetus, and the fetus into an infant, its environment has few surprises. The temperature is uniform. The sounds are repetitious. There is no need to take action for nutrition, elimination, or breathing. The constancy leaves the embryo unable to distinguish self from not-self, any one event from any other event. As far as it could know, it simply is, not temporally, but eternally. The universe and the self are the same, and hence there is no concept of either self or universe. Perhaps it is the only time when the individual *is* the "universal" and the "universal" *is* the individual.[45] Yet to recognize the shareable, the individual must first recognize the uniqueness of individuals, which requires the ability to distinguish self from not-self.

So how is the individual fetus or infant able to differentiate self from not-self, when its only experience has been within the safe confines of a mother's womb? Without recognition of differences, how would the unborn infant know that *it* and the universe are not one and the same? The beating of the mother's heart, the temperature of the environment, the constancy of darkness, cannot reveal to the infant that there is a world outside itself—because these events are too regular to be noticeable as unique individuals.

But the birthing process is sufficiently startling and unique to call the infant's attention to the possibility that there is more than one individual, for the universals in the events preceding birth are startlingly different from the universals that characterize the birthing event itself and its immediate aftermath. This is not enough to distinguish self from world, but it is enough to distinguish one individual event from another individual event, to break up the formerly homogenous unity into distinguishably different parts. Is the birthing event the origin of the dawning of the idea of individuality and of the self? Is this also the dawning of consciousness?

The contractions of the uterine muscle, the sudden burst of light, and just as suddenly the infant's need to breathe for the first time on its own, the sensation of the slamming permanently shut of the pulmonary aortic opening in its heart—all of these are unfamiliar experiences that highlight the differences needed to notice individuality. Such startling dramatic changes highlight the uniqueness of the new event in contrast to the nearly uniform warmth and peace that had always existed before. Perhaps consciousness dawns when the infant becomes aware that there may be unique individuals in the world, that it is only part of the universe, not the universe in its entirety. What also dawns explosively is awareness that it is able to act—to breathe, to make sounds, to see, to touch, to smell. It is no wonder most infants cry at the moment of birth, whether it be from joy or distress, or both!

Perhaps the first event the individual the infant is conscious of is the birthing event itself. This is an event blindingly bright rather than dark, cold rather than warm, characterized by a sudden need to breathe for the first time, and accompanied by an assault on the ears such as had never been experienced or dreamed of before. Perhaps it is the contrasts that awaken consciousness: the differences between new bright and the old dark, the new cold and the old warmth, the new noisiness and the old muffled quietness, the new need to struggle for breath.

And as the infant is aware of contrasts, this contrast between what it is experiencing now and what it had experienced before, it becomes aware that there is a present in contrast to a past, a now in contrast to a before. Perhaps this is the dawning of the infant's awareness of time. The fact that gratification of the infant's needs will be delayed many times during the next hours and days will deepen its awareness of time. Waiting and anticipation are temporal experiences.

This past is present in a new present characterized by cold, brightness, and the need to breathe. Consciousness requires recognition of differences in universals as a means for recognizing differences in the grounds of singularity that distinguish one individual from another. Conscious awareness requires recognition of shared universals, as well as universals that distinguish one individual from another. Equally intriguing is the role of temporality for singularity. But the individuals the infant has become aware of are events rather than persons. The infant is not yet aware of the difference between self and not-self; rather the infant is aware that change has occurred in events, that one unique event has given way to another. So when does the infant recognize the difference between singularity in self and singularity in other persons?

In the example of the newborn above, the infant begins to recognize himself as an individual. It is only through the consciousness of the individual that there is an "other," that universals, such as warmth or cold, darkness or light, are known. The infant must recognize that there is more than one individual, before the infant can realize that aspects of reality may be shared, or not shared, by different individuals. But how is a universal recognized? By the conscious recognition of the universals presence in more than one individual event? Or is the infant recalling Forms (as they exist outside of consciousness) and noticing that the individual events resemble or imitate them?

The example of the newborn infant illustrates the interdependence of universality and singularity. One cannot be noticed by the infant without the infant at the same time noticing the other. But the example suggests that it is startling differences in the universals that ingress into unique events that may call the infant's attention to the fact that the events are individuals, different from one another. Periodic processes, such as the beating of the mother's heart, do not underscore uniqueness. The infant does not notice something that from his perspective has always been. But birth is noticeably unique. Not in the nine months of existence in the womb, did any such thing happen. Birth is not just one more event like the individual beats of the heart. It is undeniably unique, different from anything the newborn infant has ever before experienced.

As jolting as the experience of birth is, the infant cannot go back to the womb, but must learn to cope with its new environment. But the contrast between what is and what was sets up a dialectical tension within the infant. It is a tension between the wish to return to the interconnectness, the oneness with a larger one, and the need to make sense of the new world sufficiently to be able to exercise some control over it.

The experience of the newborn infant desiring both to return to the comfort of connectedness while needing to learn to control a much more "external" environment is similar to that of the vulnerable patient in St. Francelyn's. Hospitalization forces an interruption of the normal distracting everyday activities under conditions that emphasize the relative lack of power of the patient. Though in everyday life the power of the patient was real, it was limited in ways the patient failed to realize until hospitalization occurred. The result is a major shift from a sense of "omnipotence" to a sense of "impotence."

As long as science is able to fix the patient's problem, the patient can overcome and perhaps even forget for a time the sense of impotency that occurred upon hospitalization. But when science cannot fix the problem, the sense of impotency returns. For many, the initial result is despair. The despair becomes deeper if the recommended treatments fail to produce results after multiple attempts. The patient realizes that the general universals are failing to apply to them in their individuality. The failure of the recommended treatments emphasize the cut-offness and uniqueness of the patient as an individual. But for many there is an "awakening from despair" when they realize that their individuality is interconnected, is part of, a much larger and comforting individuality. When this is realized, sickness and death are no longer the disasters they formerly appeared to be. The fundamental question is whether this frequent experience of patients is merely a reversion to the comfort of the womb, and hence is an illusion, or whether the patients are experiencing something real. If the latter is the case, it is a very important truth.

MYSTICISM

Plato's introduction to a world beyond this world, a World of Forms, and Aristotle's interest in an element within the individual that was completely general, perhaps eternal, and my own experiences with vulnerable individuals in St. Francelyn's Hospital, makes me curious about a special feature of the relationship between universals and individuals. What is the connection between a vulnerable individual and the possibility of a world beyond what can be known through reason, the senses, and science?

As I wander through the halls of St. Francelyn's, deep in thought, absorbed in what I have learned from Plato and Aristotle, I become aware of a distant choir of angelic voices that seize my introspective thoughts and carry them away to a room just around the corner. The music is enrapturing. As I enter the room the heavenly choir is finishing. And the person who is the director of the choir greets me cordially. She is Hildegard of Bingen.[46]

The ecclesiastical music is so beautiful and timeless that though the choir has stopped singing there is a sense that the music is still present. Hildegard has been called a mystic.[47] My curiosity about universals and individuals in nursing, together with special experiences in nursing, prompt me to turn to mysticism for the light it might shed on the nature of universals and the element of singularity within individuals in nursing experience.

Spirituality is among the special experiences in nursing that are an important factor in health and illness. Because of the more intimate nature of the relationship between nurse and patient, nurses are more aware that spirituality is important in the perception of health and illness by the patient than is acknowledged by more scientific approaches to health and illness. Yet, health and illness cannot be defined strictly in terms of the presence or lack of a disease process. Nor can it be defined by reasoning alone or by reasoning in combination with science. And when health and illness are defined by these means alone, the patient may be thought of as having another sort of pathology. If he has a serious disease process and feels healthy, he is thought to be in "denial."

And if he is ill yet without a discernable disease process, he is thought to be "psychosomatic." Both categories are denigrating to the character of the patient. But an examination of religious experience and mysticism may help in understanding how such diagnoses may not only be challenged but be argued to be wrong. And finally, are spirituality and mysticism related?

I am assuming that religious experience is a less intense version of the experience that the mystics describe, and that spirituality includes both forms of experience. Since mysticism is more extreme, stronger or intense, and some of the mystics have been very articulate, I examine mysticism for insight into spirituality in general.

Is the mystic experiencing unusual universals or a very special kind of Individual? If I can establish through an examination of the relationship between universality and singularity, and their functioning in experience, that a case can be made for a mode of knowledge in addition to reason and the senses, then this could explain the nature and importance of spirituality in some of my patients, and even the mystical element in nursing. Further, this would resolve some of the mysteries about health. For one thing, it would become apparent that science and logic, though important, provide only partial explanations of health and illness.

As a nurse I have often noticed that though science has a role to play in curing disease, healing is accomplished by something other than science. What is this other?[48] Patients whose actions and statements express spirituality challenge the older notions of health and illness, especially the notion that health is simply the absence of illness, and illness the presence of disease. Patients who have a spiritual life are able to feel healthy in spite of a diseased body. In fact, it is possible to be healthy even in the face of a terminal illness. Conversely, in the absence of spirituality, patients often feel sick or in despair, even though from the point of view of science there is very little wrong with them. How do I account for these paradoxes? What is spirituality, and why does it make such a difference? How is it possible for good health to be compatible with critical illness, and for poor health to be possible without illness? Again, does mysticism help in understanding spirituality? Are they connected?

Does the type of spirituality enjoyed by the mystic involve a relationship between individual and Individual, a relationship between the finite person and the larger Whole, the One, perhaps God?[49] Or, is the mystic experience experience of a special kind of universal? I remember what I learned from Aristotle about universals. They are incapable of separate existence. They only exist in individuals, not by themselves. Hence a universal that is an object of experience exists or has actuality in the mind of the person experiencing it. It may or may not have actuality in something outside of the mind of the person experiencing it.

Individual mystic experiences seem to involve a common set of universals.[50] Though the experience itself is ineffable, there are many attempts at describing aspects of these experiences by means of such universals as words and other symbols. Further, the truth revealed in the mystical experience seems to be a fundamentally important truth about all of reality, though it cannot be conveyed in true or false statements (propositions). But is what is revealed in a mystic experience really a fundamental truth or is it a grand illusion?[51]

The common features of this fundamental truth or grand illusion are several. First, the content of this truth (or illusion) is largely ineffable. Words, visual symbols, and auditory symbols are woefully inadequate for conveying the nature of the Reality that is experienced. Second, the experience is a direct intuition of Reality only mediated or catalyzed by symbols. Third, since the experience is direct (intuitive) and only mediated by symbols, if it is true, it is true without conveying propositional truths. Fourth, the mystic needs no verification of her experience; it is self-verifying. If the experience is not an illusion, it is an intuitive experience of an infinite One, not separate from finite individuals, but of which finite individuals are a part. It is knowledge by direct acquaintance. Fifth, the truth of the experience is more fundamental than any that can be conveyed through the senses or empirical sciences. Sixth, because the experience conveys no propositional truths, it cannot be used to support the claims of any particular theology or religious tradition. Seventh, nevertheless, the ineffable Nature experienced is known to be individual rather than universal, living rather than lifeless, transcendent of the world and yet present, different from the self and yet involved in the self, loving and interested without being interfering or controlling—a gentle companion and a larger Whole of which every finite one is a part. The mystic vision is the antithesis of mechanistic atomism. If the mystic vision is true, then though evil is real, Reality is ultimately good. No matter how bad things are, the world is on balance good.

But now I see that there are several possibilities to be considered. Suppose that the universals associated with the mystic experience exist *only* in the mind of the person having the experience. Then the revelations about reality or the universe that seem to be grounded in the mystic experience are really only revelations about the individual's experience and reveal nothing about the universe. In this case the mystic's conviction that the mystic experience reveals an important truth about the universe or the Whole is mistaken. The mystic experience is just a pleasant illusion, perhaps the result of hypoxia or some other physical or psychological factor.[52] This is one possibility.

The second possibility is that the universals experienced in the mystic vision are experienced by more than one person, but that the universals still exist only in the minds of those who experience them. That would mean that the mystic vision remains an illusion, not something indicative of the nature of the world outside of the experience of the small group of people who are called mystics. But this possibility is different from the first in that questions can be asked about special circumstances that set the group of mystics apart from the "normal" population. For example, are the mystics individuals who have experienced a special kind of stress prior to their experience? Many of them talk about a "dark night of the soul." Some of them try to precipitate the mystic experience by fasting, drugs, or special breathing.

The third possibility is that the mystic experience is what it appears to be to many mystics, a direct intuition, catalyzed by, but not mediated by, universals, of an Infinite and unique One to which the individual both belongs and does not belong.[53]

But if the experience is not an illusion, do universals play a role in the special relationship between the one and the One, between the individual and God? Is the singularity of the finite person "taken up" into the singularity of the infinite One, or does the finite person remain a one in addition to the One? Or both? What role do other finite persons play in the spirituality of the mystic? What is the source and nature of the special invulnerability associated with the spirituality of the mystic? Is this the invulnerability that spiritual persons possess even though they are physically very ill?

Hildegard is happy to respond. She begins by explaining the relationship between an individual and God. "I don't think that the fact that people who have physical illnesses and at the same time feel healthy constitutes such a paradox, if you understand the nature of what your patients are experiencing. Those that welcome God into their souls become a part of God, and share in the invulnerability and blessedness of God. Consequently, even though their body may be dying, they know that they cannot be harmed."

Plotinus overhears the conversation and approaches. "I agree with Hildegard. Though *I prefer to talk about the supremely real as The One rather than God, this is a mere verbal difference. All individuals are in the One individual. Those that experience their unity with the One, enjoy the invulnerability of the One*" (O'Brien 1964, pp. 90–105).

"I too agree that the sense of oneness with God results in an awareness of invulnerability," says St. Francis of Assisi. "But in answer to the question about how one knows about the existence of the higher world, this occurs through submission of one's will to God and through loving others and doing service to others." Teilhard de Chardin enters the conversation. *I see no conflict between science and religion. Evolution is teleological. Change is in the direction of God as Omega Point. It is not a matter of random variation and selection of the fittest. Humans are the bond between the rest of nature and God* (Teihard de Chardin 1959).

I notice that all of my consultants on mysticism are at peace, are joyful, like the spiritual patients I mentioned earlier. As a nurse I want to invite peace and spiritual comfort to all of my patients. But how do I do this?

Hildegard answers first. "You really cannot bestow to another a sense of peace. Each individual must open up his or her own being to receive the Divine Light. *Joy and peace are the result of the infusion of the Divine Light into the soul of the individual. Once the Divine Light has entered into an individual the experience is difficult to express in words. I find expression in art and music and to a lesser extent in my writing. I can't speak for the others but I have had visions that gave me insights about the connectedness between the world, the individual, and God* (Hildegard 1986).

Meister Eckhart agrees with Hildegard about the change that occurs when one is open to the inner voice of God. *Unlike St. Francis, my experience of God was through contemplation rather than submission of the will and service to others. I agree with Hildegard that there is a sudden knowledge more certain than from the senses about a truth that is most important—that God is in the individual and the individual is in God.*

St. Francis of Assisi reasserts his position concerning the path to the special and all important knowledge. *I believe that it is in the submission of the will to God, and not the intellect, that this spiritual union of the individual and God takes place. The expression of this submission of the will is in love for all of God's creatures and service to His neediest. Satan had knowledge. What he lacked was submission of will.*

"I agree more with Eckhart," Plotinus adds. "The intellect is the path to this knowledge or union, not the body. *The body is furthest from being and goodness, the intellect is closest to the One*" (O'Brien 1964, pp. 90–105).

Putting aside the disagreement about the path to this truth, I ask the mystic consultants if this knowledge they possess is really knowledge, or is it perhaps faith instead. All are quick to answer in chorus, it is knowledge, but not such as one gets through the senses.

The experience is ineffable, Plotinus contributes. It is knowledge, not faith but *it cannot be described. Further it is not theoretical knowledge, but awareness of oneness with the One. Words are mere approximations. They are never adequate.* In my desperation to share this Truth with others, *I have tried to describe this knowledge by what it is not. For example, the One is not many, and the One is not changeable. But if I assign attributes to the One, I introduce multiplicity into the*

One. This is false, because the One is one and not many.

At these words of Plotinus, Meister Eckhart was stirred to speak. "I tried to do the same thing, Plotinus. I tried to avoid assigning attributes to God that could be shared by others, because that would introduce multiplicity into God. But I was accused of heresy by the Catholic Church. I wanted to say that describing God by any word that could be shared with others would be tantamount to saying that God is like any other, to relegating God to a string of universals, or particulars, to use the expressions of Aristotle. I knew this was not true. So all I could say was that God is not light, not good, not just. I said that God is darkness. But history shows the reaction I received from those who could not follow my thinking. I was accused of blasphemy.

The truths revealed through the mystical experience are so illuminating that having experienced them changes the individual profoundly, added Hildegard. Perhaps this is what you notice about your patients who are at peace while suffering tragedy.

Pain and suffering are the highways to the union with God (Underhill 1967, p. 222), Hildegard continued. It is the imitation of Christ's suffering that is the beacon lighting the dark path to the Divine presence. When your suffering patients become aware of this meaning, their suffering takes on a new life.

St. Teresa of Avila portrayed the difference between the closeness to God in prayer from that of the mystic experience. In prayer, she said, certain inflowings of the Godhead are present. But in the vision, the Sacred Humanity is our companion (Underhill 1967, p. 283).

The mystics describe *being* as greater than *doing*. Meister Eckhart cleared his throat as he spoke. If the soul knew the very least of all that Being means, it would never turn away from it (Underhill 1967, p. 93).

What Hildegard and the others were saying made sense to me. It seemed a plausible explanation for the experiences of some of my patients who, though they suffer, are not in pain, and though they are alone, are not lonely, and though they are away from familiar surroundings, are at home.[54] Yet I also recall others of my patients who have had "near death experiences." Their descriptions of an enlightenment so profound that it changed their lives in significant ways is similar to what the mystics are describing. After their experiences with near death, worldly pleasures have much less value. They may give away their material wealth to pursue a life of service and contemplation. Often family and friends are baffled by the change. Family members may even begin to think that the individual has lost his mind.

A similar situation happened to me and my family after my experience, said St. Francis. My father thought I had lost my mind when I renounced my worldly possessions and began caring for lepers and others whom no one would touch. Yet it is a calling that you cannot ignore. It consumes your life.

But how is that not the same as losing one's mind? I was still curious. Some of my patients have been consumed by voices, unable to provide for the minimum of self-attention necessary for survival.

I have never lost my mind so I can't say from experience what it is like, said St. Francis, but I will take a guess at an answer. The difference is the state of distress or ecstasy. An individual who has lost his mind is in distress. The voices are punitive and disturbing, deprecating to the individual. In contrast, the mystic experience is one of utter joy and ecstasy. The conversion experience brings to the soul a recognition of the union with God. The union always existed, but was unrecognized before the mystic experience.

Oh what a joy this is, to recognize one's union with God! Hildegard was quick to add. All the others agreed.

But you all tell me that these truths are undeniable, unequivocal, yet none of it can be known through the senses or measured. It is ineffable. As a nurse, I am interested in understanding the experience of my patients. I have recognized that there are ways of knowing that have little to do with the senses and with science. I have known many patients who are unable to converse in ordinary language because of psychological or neurological problems, yet there is a bonding between us that is also ineffable, a connectedness in spite of language and other difficulties. But the bias in favor of science and knowledge through the senses is an obstacle to talking about this other "dimension" of connectedness. I ask the mystics how they reconcile the Truth as known through their recognition of union with God or the One with the beliefs of science?

Perhaps I can help, said Teilhard de Chardin. I too felt the sting of rejection by the Catholic Church for my writings. I wrote that science and religious experiences are not contradictory. They emanate from the same Creator. Human beings are the links between science and religion. God gave human beings the intellect to discover things about this world that will bring them closer to God. Your patients can make use of the greatest discoveries of science to help them get well or to conquer disease and yet come closer to Him Who, as Creator of all things, has allowed discoveries to take place.

I have been thinking about your comparison, said Hildegaard, between the experiences that we here all have been describing and the near death experiences of some of your patients. As she speaks, all of us turn in the direction of Hildegard. I have been curious about it too, Hildegard continues. From what I understand, persons in occasions of near death have had "out-of-body" experiences, is this not so? I agreed that the out-of-body phenomenon was a common description.

Well there is one difference between my own experiences and those of your patients, Hildegard continued. In my experiences, God's light fills the soul suddenly and violently. Through this divine light I am given Truth. The connectedness between God's creation and God is suddenly evident in what had appeared to be an ordinary physical world. My body is in my soul. My soul is in God. I have never experienced out of body phenomena, but rather a great and wondrous connection with the universe of God's creation. I had renounced material possessions, yet at the same time, I administered the daily necessities of the convent. It would be foolish not to recognize that secular responsibilities are also necessary. The body would not be able to survive long without providing for corporal needs.

I could not agree more, St. Francis added. I compelled those who would follow my ways to take the vows of poverty, chastity, and obedience, yet I also required that they be self-sufficient. Living by handouts was sanctioned only when necessary. But despite my insistence on living within our means, some of my brothers were unable to understand the boundaries between those material things that were necessary to sustain life and those that were excess. The differences between want and need were difficult for some to recognize.

I agreed that it is not necessarily easy to set those kind of boundaries successfully, that is, between the needs of the of the body and the pleasures of the world.

Apparently this is the same for many, said St. Francis. It is a troubling, unresolved problem. If the Divine Presence reveals the Truth to one who is open to it, others who do not hear it are unable to recognize the differences between need and want. They must learn through the modeling of others.

The mystics have introduced me to an interconnectedness between the unique individuals I call persons, and a much larger unique entity that they variously refer to as "God" or the "One." Once the connectedness is experienced, it is impossible to feel alone or ill. But I wonder what the life of the mystic was like before the mystic experience?

This is what some have called "the dark night of the soul," said Hildegard. The others agree with Hildegard. Before the mystic experience an individual feels alone and cut off from all other individuals. The individual is alone even when in a crowd, maybe especially so when in a crowd. No place is home. Value is to be found in nothing and in no one.

Is the experience of the dark night of the soul something like the suicidal thinking expressed by some of my patients? I wonder.

I have not felt suicidal, St. Francis responds. But I have felt a great despair, perhaps like your patients express. It is a despair so profound that I am in isolation from all others and there exists a sense of meaninglessness so far as the value of my life or anything else is concerned. Yet I have never thought to end my life by my own hand. Perhaps the despair is so deep that there is no energy for that type of action or any other type of action. Or, perhaps it is because nothing attracts, not life, not death. Do you remember the story of the donkey (Buridan's ass) who starved to death because he could not decide between two stacks of hay, both equal in size and both equally distant from him?

I admitted that I was familiar with the story.

In both the story of the donkey and the dark night of the soul, there is immobilization. But the donkey could not choose between two pleasures. My immobilization was the result of despair, of utter lack of vision. Nothing or no one could make a difference. That donkey could not move because two things were equally desired and he could not have both. I could not move because nothing was desired.

The others nodded heads in silent affirmation. St. Francis continued. Then came the enlightenment. It was a jolt so intense, that it was almost unbearable. Perhaps as unbearable as the despair, but in a different sense. Ecstasy and despair. Both are unbearable. Both ineffable. But unlike despair, when no light provides a beacon, the enlightenment at once revealed to me the Truth. And with the truth came the way to serve God and to travel the pathway in the Divine presence. All in concert with the One, the One in all. As a creation of the Creator I am one with Him and with all in the universe. The vision is so beautiful that at once I understood that care of myself and of all of God's creation was also care of God. Love of myself and love of all God's creation was love of God. Service to myself and service to all of God's creation is service to God. (*Cf.* Underhill 1967.)

What St. Francis and the others were revealing was that the interconnectedness of the many in the One is a truth known through enlightenment, not through science. And that when my patients experience this enlightenment, they abandon the despair of isolation and meaninglessness in their lives. The frailty of the finite one is surrendered to the power of the infinite One. The unenlightenment of the finite one is surrendered to the omniscience of the everlasting One.

Yet Hildegard again asserts that this enlightenment is something I cannot give my patients, let alone give them a mystic experience. Each person must find it for herself. So how might I participate in a milieu that would catalyze such an event for my patients? Is it possible to prepare such an environment? Or do I simply abandon the effort altogether? It would be easy to dismiss the world beyond the world as hokey and leave my patients to their own resources. Hildegard warned me that I cannot make the mystic experience happen for my patients or for myself. The individual is the recipient of a rare gift beyond their power to control. But I am not speaking here of mystical experiences. Those occasions are extremely rare and happen to a select few. But mystic experiences and near death experiences aside, as a nurse perhaps my role in the spirituality of my patient is simply to run interference for him in the sterile and mechanistic medical world, to create opportunities for him to achieve self-discovery through spirituality. Illness is an opportunity for reflection and the nurse must help the patient have the time to do the reflecting. If illness is considered to be only a "speed bump" to be gotten past quickly, the opportunity it provides for spirituality will be lost. The theme of greeting cards that have a "get well quick" message implies that illness is an annoyance and serves no positive purpose. The nurse, who recognizes the opportunity for self-reflection that an illness provides, understands her role in this process as a continuing one not to be completed by a simple referral to a clergyman.

This time it is Meister Eckhart who notices my bewilderment. I have observed, he said, that in your modern hospital the value of persons is often ignored in favor of the expediency of the treatment you have evolved through the efficient application of modern science. This is not to say that science is not truly wonderful. Your modern science has cured so many of the plagues and illnesses that destroyed many people in my time. Yet is it not true that despite the longer lives and varieties of experiences that your world offers to a person, the angst of the dark night of the soul remains as mysterious to you as it was to us?

I had to admit that this is true. Our modern concern with quantity of life instead of quality of life has not been resolved despite the healthier lifestyles we advocate.

Eckhart continues. Perhaps your science has been able to mend the body but has been unsuccessful in mending the human soul. The cure to the sickness of the soul is not more and better science. Perhaps that is why your medications which alter thought processes and moods do not have lasting effects. I cannot give you directions on the path to spiritual enlightenment. Only God as the Great Cartographer can do such a thing. Yet I see that in your speed to discover new things or to rush to cure a person of a disease there remains little time for self-reflection. Perhaps the meditation rooms and chapels at St. Francelyn's are an attempt to induce the healing of the spirit. But healing of the spirit cannot take place at some designated room or at a time convenient to a treatment team. God makes Himself known at different times and at the oddest of occasions. I have found that silent contemplation and writing have been my guides. And then only after the dark night of the soul. I cannot imagine what it would have been like had I been given antidepressants or antianxiety medications to resolve what I now know was a spiritual sickness. Such medication would have prevented the enlightenment upon which my real health has depended. When does your world leave time for contemplation? Or for silent reflection for that matter? Self-discovery is as important as any scientific discovery.

The mystics' experience with a Presence brings to mind a puzzle connected to my earlier question about whether the mystic experience conveys an ultimate Truth or whether it is a grand illusion. What is the difference between the mystic experience and some forms of hallucinatory experiences? As a nurse I have encountered both the spiritual individual and the hallucinating individual and have listened intently to their descriptions of their experiences. What I discovered are commonalities and differences between them.

The common feature is that both experiences are to a degree ineffable. Though both experiences are ineffable, the individuals make use of verbal and other types of symbols in the attempt to talk about their experiences with me. Both experiences involve data of sensation. And in both cases these data of sensation are *not* experienced by others; there is a lack of intersubjective validation, especially so for the hallucinatory experience. Both experiences are largely involuntary: the mystic experience and the hallucination are something that happen to an individual, not something that the individual does, though the individual with hallucinations may try to avoid circumstances associated with hallucinations, the person with a spiritual or mystic experience creates circumstances that may precipitate a mystic vision or spiritual experience. But perhaps the most riveting similarity between the mystic experience and the hallucinatory experience is the religious component. Many individuals who have experienced hallucinations have been absorbed with religious thinking.

That the mystic experience is sought and the hallucinatory experience is avoided is the first hint concerning the radical difference between the two kinds of experience. The mystic experience leaves the individual with a sense of peace and "at homeness" lingering for a lifetime. The hallucination is disturbing and isolating. Mystic experiences make it easier to relate to others because of a heightened sense of community. Hallucinations result in a feeling of detachment from others and the world. The withdrawal is not comforting but frightening with lingering after effects quite the opposite of the mystic experience.

The listener to the person with a mystic experience and to the person with the hallucinating experience can probably remember similar experiences in his own life. The mystic experience is not dissimilar to religious experience or spiritual appreciation of nature. This similarity in the accounts given by most mystics provides indirect intersubjective validation of the mystic experience. This is strengthened by the insight from the mystic vision that all ones are present in the same One. If so, the unique One experienced by any one mystic can reasonably be supposed to be the same as the unique One experienced by any other mystic or religious person. Those who study mysticism notice that mystics, though from different cultures and religious traditions, speak the "same" language. In contrast, hallucinations are similar to nightmares, or brief hypnopompic and hypnogogic hallucinations that occur when one is fatigued or in the dreamlike state between slumber and wakefulness. But here there is no common language: one is reminded of Heraclitus notion of the "wet souls"—each lives in his own private world, cut off from the world at large as well as the other private worlds.[55] The spiritual experience of the mystic is a desired and ecstatic state, whereas the hallucinatory experiences are frightening and undesirable. The effects of the two types of experience are opposite spiritually.

Does the distinction between universality and singularity shed some light on the differences between mystic experiences and some hallucinatory experiences? In mystic experience the universals in the symbols, such as visual images or words, are a bridge that connects unique ones with the unique One. In hallucinations, similar symbols and similar universals fail to allow the one to connect with the One. Hence, it is not surprising that hallucinations result in strong disappointment, feelings of unworthiness and alienation. It is also not surprising that there is a powerful yet distorted "religiosity" in the experience of some hallucinating patients. In these accounts, it is as if "God" and "Devil" were fighting for control of the individual soul. The individual perceives himself as deity or demon, to be worshiped or reviled. The "visions" of the hallucinating patient not only fail to relieve the dark night of the soul, but tend to cause a "hang up" in a state of spiritual angst. In such angst God or the One becomes the Devil or ultimate evil. In contrast, for the mystic neither the Devil nor ultimate evil exist. Those of us who work with patients in this condition of spiritual angst have discovered that, with many of the patients, any attempt to "talk through" the spiritual problem only deepens or worsens the condition. We know that the words and symbols associated with positive spirituality will have the opposite effect on this kind of patient. Here medication seems to be much more helpful than any use of language.

And what can be said about the affective element in the mystic experience compared with the affective element of someone with a bipolar disorder? Is the dark night of the soul and the joy and elation of union with the One that the mystic experiences the same as the depression and elation experienced by individuals who suffer from a bipolar disorder? Like the individual with hallucinations earlier described, and unlike the mystic, the person experiencing depression or mania does not describe a sense of connection with the infinite One. Though the level of energy of a person in a manic state might be confused with the energetic actions of many mystics following the joy of mystic vision, the manic does not say that he is at peace with himself as the mystic does. Further the uncontrolled energy of persons in a manic state too often results in self-destructive actions. For example, they may spend too much money or take unnecessary risks. Their gregariousness results in them "talking at" rather than "being with" other persons. Persons with bipolar disorder often express an underlying loneliness rather than connectedness between self and others and between self and world. Could it be that lacking connectedness with others they find some solace by influencing others? If so, this may help to explain why some persons with mania give extravagant presents, deliver eloquent speeches or even control or dominate the more submissive individuals in their lives, yet still feel lonely and isolated.

In contrast, the elation of the mystic springs from an awareness of being a part of an all-embracing living One along with all others persons. This awareness allows much greater openness with other individuals because of the sense of peace and invulnerability. The person in a manic state thinks that his power comes from himself, and has a false sense of invulnerability as an individual. In contrast, the mystic experience does not interfere with everyday activities, and may in fact enable the mystic to perform these functions with a high level of excellence. For example, Dag Hammerskjold was a very effective secretary general of the United Nations (1953–1961). It was only posthumously discovered from his diaries that he had mystic visions.[56] Far from feeling lonely, the mystic feels very connected with other persons and with the world. The mystic functions much better and the manic much more poorly when in their states of elation. Could this mean that some psychiatric conditions stem from spiritual problems?

If some psychiatric problems stem from spiritual problems, what happens when the nurse tells the patient "just take your medications and you will be OK"? Medications are useful for controlling extreme psychoses. In this sense, when we advise the patient to take the medication and they will be all right, this is in one sense true. But despite this why do so many patients quit taking their medications? And why when patients take their medicines and treatments as prescribed, do they still say that something is missing? The question is what do the medications leave undone?

I remember being chided gently by several of my "treatment compliant" patients that, though the medications have helped to control or diminish overwhelming and disabling anxieties and hallucinations, the medications are unable to give the patients a connectedness to the larger community. One of my patients expressed the experience aptly when she said, "the medications have robbed me of feeling human. I look at my children and I know I love my children, but I can't feel the love for my children." Another of my patients described the problem this way, "Why do I feel so alone in the company of others. People laugh at jokes, and I don't understand the jokes. I cannot laugh with them. Yes, the medications keep me out of the hospital, but they cannot connect me with others."

Is it fair to tell the patient to take medications and everything will be all right? Or can the nurse, knowing the limitations of the medications, empathize with the patient in such a manner as to begin the connectedness the patient is seeking? If the patient is experiencing spiritual angst, as the earlier reasoning indicates is likely, then feeling will be an important part of getting well. Medications that dull feeling may get in the way of the patient's progress beyond a certain stage. Patients who stop taking their medications may be giving us an important insight into possibilities for better treatment.

Mysticism reveals the importance of feelings in the relationship between the one and the One. And the relationship of the one with the One is important for the health of the finite and unique individual. But what are the factors that diminish feelings and hence diminish opportunities for the realizing the relationship between the one and the One?

When the patient's feelings are dulled by medications or ignored and interrupted by a harried environment, the patient is unable to draw on the healing power of the relationship between the one and the One. The nurse also needs to draw on the power of the relationship between the one and the One. If she has a harried schedule and there are other factors that diminish her ability to feel, there is interference in the relationship between the one and the One. This in turn diminishes both her health and her ability to help the patient. Empathy is one of the feelings that can be lost in such an environment. The mystic experience suggests that a healthy relationship between the one and the One is essential for healthy relationships between one person and another; that is, unless an individual is spiritually healthy, it is very difficult or impossible to be "with" other individuals. Hence, anything that dulls feeling—either medications in the case of the patients or a harried work schedule forcing detachment from the patient in the case of the nurse—diminishes health. Feelings are important to health. Treatments that are impersonal and medications that merely blunt feelings cannot restore health.

From the foregoing I conclude that an environment that facilitates contemplation, or at least does not interfere with it, and nurses who are able to maintain a high level of spiritual health for themselves, are very important for promotion of the health of the patient and of the nurse.

What has been said about mysticism also helps understand how a patient can be healthy even in a condition of terminal disease. When the nurse tailors treatments with the spiritual health of the patient in mind, she attempts to achieve a delicate balance between relief from over-whelming feelings that restrict the patient's ability to experience others and the One, with the blunting of feelings that are just as restrictive.

DESCARTES

While deep in thought about the message of mystical experience and its relevance to nursing, I almost bump into a figure sitting alone in the main hallway in St. Francelyn's. I looked up and saw that it was the fig-ure of a man. His face was familiar from pictures I had seen in philoso-phy books.

Can René Descartes shed light on the relationship between univer-sality and singularity as it is encountered in nursing? Further, what might his views be about the mystics?

Descartes brushed off his clothes as he spoke and composed himself after our barely missed collision. I heard your conversations with the mystics. Had I had been there, he said, I would have asked some impor-tant questions that were left unaddressed. For example, how is it possi-ble to *know* anything? For that matter, how can I be assured that even my own existence is real? I, for one, am not convinced of the "truths" to which mystics lay claim. My reflections about truth led me down a completely different path and to different conclusions. Incidentally, did the mystics talk about some of the untoward consequences of the "truth" according to their visions?

Descartes aroused my curiosity. What untoward consequences? I asked him.

Holy wars, for one, came the clipped and direct response.

Holy wars, what do you mean, holy wars?

The kind of holy wars that leave thousands dead and injured fight-ing to establish the "real truth" revealed to one group opposing the "heathen truths" revealed to another group.

Descartes was talking about the bloody wars fought in the name of God. The Crusades were an example. Hildegard of Bingen supported the Crusades as necessary to convert those who did not hold the same truths as the Catholic Church. And the Inquisition is notorious in the history of human cruelty in the name of a spiritual good. Descartes' observations about the manner in which one group imposes "truth" on another calls attention to the possible misuses of the mystic vision. Though the vision is neutral with respect to particular religious traditions, it has sometimes been used to support the intolerant views of particular traditions or religious organizations. Such misuse of the "truth" extracts its toll in human suffering. Descartes noticed that his remarks had an effect on me. He had my full attention.

Descartes continued. When people claim to "know," they have a tendency to act on their professed knowledge. But if what they profess to know is not really knowledge, too often it is the case that what one person "knows" is in conflict with what another person "knows." If there is a conflict, at least one person has to be wrong. In my experience almost all who profess to know are mistaken. This does not mean that I disagree with the mystics when they claim that some knowledge is based on direct awareness. On the contrary, I believe in the usefulness of intuition. What I call intuition is direct awareness, and it is the ground of the little knowledge I can say that I actually possess. Only when the object of the direct awareness is clear and distinct is it possible to make a knowledge claim on the basis of the awareness.[57] But the mystics claim direct awareness of a Presence that they call God or the One. If the Presence is God or the One, then It is infinite. And if it is infinite how can it be clear and distinct to a finite mind? But unless the object of intuition is clear and distinct, knowledge is impossible. I have no problem with the mystic who is careful not to make claims about the truth of his religion or dogma on the basis on the mystic experience; my problem is with those who make the leap from the mystic experience to the claim that it validates their particular religion or doctrine. In my time too much blood has been shed by individuals who failed to properly limit their knowledge claims. Be careful that such does not happen in your time.[58]

Descartes continues. *One avoids extremes by limiting knowledge claims to what is actually known. I am interested in science.* I think nursing is interested in science too. *One of the hopes I had in my time was that science could be developed in the areas you call physics and perhaps, biology.*[59] If so, I additionally hoped that discoveries in these new sciences might help in relieving many people of their physical problems.

I ask Descartes what he means by "knowledge," and how does knowledge differ from belief? What is the difference between knowledge and science? Does knowledge come from the senses perhaps?

Descartes assures me that knowledge does not come from the senses. The senses are unreliable. Haven't we all one time or another been fooled by the senses?[60] The artist, Escher, in your time, made a career out of enabling the senses, especially the sense of sight, to fool persons. Furthermore, the information provided by the senses is too vague to be a foundation for knowledge. The information is too qualitative and subjective. There is no way of knowing whether two people see the same thing in the same way. Information from the senses will not help you in your search for universality and singularity in nursing experience. You cannot get much more subjective than information acquired through the senses. In fact, sense experience is not much less subjective than the mystic experience. The problem is the same in both cases. No one person can know what another is experiencing, especially when the object of experience is unclear and indistinct. The result is that both mystical experiences and sense experiences are too uniquely individual to be a basis for knowledge. So, if you want to understand that which is repeatable and shareable you will have to find something else other than mystical experience and sense experience.

Now Descartes really has raised my curiosity. I always thought information coming through the senses, although somewhat subjective, was shareable—that others heard the same sounds I heard, saw the same colors I saw, felt the same textures I felt. What does Descartes mean that this is subjective, not shareable or repeatable?

Descartes responds as if he were reading my mind. *Information through the senses is subjective. Although there may be agreement between two or more persons about some sensory phenomenon, another person might come along and disagree. Disagreement means lack of certainty. Lack of certainty is inconsistent with knowledge; one only knows what is indubitable.* Again, *there is no way for one person to know what another person experiences.*[61] There is room for doubt that you see the same color that I see. Although we may both use the same color term, for example "green," there is no way of knowing that we are experiencing the same color. I may see green a little differently than you see green. We learn to use the color terms by noticing what other people call "green." But I cannot know that the object I am looking at is really green, or if it is, that the shade I see is the same as the shade you see.

Descartes continues. *I looked for something indubitable in the hope that if it were indubitable for me, it would be indubitable for everyone. Unfortunately, my best example of something that was indubitable, was my own existence as a thinking thing. At any time I was capable of doubting my own existence, I could safely conclude that I existed. Because if I did not exist, I would be incapable of doubting my own existence. Therefore, the proposition "Descartes does not exist" must be false at any time that I, Descartes, question its truth or falsity.*[62] *I think therefore I am.* In this argument I am using both intuition and logic. The intuition allows me to know my unique existence in a unique moment of time. Logic allows me to draw the conclusion that I must exist. But of course this provides no ground for others to know that I exist, or for me to know that others exist. Someone else can doubt my existence. Therefore, the knowledge that I gain from the cogito argument is private and unique rather than public and general. But my worry is how to get from the private and unique to the public and general.

Remember, a science is a body of systematic public knowledge (not just private knowledge as in my cogito argument). Again, *knowledge is not knowledge unless it is indubitable.* And nothing can be indubitable and public, unless it is universal and necessary. The universal and the necessary is that which is true for all times, all places, and all people. Aristotle was wrong in his belief that science could be about that which was for the most part. This allows doubt. *In my time the only sciences were arithmetic and geometry. That "triangles are three-sided rectilinear plane figures" is part of geometry. This example of knowledge follows from the clear and distinct idea of a triangle. And the proposition "2 + 3 = 5" is also indubitable, and part of a body of knowledge, arithmetic. I had hoped to convert private knowledge into the public knowledge in other areas, such as physics and biology, thereby creating sciences of physics and biology. This had not been accomplished in my time.* I am sorry to say that physics and biology have not become sciences in your time.[63] Further, from the vantage point of your time, I doubt that they will ever become sciences. It has become clear that there will never be any empirical sciences, for the use of the senses introduces doubt into all of the theories and propositions of these so-called sciences.

Descartes' narrow view of science is puzzling. If we have to wait for certainty before a discipline becomes a science, then many of the life-saving discoveries of biology, anatomy, chemistry, physiology, neurophysiology, and so on, were not discoveries of science. But if they were not discoveries of science then what do we call them? And if they are not part of science, how can these discoveries be as useful as they are? Does their usefulness indicate something about their truth?

Perhaps Descartes' reluctance to acknowledge that the biological disciplines were sciences originated in part from the morally offensive nature of the means used to obtain information in these disciplines. Galen's original work in anatomy and physiology was updated in the sixteenth century by Vesalius. According to at least one account, Vesalius practiced vivisection on condemned criminals, with the excuse that they were scheduled for execution anyway.[64] What does one do with information obtained by morally abominable means? Note that much of our twentieth-century information about blood flow in particular and human physiology in general stems from the work of Vesalius. Descartes may have been unwilling to dignify it by calling it science. However, Descartes' insistence on indubitability was still probably his primary reason for rejecting empirical science. It has become generally accepted, since Descartes' time, that no body of information obtained through observation and experiment can be indubitable.

There are related ethical problems in health care and the health sciences. For example, does experimentation on living animals make us insensitive to pain and suffering, and hence less likely to be moral? That which ought to be done to cure disease and advance the health of the patient is often in conflict with what ought to be done to advance knowledge. The goals of the professional practitioner and the goals of the scientist are very often incompatible. Quest for knowledge of those universals that are general is in conflict with the needs of the individual in his uniqueness (Brencick and Webster 1994).

The nurse has two problems in this area. Remembering Vesalius, was the information used by the nurse obtained by morally acceptable means? And if not, what should be done with the information? The second and equally important question, raised by Descartes and the philosophers that follow him, is whether the information is knowledge. If the information is only likely to be true, but not indubitable, the nurse needs to be aware of this in using the information in the care of a patient. Knowledge of the techniques used in the particular research that provides the information used by the nurse is perhaps even more essential for evaluating the trustworthiness of the information.

I ask Descartes what he means by "thinking thing," and whether this sheds any light on the problem of the uniqueness of the individual.

Descartes continues: *the mind is a thinking thing, a res cogitans. The biology of my time was unable to find the thing that thinks. It made considerable progress in learning about nerves and the brain. But it was apparent that ideas and minds were not going to be found from that point of view. This is because biology is only capable of exploring that which occupies a finite volume of space, that is, is spatially extended. But on reflection I became convinced that minds cannot meaningfully be said to be of finite size. Though they may have a spatial position,[65] they do not occupy finite volumes of space; that is, minds are unextended.* Further, biology could discover nothing that was capable of thinking. *And as a philosopher I thought I understood why the biologist could find no mind in the body. The essences and properties of bodies and minds were inconsistent, so that nothing that counted as a body could be a mind, and nothing that counted as a mind could be a body. To put it more simply, the "I" of the "I think" couldn't possibly be a corporeal substance. It seemed reasonable for me to generalize and say that nothing extended could think; that is, that no corporeal (physical) substance could be a thinking thing, and no thinking thing could be a corporeal substance.[66]*

I ask Descartes, what about the brain? Is this not where thinking occurs?

The brain is a machine that is useful in processing signals from the sense organs and other parts of the body. It may even be useful in storing physical traces which are needed for memory. But the brain cannot think; it is only a compound corporeal substance.[67] *But if injury occurs to the brain, the signals from the outside world to the mind are improperly processed and the mind may be mislead or deceived. The body can trick the mind as in the phantom limb cases that I and my friends encountered on battlefields*, when I spent a few years as a mercenary. *But the brain does not think. The brain merely processes signals for the convenience of the mind. It is the mind that does the thinking, and which is the "I" of the "I think."*

Correct me if I am wrong, Descartes. What you are saying is that the self is really the mind, and that the mind is an incorporeal substance. This substance may dwell in a body during the life of a person, but the body is extraneous to the self. This raises questions about when the self begins to exist, and what happens to the self after the death of the body. Since the brain and the mind are two different things, the death of the brain is not necessarily the death of the self.

In addition, I ask Descartes, can you be of help with my question concerning the nature and ground of the element of singularity that guarantees the uniqueness of an individual person? Why is it impossible for a mind to be duplicated? Your notion that minds are simple incorporeal substances seems to undercut their uniqueness one from another. What I mean by that is the "I," the self, the soul, the breath of life, or whatever aliases this incorporeal substance is called, cannot be distinguished one from another. A breath of life is a breath of life is a breath of life. It seems to me that the notion of a simple incorporeal substance leaves unsolved the problem of the ground of the uniqueness of individuals.

My follower Leibniz wrestled with this question. You might ask him about his Principle of the Identity of Indiscernibles, which holds that any two things that are alike in all respects are actually the same thing.

This sounds exactly like what is bothering me about your concept of simple incorporeal substances. Each mind would be indistinguishable from any other mind.

Descartes continues: I rather like what Leibniz did. It fills in a gap in my own thinking. I have to admit that my original presentation left this problem unsolved. How do I account for the irreducible uniqueness of each mind in comparison with all other minds? Initially I thought I resolved the problem by placing minds in different spatial and temporal locations, that is, in different bodies at different times. But I was disappointed by this attempted solution because what made one mind different from another was a spatial-temporal location. *I wanted a clean distinction between mind and body.* What is somewhat disconcerting to me is that space and time may be needed for distinguishing one mind from any other mind. Different minds perceive the physical world from spatially different points of view, and often from different times as well. These differences in perspective guarantee that the thoughts of any one mind will differ from the thoughts of any other mind (in Leibniz's words, different spatial standpoints result in different mirrorings of the universe.) *I admit that I view the mind as a simple incorporeal substance.* As simple incorporeal substances, no one mind differs from any other finite mind. It is disconcerting that it is only the thoughts of minds that distinguish one from another, but not the substance of the minds.

I ask Descartes to comment on the distinction between universality and singularity and its application to nursing.

Descartes responds: What makes a person singular or unique is that his body occupies a space and a time different from that of any other body. While a person is living, the mind enjoys a union with the body. Part of what makes a mind unique is that it is in a body occupying a space different from that of any other body, during a time shared with some persons but not all persons. But here I run into some problems. I do not want the uniqueness of an individual mind to be entirely dependent on or reducible to the uniqueness of an individual body. Because if the mind were dependent on the body for its uniqueness then when the body died, the mind would die. *But the mind as a simple substance will survive the death of the body.*

Hence, Descartes continues, there must be an additional ground of singularity for a mind, in addition to that which is derived from its occupancy of a particular body. But I cannot say what this additional ground might be. I am torn between believing that it is the distinctness of one finite mind from all others just as substances, and thinking that it is difference between the thoughts or experiences of each mind that grounds their uniqueness or singularity. The problem with the first option is that the stuff of any one mind seems indistinguishable from the stuff of any other mind. The problem with the second option is that I regard thoughts or experiences as merely accidents of minds. Hence I cannot solve this problem.

Do you have any guesses concerning when the mind first enters the body? And do you have any guesses concerning where the mind goes and what it does after the death of the body? In my time abortion is thought by some to be murder because they believe that the soul is present from conception or from shortly after conception. Is the soul the same as what you are calling the mind? If the soul leaves the body, when does it leave the body? I am assuming that to be human is the same as having a soul or a mind.

Descartes replies. *I mean by the word "mind" a thinking substance.*[68] If so, the thinking substance may not exist until birth. Before that time, the fetus might possess a soul in the sense in which any animal has a soul. If so, that kind of soul is part of the body and dies with the body. If one means by a soul a thinking thing, a mind, then a soul does not exist until about the time of birth. I, Descartes, do not like the word "soul" because it is ambiguous, and also because I do not find it useful for making sense of animals. In the case of persons the word "mind" is clearer and hence more useful. *Humans have minds. Animals are just machines.* As to where the mind goes after the death of the body, I have no idea. *But I am convinced that it will continue to exist.*[69] But just where it will exist and what it will be doing I have no way of knowing.

Descartes' account of the ground of the singularity of minds leaves me puzzled and unsatisfied. I have several lingering questions. I am not sure I understand Descartes' notion of a disembodied thinking thing. Without senses and a body, what would such a mind think about? A subject without objects of experience is impossible. Descartes has defined minds as thinking substances. If so, a mind ceases to be a mind if it ceases to think, and is not a mind until it begins to think. Does he mean to imply that the prenatal infant and the comatose patient are not human because they do not possess minds? Or is the potentiality for thought sufficient to allow that something is a mind? Perhaps there is something wrong with Descartes' mind-body distinction? Could it be that mentality is after all a function of the body? But this would require that the body consist of more than just the mathematical qualities that Descartes ascribes to it. Mathematical qualities can't think.

And there is another problem, empathy. If I can only intuit my own existence as a mind, but not the existence of any other mind, then how can I truly empathize with the feelings of another person? Is it not the case that empathy presupposes direct awareness of the feelings of the other? But in Descartes' picture of reality each substance is independent of the other substances. Consequently experience is private, not a possible object of experience on the part of another mind. But this extreme disconnectedness of one person from another is not only inhuman, but is inconsistent with nursing experience. If I were a Cartesian nurse, I would have no way of knowing whether my patient was suffering from experiences similar to ones I have suffered from in my past. Inferences from facial expression and body movements cannot be relied on. I have no direct awareness of the mind of any other person. Since other people have bodies that are similar to mine, I guess that they also have minds. But for all I can know they may be just clever automata.

THE EMPIRICISTS: HUME

Perhaps I may be of some help with the problem of distinguishing the elements of universality and singularity in individuals, says David

Hume. *First I would warn you not to try to solve the problem too easily by engaging in speculative metaphysics.*[70] Descartes engaged in speculative metaphysics when he described the self as a thinking substance (Hume 1978, p. 251ff.). By the way I can appreciate what you are trying to do in nursing. You are trying to make sense of the knower, which is a metaphysical problem, and what the knower can claim to know, which is an epistemological problem. I concentrated on the epistemological problems, limiting my forays into metaphysics to what could be justified epistemologically. Perhaps nursing is bothered by similar problems because of the relationship between nursing and the so-called medical sciences.

What do you mean by "so-called" medical sciences? I ask.

First of all *I agree with Descartes that in order for something to be a science it must be a systematic body of knowledge. And to make a knowledge claim, the evidence must be sufficient for certainty. A mere body of information, when the information is less than certain, is not a science. Descartes is right. If you did know, you would never have to say "sorry, I was wrong."*[71] Since your so-called medical sciences are merely bodies of uncertain and changing information, they cannot be systematic bodies of knowledge. And hence, they are not sciences.

If they are not sciences, what are they? I ask.

At best, *these are bodies of reasonable belief.*[72] But I have to admit that it is necessary to act on mere reasonable belief. Otherwise, it would be impossible to help anyone or provide them care, as you need to do in nursing. But it is wrong to claim the authority of knowledge when one's information constitutes at best a body of reasonable belief.

If we cannot obtain knowledge in the so-called empirical sciences, why are some beliefs preferable to others? What makes them reasonable? I ask Hume.

Beliefs concerning matters of fact are reasonable to the extent to which they are based on past experience. For example, in my past experience I may have noticed that two events have always accompanied each other. If the two events are contiguous, and one always succeeds the other, I am apt to believe there is a causal connection. It is reasonable to expect them to be connected in future experience. But it is impossible to know that this will be the case. This is because the idea of necessary connection is merely subjective. It is due to habit or association of ideas. Objectively we only experience constant conjunction (Hume 1978, pp. 69–176).

What about statistically significant correlations? I ask Hume. We settle for far less than the constant conjunctions you were seeking. What I mean by that is there is an accepted margin of error, and if the correlation is greater than the margin of error, we suspect that there might be a causal connection between the two factors. We seldom, if ever, find 100 percent correlations.

Hume answers. *It was my strong belief, and I thought it was a natural belief, but not something I could claim to know (for certain), that real causes and effects were always constantly conjoined. If so, then if one had identified the real causes and effects, the correlation would be 100 percent* (Hume 1978, pp. 75–78). Perhaps I had better distinguish knowledge from belief more fully. And in turn, belief in general from reasonable belief. My standard for knowledge is similar to Descartes'. In order to know that a proposition is true, the argument or evidence must be sufficient to remove the possibility of error. But the only realm in which knowledge is possible is that of relations among ideas.[73] The unit of knowledge is the proposition, which is the meaning of a descriptive statement. Propositions are either true or false. *But there is an important distinction between propositions whose truth or falsity depends on relations among ideas, many of these can be known to be true or false, and propositions whose truth or falsity can only be ascertained through experience. The latter I call "matters of fact." The former I call "relations of ideas"* (Hume 1978, p. 94).

Is this something like the relationship between nursing theory and nursing practice, with theory being concerned with relations of ideas and practice with matters of fact?

Hume continues. Before I answer that question more specifically, let me tell you what I mean by relations of ideas. My predecessor John Locke used the word "idea" ambiguously. I try to be more consistent. There are puzzles I have not resolved. *Ideas are copies of antecedent impressions* (Hume 1978, p. 1). *But once an individual possesses an idea, it can be noticed that some ideas are related to other ideas in such a manner that it is possible to know relations among the ideas* (Hume 1978, pp. 70–71). For example, if one possesses the ideas *two, three, five, equals,* and *addition,* one can then know that "2 + 3 = 5" is a true proposition. But what I mean here by the notion that "2 + 3 = 5" has nothing to do with things in the physical world is that in the relations of ideas, the concepts *two, three,* and *five* can be added, subtracted, multiplied, divided without any relationship to things in the physical world.

Hume continues. But as soon as I add two, three, and five sticks, I have a very different matter. In the second situation, I have reasonable belief that two sticks plus three sticks equals five sticks, but I cannot be certain. I must add to my knowledge about the relations between ideas some reasonable beliefs concerning the nature of sticks. In this case I am "contaminating" the complex idea "two plus three equal five" with "facts" in the world. "Facts" in the world are not certain. They are tentative at best. It is interesting that sometimes adding two things in the world with three things in the world you can come up with five things. *But such is not always the case. Information concerning events in the world is not certain. That is why I make a distinction between "relations of ideas" that can result in knowledge and "matters of fact" that are about things in the world and as such are always tentative. And that which is tentative is not knowledge. It is belief.*[74]

But I object to what Hume is saying about the uncertainty about two sticks plus three sticks equaling five sticks. I have seen it myself. Others have seen it too. Why cannot this be considered knowledge?

Hume says, Aha! Have you ever added two cups of sugar to three cups of water? What happened?

As a matter of fact I have, and the result was only three cups of syrup. You are right. Two plus three does not always equal five when the numbers are applied to things in the world.

I am glad you understand my point. It is also interesting that you used the phrase "matter of fact" to preface your last comment. *Matters of fact always spoil the certainty that exists among relations of ideas.* But in nursing you must include matters of fact, even in your theories. By that I mean that you want your nursing theories and practice to be related to the world. If you restrained yourself to relations of ideas, your knowledge would be certain but *trivial*. Let me give you another example with more meaning for your nursing practice. The number ten is an idea. As an idea it is always the same. But when ten is related to matters of fact the meaning of ten changes. For example, a loss of ten pounds for an overweight adult is very different from a loss of ten pounds for a newborn infant. The idea of ten remains the same, but this is trivial. What is significant is that the loss of ten pounds would improve the health of the first individual and kill the second individual.

Ah, I understand, I tell Hume. But may I change the subject? There is a related matter that still confuses me. Why are you called an empiricist?

There are several reasons why people call me an empiricist. First, my predecessors are John Locke and George Berkeley. The three of us are called British Empiricists, because first of all we are British and secondly *we believe all ideas are derived from sense experience, and that any significant knowledge we might happen to have is founded on experience.* The root meaning of the word "empiricist" comes from the Latin and Greek words that mean "experience." In fact there was a school of medicine that practiced solely on the basis of experience without the aid of theory or science. They were also called empiricists.[75] However, this is too narrow a meaning of empiricism. I believe that nursing needs both theory and those bodies of reasonable belief based on past experience that you call the empirical sciences. But be careful when you use such phrases as "actual truth." Actual truths are empirical truths, that is, contingent truths. But no matter of fact or actual truth is demonstrable, because all matters of fact are contingent. I have observed what you call medical sciences in your century. I am bothered by the fact that authority is claimed on the basis of knowledge, when there is no knowledge, but only reasonable belief.[76]

Yes. I have observed that a tentative suggestion from a research study, often statistically significant but with a small population sample, is sometimes used by the health care practitioner as a ground for ordering everyone in a certain population group to accept a prescribed therapy. For example, all elderly persons may be prescribed baby aspirin, because a study suggests this might be helpful in reducing the incidences of heart attacks and strokes, or all newborn babies in a hospital are required to sleep on their backs or sides, because a study has suggested a significant positive correlation between SIDS (sudden infant death syndrome) and sleeping on the stomach. When authority is based on such tentative information the authority is unfounded. Further I have noticed that if a patient objects, he or she is branded as noncompliant. In fact these research studies are only preliminary, and must be supplemented with many further studies investigating undesirable as well as desirable correlations with the practice being investigated. For example, with infants, if there is a tendency to vomit, the risk of suffocation from emesis may well be greater than the risk of SIDS. Or with the elderly, the assumption that pills will solve most problems might lead to an overreliance on medications instead of the healthier life habits that are needed.

I (continuing) just thought of something in relation to what you were saying. If medical knowledge is merely tentative matter of fact or reasonable belief, then why do we have such phrases as "doctor's orders"? It seems to me that "doctor's orders" implies authority. But you say that this authority is unfounded because of the nature of matters of fact. So how would you change the wording of "doctor's orders" to reflect the actual status of medical knowledge?

Hume answers that the phrase "doctor's suggestions" would be more appropriate in reflecting the tentative status of the reasonable beliefs that exist in this area. Of course, no such diagnosis as "noncompliance" would make any sense.

I know we have digressed a bit. But this is helpful to me as a nurse. I have been worried about the implications of the term "noncompliance," because it seemed to me that there was no knowledge base sufficient to ground the authority presupposed by the term "noncompliance." Morally it is important to allow an individual to take his own risks, to apprise him that the treatment recommended is a gamble, and give him reasons why the gamble is thought to be reasonable, and to give him alternatives, if possible. I have also been confused about the relationship between scientific research and clinical practice. Somehow the words "this study *suggests* that" is translated by the clinician to read "this study *proves* that" and that therefore anyone who resists this conclusion is doing themselves harm, is incompetent, is noncompliant, and is in denial. I appreciate your helping me be a little clearer about these matters.

Hume says that he is glad that he could be of help. But I want to caution you about tilting too far in the opposite direction, of holding that all beliefs are equal. *In my opinion, reasonable beliefs have to be based on past experience. Beliefs that are not based on past experience are mere superstition. I also mean by experience, sense experience* (Hume 1978, book 1). I do not know what to make of the mystics claim to another kind of experience, direct awareness. To their credit, I know of no reputable mystic who has tried to base specific reasonable beliefs on the mystic experience. I cannot claim to know that God or the One does not exist.

I ask Hume, if it is past experience that makes a reasonable belief reasonable, does this not imply that you have memory of past experiences, and if that is so, does this not imply that in some sense the past is present in the present?

Present in the present? I am not sure what you might mean by that. In my opinion each event is a unique individual, separate from all other events. This applies to impressions and ideas as well as physical events.

Doesn't that create problems with memory? I ask Hume. How is memory possible unless in some sense the past experience is present in the present experience?

I admit that memory was a problem for me, says Hume with a sigh, as was personal identity (Hume 1978, pp. 189–191, 251).

Are these problems connected with the problem with universals? I ask Hume. I understand that you followed your predecessor George Berkeley in his position that the only universals were words, that aspects of actual events could be referred to with the same word because of *resemblances* between what were otherwise unique individuals (Hume 1978, pp. 17–25). Since I am concerned with the contrast between universals and the element of singularity in individuals, I wonder if you can shed further light on your position concerning universals.

My followers in the twentieth century were able to articulate more fully the problem that Berkeley and I found with words, a problem that forced us to admit that there were some universals, namely words. But to admit that there were universals beyond words seemed too speculatively metaphysical for my taste. The distinction of my twentieth-century followers that helps is that between *types* and *tokens*. In my view, every actual event or thing is a unique individual. This includes each occurrence of a word, whether written or spoken. The individual occurrences of words are called *tokens*. But to understand a word it is necessary to understand the *type* that the token represents. For example, in this paragraph the word "word" occurs more than once. Each occurrence is a distinct *token*, but all occurrences of the word "word" are occurrences of the same *type*. Hence, I was forced to admit that there was at least one species of universals, words.[77]

If there is one kind of universal, why not other kinds? Also, why are you so convinced that existent events and things are uniquely individual? What grounds the element of singularity?

Hume frowns and answers, it is not just persons or things that are unique individuals, but each event is also a unique individual. This is part of what I had in mind when I wrote that I had an idea of personal identity but no notion of how the idea originated. But I should explain that by personal identity, I had in mind the ability of an individual to be the same individual in spite of having changed as time passes, but also the fact that each individual is different from all other individuals. The element of singularity that you are searching for would account for this sameness and differences. But I have no clear notion of the origin of this idea, of the singularity for which you are seeking. My suspicion is that it may have something to do with space and time as Descartes has already speculated. Also, my predecessor John Locke speculated that it was memory of past personal experiences that allowed an individual to be the same individual as time passed and changes occurred. This same continuity of memory he tried to use to distinguish one individual from other individuals. I suspect that memory will be inadequate for solving your problem, because memory can be false. Note the controversy in your time about the validity of recalled suppressed memories.

What I have learned from David Hume that applies to nursing and the problem of universality and singularity is that the results of empirical research are always tentative, though they provide the best or most reasonable grounds for action. Since these results are tentative, they should not be used by the health care provider as a ground for authority in decision making. Given the tentativity of empirical research, it is only reasonable that the health care consumer be afforded the opportunity to take his or her own risks. The health care provider makes suggestions, but does not give orders. The health care consumer has the right to ignore the suggestions of the health care provider without being labeled "noncompliant" or "in denial." Also, by being more honest about what is known and not known, and especially what is only reasonable but not known, the health care provider may reduce exposure to litigation.

With respect to universality and singularity, Hume has left me with the positive insight that events, not just things and persons, are unique individuals. But he has not been very helpful in explaining the ground of the singularity that makes individuals unique. He has also not been very helpful about the problem of universals. His nominalism is too extreme to be useful. His insights about both memory and personal identity are frustratingly unsatisfactory. But his debunking of the claim of the empirical sciences to be sciences in Descartes' sense seems fundamentally correct.

CHAPTER 4

Universality and Singularity in Nursing Practice as Illuminated by Imaginary Discussions with Modern and Contemporary Philosophers

IMMANUEL KANT, MARTIN HEIDEGGER

May I be of some help in your quest? asks Immanuel Kant. *I too have been troubled with the relationship between universals and what you call the element of singularity that makes individuals unique. I have also been troubled by the status of science, especially physics. Further, I was troubled by the fact that we possessed everyday nonscientific knowledge, which should have been impossible on Hume's account.* Since these issues overlap in nursing and other areas, I will discuss them together.[1]

Please do, I said.

Kant continues. Perhaps the easiest way to understand some points on which I differ from Hume is to return your example of the newborn infant. You know, I never had any children, and some say that I died a virgin having never left Konigsberg. I will only confirm that I never left Konigsberg, the rest is for me to know and you to find out. But continuing with the dawning of experience in the transition from the womb to the outside world, let's pretend that there is a Baby Kant and a Baby Hume.[2]

Baby Hume and Baby Kant are both startled by the birthing experience, and both cry. They both notice that a sudden change has occurred, and for both this is about the first event they are consciously aware of—consciousness dawns at this moment in time. But notice what I said here that in both infants there was a change noticed. For Baby Kant change implies that there was a before in contrast to the now, and that will be an after (future). At this moment of the dawning of awareness—before, now, and later—the structure of time is already present.

Next Baby Kant notices freedom of movement compared to the vague memory of enclosedness in the womb. Opening his eyes, but struggling with the blurredness consequent on the medication that has just been put into his eyes, he notices the difference between the light in one direction, and darkness of the door in another direction, the moving figures hovering over him. *But to say "his eyes" is a little misleading, because he does not yet distinguish "himself" from the "world" and as a consequence he does not yet have the ability to distinguish (empirical) reality from dreams.*[3] But in noticing the difference between an object in one direction and objects in other directions, some of which are moving, he begins to be aware *of space as well as time*. But just as with time there will be something happening later than now and something that happened earlier than now, so with space the infant is vaguely aware that there must be something beyond anything in sight, and something even beyond that, though none of these things are in his present sight. *But the full dawning of this awareness awaits the unfolding of other aspects of experience such as ability to distinguish self from world* (Kant 1965, p. 244ff).[4]

The newborn infant is initially unable to distinguish self from world. This is something that becomes possible only when the infant starts to impose a concept of permanence on things in the world, by this I mean that things do not just appear and disappear (Kant 1965, pp. 212–17).[5] The infant becomes confident that when he turns his gaze away from his mother, that she will still be there when he turns toward her again. And by the way, Baby Hume might not be so confident that his mother doesn't disappear when he is not looking. Though he also soon comes to believe in her permanence. *Finally Baby Kant learns to see events as involving connections* (Kant 1965, pp. 218–32).[6] If I cry, mother or someone comes. And if I vary the manner in which I cry, different things happen. I can be fed. My diapers can be changed. Or I will be cuddled. *But Baby Kant doesn't yet know what the word "I" means in this context, though the beginnings of meaningfulness are there* (Kant 1965, pp. 244–51).[7]

I am following you, I said to Kant. But I am curious, how does the word "I" become meaningful? How does the infant come to an awareness of self?

This is a very important question. It is central to understanding my philosophy.[8] Return to the baby in the crib. I don't mean to say that a baby is born self aware, nor that a baby has understanding of such things as space and time, and the manifold of space-time. The baby becomes initially aware of chair there, and mother sometimes in chair, and of the difference between crib here and chair there. A bit later comes awareness of room around crib and chair, and of house around room. Eventually the house is experienced as part of a neighborhood, the neighborhood of a community, and the community as part of the world. But this is done not in terms of actual experiences of all of the different places, but of realization that all places are within the one space.

Now let's look at time. Any new mother of Konigsberg will tell you that infants are born with no sense of time. When they are hungry, they want to be fed, and it doesn't matter that it is the middle of the night or in the middle of some important social event. But eventually the infant recognizes that some times are better for getting food then other times. He notices, for example, that when the sun is up and light floods his room, mother is more apt to answer his cry for food than when it is dark. When it's dark, and all is quiet, it is time to sleep. And when it is light, it is time not only to eat but to engage in other pleasant experiences like playing and going for walks outside. But the infant also begins to notice that day follows night. Then spring follows winter, year follows year, birthdays mark remembrances of his personal past.

Time like space is part of a continuum.[9] *There aren't two different times, rather all times are part of the one time of the world. Nor are there different spaces. All places are within the one space of the world. This space-time manifold (Kant 1965, Aesthetic) is necessary for consciousness and it is universal for experience. You cannot have awareness of an object of sensation without awareness of place in the one space. By the same token you cannot have sensuous intuition of an occurrence without awareness of its date in the one time. Since the one space and the one time of the world are singular individuals and combined are the container within which one places any object of sensation (sense datum), I call them the pure (empty) forms of sensuous intuition. Because space and time are universal and necessary I call them "a priori." While the space time manifold is the only pure form of sensuous intuition, it is not the only thing that is a priori (Kant 1965, Aesthetic).*

Let me explain the *a priori*, especially the synthetic *a priori* by returning to the example of Baby Kant. Baby Kant is now a toddler, sitting up in a high chair with a cookie and a glass of milk. I do not mean to say that Baby Kant is aware of the space time manifold itself and of all of the nuances of substance and causal connectedness. But just the same, as he experiments with the cookie and the milk, *he finds it necessary to use the forms of intuition, space and time, and the a priori concepts of substance and causality, which become categories when time is added to them, for making sense of what he is witnessing* (Kant 1965, 107, 113).

Baby Kant dips the cookie (substance) in the glass of milk (another substance) and sees and feels the increasing mushiness and shrinking of the cookie (causality with time and space). What happened to the cookie? (Substance and causality) He looks (visual sensuous intuition) at the milk and doesn't see (visual sensuous intuition) the other half of the cookie in the milk. (Puzzle raised by the category of substance.) But when he takes a drink of the milk he discovers that it is thicker and tastes like cookie. Further he feels actual fragments of the cookie in the milk. The situation becomes clearer to Baby Kant when he learns to impose the *a priori* concept of substance on the cookie. *This concept really amounts to permanence in time.* This concept allows him to understand that half of the cookie merely changed form, it did not disappear. His *understanding* is confirmed when he drinks the milk. Another *a priori* concept is also useful, that of causality. Baby Kant has discovered that he can cause a change to occur in the cookie by putting it in milk.

Then he puts his hand in the milk. He is surprised, and somewhat relieved, to discover that the milk does not dissolve his hand as it did the cookie. Baby Kant's understanding of both substance and causality is improved. Though the *a priori* concepts of substance and causality do not change, his consciousness of them sharpens as he understands them better.

Now Baby Kant drops the cookie on the floor. He learns a number of things by this type of action. As he gently lets go of the cookie, he is surprised to notice that it doesn't just float in the air or rise like a balloon. It falls rather rapidly toward the floor. In fact it falls rapidly enough so that he has to perform the experiment a number of times to figure out just what happens. *What is universal and necessary in this situation are space and time and causality and substance. But just how the latter two apply to this situation can only be learned through careful observation* (Kant 1965, pp. 180–87).[10]

If the cookie should break as it hits the floor, Baby Kant discovers that, in addition to soaking it in milk, there is another way to change the cookie, consistent with both causality and substance. *All change requires a cause* (Kant 1965, p. 185). But the cause of hitting the floor at sufficient speed results in a different kind of change than the cause of soaking in milk. And if his mother is sufficiently patient, and the supply of cookies sufficiently large, Baby Kant may eventually confirm the Newtonian law of gravitational acceleration.

Now suppose that the family dog enters the kitchen area just at the time Baby Kant is performing his experiments with gravity. It isn't long before the dog discovers the cookies and consumes several. Now the cookie has disappeared. *But the category of substance reassures Baby Kant that the cookie still exists* (Kant 185, p. 184). It is just inside the dog.

But then the dog wants more cookies. Baby Kant discovers that he has the power to affect the behavior of another living thing, the dog. That he *can* affect the dog, making the dog sad or happy, by withholding or sharing cookies, allows Baby Kant to begin to understand what it means to be a self.[11] The dog illustrates the concept of substance in being permanent in time. Baby Kant notices that he himself has a body somewhat like that of the dog. Both have eyes, ears, and limbs, and live and move. He concludes that he, Baby Kant, also has permanence in time. Yet there are differences between Baby Kant and the dog. For example, Baby Kant notices that he has hands and the dog doesn't. And he also notices that both have the power to affect events outside their bodies. By pleading, the dog gets a cookie. Baby Kant can please the dog by giving it a cookie. The dawning of self-awareness begins in this recognition of others and in the relationships between self and other (Hegel 1966). This is the beginning of Baby Kant's *understanding of himself as empirical ego,*[12] from the standpoint of theoretical reason, because he is beginning to understand or know that he and the dog exist together in the same world and both endure through time (Kant 1965), and of himself as a noumenal ego with the power to act, from the standpoint of practical reason, because he can bring about changes in the world around him (Kant 1956).

And what about Baby Hume in the same situation, I ask Kant?

Kant says that Hume would claim that Baby Hume has *no ideas except those that come from individual experiences.*[13] As a consequence Baby Hume initially has serious difficulties in connecting one experience with another. Baby Hume cannot know that there is place beyond his room or that things will be happening later than those that are happening now. In the cookie and milk experiment, Baby Hume cannot know with any certainty that the next time he dunks the cookie in the milk it will also dissolve. However, Baby Hume comes to believe that this will happen after a few experiments with the cookie. What is puzzling is why Baby Hume comes to believe this, since he lacks *a priori* concepts of causality and substance as well as *a priori* intuitions of space and time. Without the synthetic *a priori* I (Kant) am puzzled by Baby Hume's ability to survive; because even a piece of food, like a cookie, cannot be known to be there (on Hume's theory) when he is not looking at it. But Baby Hume has *"natural beliefs"*[14] that are surprisingly like my *a priori* concepts and intuitions, and also surprisingly like Descartes' notion of an innate idea. These "natural beliefs" allow Baby Hume to grow up and write books in philosophy.

How do the natural beliefs arise? I ask.

On that issue Hume and the other empiricists are between a rock and a hard place. On the one hand they want all ideas and beliefs to arise from their individual past experiences. *John Locke,* the first of the British Empiricists, *rejected the doctrine of innate ideas for which René Descartes had been famous.*[15] On the other hand some empiricists in the twentieth century are tempted to extend the insights of biological evolution into the realm of "natural" beliefs, such as the belief that ordinary things don't disappear without a trace. Some beliefs have more survival value than other beliefs. For example for their survival our early ancestors needed to believe that a charging saber tooth tiger would still be there even if the hunter hid his eyes. This is called evolutionary epistemology: "correct" beliefs are simply beliefs that allow their possessors to survive long enough to have progeny. David Hume, himself, seemed to fall back on the position that he as an individual, that Baby Hume, had been conditioned by early experience to believe in causal connections and in the relative permanence (endurance) through time of ordinary things.

Yours has been the major critique of Hume's skepticism, that there is little empirical knowledge, and especially that there are no empirical sciences. How did you happen to come to disagree with Hume so strongly?

Kant answers. *I thought physics had succeeded in becoming science, and therefore that Hume was wrong in his denial that physics was science* (Kant 1950). *Sir Isaac Newton's work was very impressive to me, especially his contributions to astronomy. His universal law of gravitation provided the explanation for the changes in the motion of planets resulting in Kepler's three laws of orbits. But how could a human being know about the laws of nature?* I realized on the one hand that these were laws that applied to all planets in all solar systems throughout the universe and to the motions of stars as well as planets. *But I also realized that such knowledge would be impossible if the objects were independent of the knower. Such knowledge is possible only if the knower is contributing to the objects that which is known; that is, if the objects are conforming to the knower rather than the knower to the objects.*[16] In this case Newton is contributing the concept of law to his observation of the motion of the planets. *By "law" I mean that which is universal and necessary, always and without exception.* On the other hand, if the objects were independent of the knower, the knower could not know that these objects had the universal and necessary characteristics needed for law and predictability. *These same universal and necessary characteristics, which allow for predictability, also allow the objects to be recognized as physically real. And what I mean by "physically real" is that these objects are public, that is objects for the experience of all persons. They are not private objects, not just objects of subjective experience as a hallucination would be, for example* (Kant 1965, pp. 120–75).[17]

Kant continues. *On the other hand, if the knower conformed to the object, that is, allowing the object to actively change the subject, then Hume's skepticism would be unavoidable. The object might effect one subject in a way differently from another subject, and there would be no way of knowing about such differences* (Kant 1965, pp. 120–75). You and I would have no common ground on which to know the object because your notion could not be known to be similar to my notion. Your knowledge of the object would be private, and mine would be private because there would be no way of knowing that any two objects would have the same effect on the two different subjects. In addition there would be no way of knowing that the same object would have the same effect on even one subject at different times. In the example of Newton and the laws of orbital motion, the fact that the Moon obeyed the laws would be of no use in knowing that Jupiter's satellites obeyed the same laws. Further, the knower would be unable to distinguish the empirically real objects from products of the knower's subjective imagination. *But if the object is conforming to the knower, then knowledge is possible concerning those universal and necessary structures imposed by experience on the object. This is because every subject can know that these universal and necessary structures will be present in every physically real object. I call these structures the forms of intuition and the concepts of the understanding. And it is exactly these structures that allow the knower to distinguish the physically real from imaginary objects* (Kant 1965, pp. 120–75). It is these structures that are the presuppositions of intersubjective validity. In the example of Baby Kant and the cookies, the fact that mother also acknowledged that the cookie had half dissolved in the milk, confirmed Baby Kant's understanding and use of the concepts of substance and causality. *It is these structures that provide us with a common or public world.*

Let me give you an example from nursing that illustrates the above matters, says Kant. Suppose you walk by a room in St. Francelyn's and see a figure lying in bed with an IV in place. Your initial response is that this must be a patient. As the subject of experience you impose the form, patient, on the figure in the bed—you see the lump as a patient. Two other nurses pass by and see the same figure lying in the bed, and concur that this is a patient. You have intersubjective validity. All three nurses see the same figure and impose the same empirical concept, patient. But the very notion of "same figure" would be impossible without the imposition of universal and necessary forms, which I call categories.

Kant continues. In the example of the figure lying in the bed, even if it were discovered afterwards that all three nurses were mistaken in identifying the figure as a patient, *your ability to correct the mistake would rest on your success in identifying the figure as physically (empirically) real. If it is physically real, you know that as time passes it is the same figure. Even when the figure did not remain in your sight, at all times, for example you were out in the hall, you knew that the figure continued to exist. It did not simply disappear and reappear, nor did it undergo unexplainable or drastic changes* (Kant 1965, pp. 212–17).[18] Hence, if at a later time you discover that the figure is a student nurse who is lying in bed pretending to be a patient as part of an experiment on what it is like to be patient at St. Francelyn's, then you know that it was a student nurse and not a patient when you first misidentified the figure. This is because *one of the universal and necessary forms is that of substance, and substance is the form of permanence in the face of the passage of time* (Kant 1965, pp. 212–17).[19] The figure on the bed can get up and move to another part of the hospital. It is possible that the student nurse and the patient changed places when you were not looking. But if proper safeguards were taken to prevent this kind of switch from happening, then you know that if the figure in the bed was a student nurse at 12:05 am, it was a student nurse at 11:55 pm. *It is the category of substance (that is, permanence through time) combined with empirical observations (figure, patient, student nurse) that makes this knowledge possible* (Kant 1965, pp. 212–17).[20]

Are you saying, I ask Kant, that knowledge is possible concerning empirically real objects, or in Hume's words, matters of fact? And if so, what are the limitations of the knowledge, if any? And one more question, do you really mean to grant that there are empirical sciences? I remember that you said that physics is a science. Are there other empirical sciences?

Yes to all of these questions, Kant answers. Hume was wrong about knowledge being restricted to immediate sense experience and memory. Time, space, causality, and substance, being imposed by experience on physical objects, allow many conclusions to be drawn about physical events and relations among physical objects (Kant 1950; Kant 1965, pp. 65–281). With the figure in the bed in St. Francelyn's, recognition of its physical reality allowed you to know that it existed continuously (substance) from 11:05 to 12:05 (time), and being physically real it had to have a determinate place in St. Francelyn's (space). *Further, if you should encounter the same person twenty minutes later in the coffee shop, you would know that to get to the coffee shop the student nurse ("patient") had to have decided to get out of bed and walk to the coffee shop* (causality) (Kant 1965, pp. 212–17).[21]

Kant continues. Categories give us knowledge, as in the above example, because the structures we impose on the objects of experience are universal and necessary. *But an immediate consequence of this anal-*

If you cannot know things as they are in themselves, how can you be certain that phenomenal objects are not things in themselves?

I call my idealism "transcendental" because it has to be based on objects of experience. By definition I cannot experience that which is not a possible object of experience. If I am to suppose there are entities that are not possible objects of experience, it must be because of deficiencies in the objects of experience—deficiencies that prove that the objects of experience are not independently real. Reason demands that there be unconditioned conditions, otherwise no explanation can be complete. Morality presupposes that persons are unconditioned conditions of their actions, otherwise persons cannot meaningfully be said to act and would not possess the freedom needed for moral responsibility. But it is impossible for the constructs of experience we call empirical objects to be unconditioned conditions. Our imposition of the concept of causality on physical events makes it impossible for there to be a physical event which is an unconditioned condition. All physical events are conditioned conditions. Hence, the physical world is a world of conditioned conditions. Since reason and morality both demand a reality where there are unconditioned conditions, they demand a reality different from and more fundamental than physical reality. Since this more fundamental reality can be thought by the mind but not known through the senses I call it "noumenal reality" (Kant 1965, pp. 257–75).[26]

What do you mean by "unconditioned conditions," I ask Kant.

Kant explains. "Unconditioned conditions" are self-caused entities. Unlike physical events, each of which is the effect (conditioned) of its predecessors and laws, *a person is unconditioned. A person is not an effect of preceding events and laws but is the condition of his own actions.* Actions are explained by reasons, not by antecedent events, and reasons are not to be confused with laws. *So you have actions flowing from the person with the person being the unconditioned condition of the action.*[27]

Do you know that such a reality, unconditioned conditions, really exists?

Your question uses two terms that are troubling to me, "know" and "exists." I would prefer to say that my hope that there is a more fundamental plane of reality is a justifiable or reasonable hope. But I admit that practical reason assures me that persons are free. What I mean by persons are unconditioned conditions. But the bodies of persons are physically real. This means that the body and all events within it are conditioned conditions while the self remains unconditioned. Can you see a problem? I certainly can, says Kant (Kant 1965, pp. 409–14).[28]

I think I understand where you are going with this problem. How can an unconditioned condition, the self, have an effect on a conditioned condition, such as an event within the body? And how can a conditioned condition, such as events in the body, have an effect on the self, which is supposed to be unconditioned?

These problems bothered me greatly, Kant admits. *I thought I could solve them by assigning freedom to the noumenal world and determinism to the physical part of the phenomenal world* (Kant 1965, pp. 409–14). Unfortunately the actions of a person involve the body. So I need to be able to see the self as the unconditioned condition of such events in the body as are necessary for the performance of an action. The self needs to be able to start chains of events within the body in order to speak, or to move the arm to eat, or perhaps to hit keys in order to use the computers of your time. Using the neurophysiology of your time, the self needs to be able to cause the firings of the appropriate neurons, which are among the causes of the movement of the vocal cords or arm. I did not want to acknowledge that in sense perception or memory the self was allowing objects in the physical world to partially condition the self. I posited an appearance reality distinction between noumena and phenomena that made it difficult for me to acknowledge that there might be reciprocal conditioning of the self by the body.[29]

Kant continues. *Freedom is a presupposition of morality* as it is a presupposition of action.[30] No one is a person unless she is the unconditioned condition of her actions and of the consequences of her actions. These insights were fundamental to my ethics. Granted that persons exist, freedom exists.[31] *If so, I reasoned, that the objects studied by physics and other empirical sciences were not ultimately real, for determinism in the world of physical events was inconsistent with the existence of unconditioned conditions.* But we have practical knowledge that selves are unconditioned conditions.[32] Therefore, our practical knowledge forces us to the conclusion that the physical world is appearance rather than reality. It is a realm of appearance that allows us theoretical knowledge. But that knowledge is restricted to this realm of appearance.

Practical knowledge? I ask.

This is not a term that I would have used during my lifetime. But I must now acknowledge that my followers were correct in one criticism they made of my philosophy. *I thought that knowledge must be theoretical; that the practical was subordinate to the theoretical, that the theoretical sciences like physics were superior* to such professions as engineering and nursing. But Aristotle before me and Heidegger after me both realize that the entities with the power to act provide us with deeper insight into nature than armchair thinking is capable of accomplishing.[33] If something can act, it must be real. Persons can act. Hence persons provide us with deeper insight into nature than the constructs of the physics of my time.[34]

Heidegger wanders over. *Achtung!* Have you been reading my *Introduction to Metaphysics?* he asks.

Yes, I have, answers Kant. In general, I find it too poetic and metaphorical for my taste. I am still not sure that a philosopher should use language in quite the manner that you do. It seems to me that you are being unnecessarily obscure. Yet I must agree with your insight that persons provide a deeper understanding of the nature of nature than is the case with anything else in the world. And I must also agree with you that it is the ability of persons to make and act that gives us the deepest insight into the nature of persons. Further, I must also agree, given history, especially twentieth-century history, that humans are *to deinotaton*, the strangest of the strange. These are among the reasons why I put such heavy emphasis on the moral law, the categorical imperative. *Freedom is terrible, though essential to human nature. It is terrible because it can be controlled only by itself.*[35] The twentieth century demonstrates what can happen when freedom fails to be self-controlling.

Please make some summary comments about the problem of universals and the problem of the singularity that makes individuals unique, I request of Kant.

The most general universals are the concepts of the understanding, which schematized become the categories. I would add empirical concepts to these *a priori* concepts. I suppose that this is what you mean by universals, for this is the formal side of physical reality. This allows you to recognize a chair as a chair and a dog as a dog. *There is another kind of universal to be found in experience itself. For example, the "I think" is the form of pure apperception. Apperception is perception of perception resulting in consciousness. All conscious experience shares with all other conscious experience, potential as well as actual, the fact of having the "I think" as its pure form. In this respect the "I think" is the most general of universals. But it has no content that would individuate, and hence distinguishes no person from other persons. As such it is not fully real. Consciousness is a universal shared by all persons, possible and actual, and hence does not distinguish any one person from any other person* (Kant 1965, pp. 135–61).

Therefore, continues Kant, *it must be the matter of sensuous intuition and the placement of the body of a self within the manifold of space and time that distinguishes one individual from other individuals. We cannot know enough about the noumenal ego to use that knowledge in distinguishing one person from another. The practical solution to the problem comes from our ability to distinguish one body from another, and to trace the history of any particular body down through time from birth to death. This access to the self I called the "empirical ego" in my First Critique.*[36] Your Mary Jones in St. Francelyn's knows herself as a distinct individual different from all other individuals, because as you have already noted, she was born at a time and place at least slightly different from the birthplace of any other individual. And the places her body has been during the time she has lived make her unique as compared with any other individual. This is one important ground of singularity. Though I admit that I would be more comfortable using the noumenal rather than the phenomenal, since the phenomenal is appearance rather than reality. Turning to our "practical knowledge" of the real self, the decisions and actions of any one person distinguish that person from all others.[37]

What about emotions?

I have a deep grained suspicion of emotion, Kant continues. *I believe our emotions may undercut our freedom.*[38] If so emotions may detract from the uniqueness of a person. I think a person is freest when her actions are determined by reason rather than the emotions.

What about reason?

Again reason involves principles that are general universals. As a rational being, each person is like any other person. But the decisions that must be made and the actions to be performed combine universals with that element of singularity the philosophers call "matter" in such a manner as to guarantee the uniqueness of an individual. If so, it is the situation of the person within the space-time manifold of the world that is one of the grounds the element of singularity, for it adds "matter" or content to the forms of reason that results in uniquely individual decisions and actions.

HEGEL AND WHITEHEAD

What I have learned from Kant and from the other philosophers is that individuals are a combination of universals and singularity. Yet that which makes each unique has so far not been fully explained. But progress has been made. The space time manifold of Kant is more helpful than Aristotle's matter (*hyle*). Descartes made his contributions prior to Kant about location in space and time—no two individuals can occupy the same place at the same time.

Yet that only tells me *where* individuals are—that they are necessarily at different places. It doesn't tell me *who* they are. Kant's concern with the self that acts (remembering the baby, the cookie, and the dog) adds a new dimension to the problem of singularity. Actions of individuals not only effect other individuals but introduce an element of novelty or uniqueness into the individual who acts. The baby could have given the dog the cookie, or not, and probably had a lot more choices than have been mentioned; for example, the baby could have eaten half of the cookie before giving the rest to the dog. The notion of many open choices leads to diversity entering the world in opposition to the closedness of causal determinism. Can singularity be partly grounded in the diversity that results from freedom of choice?

Ironically, even singularity is a universal, because all persons have singularity. Singularity as a universal is shared by all individuals. Hence singularity is in a sense a most general universal. Yet singularity is the very opposite of universality. Though singularity is a shared universal, that which is singular in the individual is unique in each individual. For whatever singularity is, it guarantees the uniqueness of an individual. It guarantees that no individual is a universal, that is, that no individual is repeatable or shareable. But if one were to be fooled into thinking that singularity was a simple add-on, like blue eyes or red hair, one would miss the true mystery of what it means to be unique. It is better to look for the grounds of singularity rather than suppose that singularity is a simple quality-like universal. For it is certainly not the latter. One does not just add a dose of singularity to a mixture of universals and get an individual.

Science produces reasonable or natural *beliefs* from the point of view of Hume. And science produces *knowledge* from Kant's perspective. But certainty is elusive to both Hume and Kant. Hume thinks that matters of fact are always uncertain. Kant believes that we can have certainty only of mere appearances, not of things in themselves. (Refer to the Baby Hume and Baby Kant passage, earlier in this chapter.) Only the mystics have found certainty, and then perhaps only at the moment of their vision. But their certainty is known by direct awareness and cannot be shared by others who have not personally experienced the direct awareness. Experience is consciousness of subject in relation to objects in the world. But what experiences? Who is the "I" in the "I think"? How does the "I" become conscious? And how does the "I" become self-conscious?

I notice an odd pair seated at a table in the St. Francelyn Coffee Shop engrossed in conversation. What is even odder is that one of them seems to be drinking beer from a large clear pilsner glass—in St. Francelyn's? The other is having tea. They are from different centuries and different countries. Gottfried Wilhelm Friedrich Hegel, the early-nineteenth-century German idealist, and Alfred North Whitehead, the early-twentieth-century process philosopher who emigrated in late life from England to the United States, are engrossed in conversation.

I ask Hegel, where did you get the beer?

Ssshh! I smuggled it in. The nuns think it is root beer. With due deference to my twentieth-century colleague, I think tea is a most unsatisfactory drink. Quite unmasculine!

Whitehead seems unperturbed by these remarks. In fact he seems unperturbed by almost anything. He is staring intently at the tiny bubbles rising to the surface in Hegel's glass. He is curious about the continuous movement from bottom to top of bubble after bubble. Could he be thinking of his theory of actual occasions? Are these bubbles subjects of their own experience or do they symbolize his actual occasions? I wonder.

I address both of my companions. I have been searching for some enlightenment about the differences between universals and individuals. I especially want to illuminate the ground of singularity that distinguishes one individual from another. My pilgrimage has raised questions concerning consciousness and self consciousness. You might have overheard my conversations with Hume and Kant. I understand that the two of you have some thoughts concerning how consciousness arises. I also understand that you have somewhat different views on the subject than Hume and Kant and perhaps even from each other. Am I right?

I guess I will speak first, says Hegel, just because I am the older. Let's start with experience, the simple kind that all living creatures share. You have no doubt noticed that animals and persons experience the events of the world around them. And you also no doubt have noticed that the experience of a human is more diverse and complex than say that of an amoeba. The common experiences of searching for food, reproducing the species, avoiding pain, and seeking pleasure are all shared experiences. What then makes the human being different from other species on the earth? Can the differences lie only in the complexity and diversity of the experiences? Is it that humans have more choices in their food or selection of mates than the amoeba? Well I for one say that it is not simply quantity of choices, but something else that explains the difference. *In my theory it is consciousness and self consciousness that are the elements that distinguish Mary Jones in St. Francelyn's from the simple amoeba in the laboratory. At some point in the evolution of human beings consciousness began. Perhaps each living human on earth carries with it the historical consciousness of the entire species. This is what I had in mind when I used the term Weltgeist. A "world spirit," if you will.*[39]

Ah, I respond. It is about your phrase "at some point" that I am curious. How and when did it happen for the species as a whole? And more importantly for nursing, how and when does it occur for the individual? Is a newborn human simply infused with consciousness at the moment of birth or does she have consciousness from the moment of conception? How does consciousness come to be, and what is it?

Hegel pauses a moment to take another sip. Well, he begins, *consciousness and self-consciousness don't just happen suddenly. Con-*

sciousness unfolds gradually by stages and degrees both in the history of the species and in the life of each new individual. Progress on the part of the species hastens progress on the part of later generations of individuals. Hence, we can expect an overall brightening or intensification of consciousness as history progresses. In turn, each new individual contributes to the history of the species as a whole. Consider art, religion, and philosophy and in your time the history of various sciences and technology. And of course, the history of nursing and the other health professions are a part of the history of the human species. *The historical context that the individual enters and develops within is different and usually richer for each generation, and is continually changing.*[40] This is an important ground for the singularity you've been asking about. In order to duplicate any one individual it would be necessary to duplicate all of history. Surely you can see the absurdity in this.

Yes. For example, those humans born in the Western world after the major computer revolution of the 1980s have a very different world and range of possibilities than even their own parents. But this tells me about what humans share in common in a generation. What then distinguishes one person from another when they are born at the same time and place?

Experience of experience of experience, replies Hegel.[41]

What do you mean "experience of experience of experience"? I ask.

Ahh, Hegel sighs. But here is the core of the grounds of singularity. Individuals become conscious by experiencing "others" that are not themselves, things and other selves.[42]

But this presupposes the individual can already discriminate self from not self, doesn't it? I ask. How does the individual come to distinguish self from other in the first place?

Through experience, Hegel affirms. Let me explain. In the history of the species and in the history of the individual, the individual notices (experiences) both nonliving objects and living objects. Consciousness begins to dawn when the self experiences inanimate and animate objects in her environment. At first the nonliving and the living objects are indistinguishable from self. As far as the infant is concerned, they are all self, or not self, since she and her world of objects are indistinguishable from each other. The concept of self has not yet dawned for her. Gradually the infant notices that inanimate objects, such as her rattle or her cookies and milk, to use your earlier example, are different from her hands and other living objects. Nonliving objects produce a different effect on the developing child than living objects. Nonliving objects produce joy or pain, amusement or boredom, but cannot inform the individual about who she is.[43]

She quickly notices that experiences with mother are different from experiences with rattle. Experiences with mother produce a range of emotions, new adventures, feelings. The infant receives praise or scolding from her mother, but not from a rattle. At the same time, she notices that some living objects, such as her pet dog, are limited in their responses to her. Her dog cannot praise her or scold her, but can produce the feelings of comfort, pleasure or pain. Her mother and other human beings who enter her experience can give her a sense of self through their variety of responses to her. And the infant in turn learns that she also has an effect on other animate objects. You have already demonstrated this in your example of the infant in the high chair with her dog.[44] The infant will also come to recognize that she has a part to play in her mother's sense of self. If the infant is satisfied, her mother can think of herself as a good mother. If the infant is dissatisfied, then the mother worries about whether she is being successful as a mother. The infant's mother in turn has a part in the recognition of the baby's sense of self too. She is good baby or bad baby depending on circumstance. In this ongoing exchange between persons the sense of self begins to unfold. *The result of this ongoing exchange, of this experience of experience, is the dawning of consciousness.*[45]

I am following your thinking thus far, I respond. Please continue with your explanation. How does the experience of the experience *of the experience* happen? And what is it?

Hegel takes another sip and continues. An amoeba simply experiences objects. Humans can operate on "autopilot" as well when they are preoccupied with other things.[46] But consciousness begins and continues as long as an individual is *aware* of experiencing an object. For example, I might be enthralled the first few times I see an amoeba under a microscope. But later, if I see an amoeba over and over again, I might lose my awareness of viewing the amoeba. I go on "autopilot" until something catches my attention because of its unusualness or importance.[47] Consciousness is associated with the ah ha! But this doesn't just occur at the moment the experience is present. It can occur later. One can become conscious of having experienced something one was not conscious of experiencing at the original time. *As you can see, awareness of awareness is different from a simple awareness of an object.*[48]

But now here is where things get a little more complicated. *When the object of the experience is another experiencing self, different from the first self, and so situated that the second self is experiencing the first self, then the first self begins to experience the second self's experience of the experience of the first self.*[49] This is what I was alluding to with the good mother, bad mother, good baby, bad baby example. This valuation of self by another self helps in the dawning of *self-awareness* or *self-consciousness*. This self-awareness or self-consciousness is what I had in mind by experience of experience of experience. *If the objects of a self were merely inanimate and inexperient, self-consciousness could not dawn. Only another self or person can provide the catalyst for the dawning of self-awareness. Thus it is impossible to become a person except within a community of persons* (Hegel 1966, pp. 1–100). Hence when we treat other persons or are treated by other persons as mere objects, which unfortunately can be a by-product of science and technology, the result is dehumanization and loss or diminishment of self. When others are treated as mere members of classes, universals, or stereotypes, the same result could occur. *And since the advancement of the Weltgeist is dependent upon the mutual self-actualization of individuals within the human species, we have a problem that extends well beyond you and me. We have the survival of civilization itself at stake* (Hegel 1966, 1900).[50]

Oh, I get it. Just like the words of the old songs, "You're Nobody Till Somebody Loves You," and "Love Makes the World Go 'Round" isn't it? I offer jokingly?

Ha! says Hegel. Something like that. *Self-actualization requires other selves.*

OK. I'm following you. But I am still a little troubled by self-perception as related to the experience of self by another. If an individual is simply how others see her, then what happens to her notion of self in the presence of people with differing views about her? And what happens when these views change or are contradictory? How does she manage to endure with some stability?

Hmmmm. May I respond to that? asks Whitehead.

Please do, says Hegel.

Whitehead pours himself another cup of tea, takes a sip and begins. *If the self were limited to present experience of the present experience of others only, a very important dimension of experience would be overlooked. What would be overlooked is the contrast between present and past experience both in self and in the other. The presence of the past in the present not only allows awareness of awareness, including self-awareness, but strengthens the stability of the self in time. It is the presence of the past in the present that grounds endurance, that allows the individual to continue to be the same individual in spite of obvious changes.[51] This same presence of the past experience in the present experience allows the individual to reflect on and compare her own experiences, because of the differences between past and present experience. But if she were to stand back from the present experience, reflect on it, reflect on past experiences, and then integrate the present with the past experiences, she is experiencing the experience of the experience. This is what I mean by an enduring sense of self. Endurance is the result of conformity of present to past experience* (Whitehead 1933). *And further, the new and older experiences upon reflection and integration, open up possible futures for her. She is also creating self through experiences with others.*

When you say "conformity" of present to past experience, you don't mean to say that you are bound by past experience, and to make choices that reflect no new contribution from the present?

Not at all, says Whitehead. *It is impossible to repeat the past. The concern of the present for the past allows a kind of stability for the self in the face of change. Permanence and flux must be balanced to be a healthy living person* (Whitehead 1978, part 1, ch. 2).

I address both Whitehead and Hegel. In my work as a psychiatric nurse I have encountered many persons who have not been able to adequately balance permanence and change. In addition, they have great difficulty with self-actualization and self-awareness. Perhaps the greatest difficulty for a psychiatric nurse is trying to engage in a dialogue with his patients, a dialogue that is genuine in the sense that both persons are open to new options. This is especially true with student nurses, who as novices are often applying textbook responses to their patients, and other new people within the field. But it is also true of the more experienced nurse. Genuine dialogue presupposes that the subjective experience of both persons is accessible to the experience of the other. When I say accessible, I am really saying shareable, because if it were not shareable, it would be impossible for the "other" to experience my experience. Only if the "other" can pull from his experience something similar is it possible for him to understand and empathize with my experience. Oddly the self actualization of both persons requires shared universals as well as their unique individuality.

But only universals are shareable. It follows that genuine dialogue uses universals to get at unique individual experiences. It is easier for most of us to do this with close friends because we have more shareable experiences. The communication about similar experiences helps in the self-validation of both persons. Each individual feels accepted as an individual through the shared experiences, which allows for further intimacy, which is very valuable for both persons.

But nearly the opposite situation exists for the nurse working with many psychiatric patients. Many nurses working with psychiatric patients, especially the hallucinating patient or the patient with no sense of moral right and wrong, find it necessary to disengage from the patient in order to protect themselves from situations that block or frustrate their own self-actualization. In these circumstances it is psychologically safer for the nurse to treat the patient as a diagnosis or an object, or a product of a chemical imbalance, rather than to treat the patient as a person.

Both Hegel and Whitehead are interested in what I am saying. They encourage me to continue.

There is another equally troubling problem, I continue. We have been discussing the importance of interpersonal relationships in achieving self-actualization. But I would like to offer an additional requirement for self-actualization. There needs to be experience of experience within a person, and not just between persons. In my nursing experience, I have encountered persons who have difficulty in being adequately sensitive to aspects of themselves. This includes their own subjective feelings as well as cues from various parts of their bodies. Such persons are often unable to accept their bodies or other aspects of themselves. It is as if they were disengaged from themselves, incapable of and uninterested in genuine dialogue with aspects of themselves. Perhaps they see themselves or their body as imperfect, or recognize that some of their subjective feelings contradict their ideal of their self. Self-actualization requires both interpersonal and intrapersonal relations that are healthy and adequate.

Whitehead says, I agree with what you are saying about intrapersonal as well as interpersonal relations for self-actualization. I do not use the phrase "self-actualization," and in fact prefer other language. The trouble with the use of jargon is that it is a substitution for the actual work of expounding a concept or working out an explanation. *I view the human personality as an enduring route of experience, which requires many subordinate routes of experiences, as well as other selves, for its ability to continue to endure.*[52]

Remember the bubbles in Hegel's glass of beer? Whitehead asks. They reminded me of *my theory of actual occasions. In* Process and Reality *I develop a metaphysics designed to bridge the gap between our understanding of experience and our understanding of physical reality. I noticed earlier in my work that the structure needed for the unity of events within a spatial-temporal world is the same as the structure of experience.* To relate this to nursing, *your experience and your physical body require the same structure. Hence, experience and physical reality are different ways of looking at the same thing. Nothing is inanimate, except that larger wholes may lack the organization to be a single living or experiencing entity.* This is what happened to the boy in your narrative. Parts of his body remained living experiencing entities after he had lost the organization needed to be a living person himself. *A rock is another example of something that as a whole is about as close to being nonliving and nonexperiencing as we can get. But the molecules within it are experiencing entities* (Whitehead 1978, 1967a).[53]

Did I hear you correctly? I ask. Do you really mean to say that molecules are experiencing entities?

Yes. But they lack the complexity for consciousness or self-con-

sciousness. Going down to scales even smaller, atoms are experiencing entities and elementary particles are experiencing entities. Our habit in the sciences of viewing these entities as lifeless and insensitive, as obeying laws mechanically, is pragmatically useful but metaphysically incorrect. An elementary particle is a route of experient occasions,[54] *with its ability to endure, in spite of the fact that its quantum events or experient occasions are always different and new, the result of conformity of present to past experience. Hence, experience is fundamental to all of physical reality.* And further, it is at least conceivable that sufficiently complex and integrated societies of experiencing entities may become conscious and even self conscious experiencing entities as a whole.[55]

Can you give me an example from nursing to illustrate your theory?

I will try, Whitehead continues. Consider the problems faced by the person with Parkinson's Disease. You will recall that learning to walk was more important to you as a toddler than where you were going. The neurons had to learn how to fire proportionately to stimulate the muscles to move in a smooth and uninterrupted fashion. The firings of the neurons had to be coordinated in such a manner as to keep the person's center of gravity where it needed to be for success in walking, and to make compensations for acceleration and deceleration, and starting and stopping of movement. Before long the coordination among these experiencing entities is so precise that the person thinks about where he wants to go rather than about how to walk. I see the living person as being a hierarchy of experiencing entities, where the many become one and are increased by one, namely the person as a whole.[56]

But with the person with Parkinson's disease, coordination among subordinate experiencing entities has at least partially broken down. Those entities that are responsible for producing dopamine are either no longer able to adequately estimate the level of dopamine needed by other experiencing entities within the brain, specifically in the substantia nigra, or they are no longer able to supply the quantity of dopamine that is required. The result is that the ability of the substantia nigra to experience adequately is diminished. These various subordinate experiencing entities continue to experience, but without the coordination that allows the person to function smoothly as a whole. They are like an orchestra tuning up, but without success in agreeing on a common key or piece of music. The first violinist disagrees with the first trumpet, and the timpanist wants to use an altogether different score. In the case of the orchestra, the conductor can get everyone working together only with the help of key subordinates. But when he is unable to get cooperation from key subordinates the result is like that of a human being with Parkinson's disease. The conductor may try to step in and do the work of some of his key subordinates.

The person with Parkinson's disease can try to consciously make the decisions that had formerly been made by subordinate experiencing entities, probably within the area of the substantia nigra. In a normal healthy person the subordinate experiencing entities take care of such tasks as uncrossing the legs or positioning the feet under the center of gravity when the person decides to stand, or changing the orientation of the body to facilitate stopping while walking. In the Parkinson's patient these subordinate experiencing entities become dysfunctional, unable to do for the person what needs to be done. Consequently the person with Parkinson's disease must consciously think about such matters as uncrossing legs before attempting to stand.

What you mean, then, I add, is that the human is a coordinated society of experiencing entities with sufficient unity to be one experiencing entity. You have heard about the phantom limb phenomenon cited by Descartes? Is this another example of confusion on the part of subordinate experiencing entities within the person? Or does it provide the evidence for mind-body dualism that Descartes thought that it did?

Whitehead answers. *The phantom limb phenomenon doesn't prove what Descartes thought that it did. Descartes' theory of physical entities left these entities incapable of any kind of experience because they couldn't enter into internal relations with anything outside themselves. In this respect they were like the atoms of classical atomism* (Whitehead 1978, part 2). From Descartes' point of view, if I were just a body I wouldn't be able to enter into internal relations with anything outside of myself, nor within myself. I wouldn't be capable of experiencing. He attempted to solve this problem by theorizing that the self was a mind radically different from bodies. In the phantom limb example, the body is fooling the mind according to Descartes. But I do not agree.

This is a very popular belief, I respond, that the body is fooling the mind in the case of the phantom limb phenomenon. When the pain from a phantom limb is treated with analgesics the nerves may be numbed, but analgesics cannot remove the impression that the limb is still there. I recall a patient of mine who had his left leg amputated. He avoided the phantom limb phenomenon in a very unusual way. Anticipating the phantom limb illusion prior to the amputation of the limb, he prepared himself by making plans for actions to be taken subsequent to the amputation of his left leg below the knee. After the limb was removed and he had recovered from anesthesia, he took his cane and moved it through the space that would have been occupied by the limb. When I asked him what he was doing, he told me that he was breaking up the energy field that would have been generated by the limb. But after learning about your philosophy of hierarchies of experience within a person, I think that he was helping the subordinate experiencing entities within himself to become aware that the limb was no longer there. By taking care of the illusion of a still existing limb, he prevented the occurrence of the phantom limb pain often experienced by other amputees.

Whitehead nods agreement. The same phenomenon can be described either mechanically, using energy fields, or in terms of experiencing organisms. *What your patient called energy fields I prefer to analyze in terms of the relations between the subjects and objects of experience; or if you prefer, I see energy fields as a special case of fields of experience.*[57] Neither analysis is right or wrong, we simply prefer different mapping symbols.

Whitehead continues. But I am intrigued by the notion of instructing the subordinate experiencing entities within one's body in order to correct or prevent an illusion as your patient did. One result of the cascading of experience, of the layering of experience, of the experience of experience of experience, which Hegel and I have been discussing, is that it opens up the possibility for the kind of illusion that your patient avoided. Shareable universals are important. When the universals experienced are not shareable, they are considered "wrong" or illusory. What I think has happened in most cases of illusion, hallucination, and delusion, is that the subordinate experiencing entities within a person have used universals not shareable with other persons for interpreting an actual object of experience.[58]

An example of using "wrong" universals is that of the patient whose subordinate experiencing entities cause him to feel a limb where no one else can see or feel a limb. Most persons faced with the phenomenon of "wrong" universals will correct or discipline the subordinate experiencing entities within themselves, rather than allow themselves to fall into error by accepting their interpretation uncritically. This activity of correction becomes so automatic that it becomes unconscious. This happens with those who wear glasses, especially blended trifocals. When such glasses are first put on, a person is apt to become sick. Flat surfaces appear to undulate like the surface of the sea on a very stormy day. Most persons say to themselves, and to their subordinate experiencing entities, the top of the table is still flat and stable. They shortly learn to see it that way once again. By the way, this is a much healthier, and more likely to be successful, approach than the prescription of analgesics to the person suffering from such illusions as the phantom limb phenomenon and hence should be encouraged by nurses.[59]

Experience at all levels involves both direct awareness of an object and mediated awareness of the same object by means of universals.[60] *Actual entities in their full individuality or uniqueness are exceedingly, if not infinitely, complex. Conscious awareness of these objects becomes possible by using a lens of universals that greatly simplifies the actual entity as an object of experience. A stone is experienced as merely a stone and not as the highly complex association of molecules that it actually is. And it is practical to experience the grey stone as merely a stone. If a person focuses on the full complexity of an actual entity, he is rendered unable to use it successfully.* For example if I am threatened by a dog chasing me I pick up the first stone I notice. I save my life by viewing the dog merely as an angry dog and the stone merely as a stone. Of course, I might have erroneously applied the universal "angry" to the dog. The dog might have been friendly, but only appeared menacing when I viewed it through the lens of universals. I will never know, because I have disturbed the original situation through my actions. Universals conceal as well as reveal.

Whitehead continues. It is very convenient and perhaps necessary that the subordinate experiencing entities within a person learn to synthesize the two modes of experience successfully. *When this is working well, these subordinate experiencing entities perform the repetitive and mechanical functions, freeing the person to concentrate on more important matters.* But like the patient with Parkinson's disease, the patient with asthma must consciously remind his subordinate experiencing entities to do what is necessary to breathe and prevent life-threatening crises. Needless to say, if one's attention is preoccupied with the mechanics of breathing or moving without falling, many of the more important human activities have to be left in abeyance. The Parkinson's patient is not going to be a successful runner and the asthma patient may have trouble making long public speeches.

These are simplified and practical examples of the application of my theory of *symbolic reference*, Whitehead continues. *In that theory I hold that experience at the higher or more conscious levels always combines two more immediate and semiconscious modes of experience, direct awareness of actual entities and direct awareness of universals. Direct awareness of an actual entity is intuition unmediated by the senses and the brain. Direct awareness of universals is awareness of pure possibilities such as redness, or flatness, or being a stone. This second kind of direct awareness is initiated by the sense organs and the brain in human beings. The first mode of direct awareness I call physical prehension, and the second mode I call conceptual prehension. The term "prehension" is chosen because the experiencing entity incorporates the object of experience into its own constitution by attending to it* (Whitehead 1978, pp. 219–35).[61]

John Dewey finishes paying for his muffin and coffee, turns and walks to our table. Excuse me, he says. I couldn't help but overhear your conversation about different modes of awareness. May I add my two cents?

All of us agree. Dewey pulls up a chair and sits down.

Dewey politely sets his muffin aside for the moment so that he can address us without a mouth full of food. It seems to me, he says, that nursing needs to make use of a lot of nonscientific practical knowledge. I heard the mystics talk about knowledge through direct awareness. I also heard Hume and Kant argue about whether knowledge could be scientific and yet, at the same time, dubitable. Now I am hearing my colleague Whitehead talk about the components of direct awareness in everyday experience, and admit that the two components may be so related as to cause error, as in illusions or hallucinations. *I have no problem with tentative or fallible knowledge. In fact I believe that most human knowledge is tentative and fallible* (Dewey 1969).[62] But as a nurse you need to *act* regardless of the lack of certainty. For example, if you have good reason to suspect that your patient is dying from a heart attack, you will need to perform actions to keep him alive, and attempt to better confirm your diagnosis that it was a heart attack later. Although you may never be certain that the originating problem was within the heart, maintaining the functioning of the heart is essential for life. This is like *your* example, Whitehead, with the apparently angry dog. By picking up the stone you acted prudently. But at the time the dog was approaching you, you could not with certainty determine whether you were angering a friendly dog, or protecting yourself against an already angry dog.

Dewey continues. I also couldn't help overhearing your talk about "right" and "wrong" universals, illusions, hallucinations, and other ways of erring cognitively. I didn't use the phrase "shareable universal" in my work, but what you were trying to say and what I was trying to say seem quite similar. *A theory or proposition is true if it allows an inquiry to continue successfully.*[63] For example, two nurses assess a patient's condition. The vital signs are stable, the patient is awake. But there is something about the general condition of the patient that worries both nurses. If only one nurse is worried, then the inquiry might stop at that point. The patient seems to be turning worse, yet without the usual visible signs. Though neither nurse is certain that this patient is getting worse, they agree that something is not right with him. They discuss the matter briefly and perhaps call a third nurse to assess the patient. They all agree that they should notify the patient's physician of their concern. This will alert the physician to begin thinking about what might be going wrong with the patient.

The more sensitive and wiser physicians will realize that the concern of several nurses, though at least temporarily unsupported by scientific evidence, such as a change in vital signs, is a source of *tentative nonscientific knowledge* that should be taken seriously.[64] At this point it would not only be practical but also prudent that the nurses and doctor decide to continue to assess the patient at more frequent intervals until something else indicates that his condition is severe enough to warrant immediate action or until everyone is comfortable with the stability of his condition. If the nurses and the doctor ignore their intuition and continue to tend to the patient routinely, the patient's condition might change radically resulting in his death before anyone could take appropriate action. On the other hand, his condition might change for the better. But I ask you, which action on the part of the nurses and doctor would be more prudent—to ignore their intuition and chance that their feeling about the patient was illusory, or to believe their intuition and assess the patient at more frequent intervals? This is an example of what I mean when I talk about practical nonscientific knowledge, and it is a common experience for the practicing nurse.

I know what I would choose, I said to Dewey. I would choose to observe the patient at more frequent intervals until I was satisfied that he was stable and not changing for the worse. If I had chosen to assess the patient more frequently and the patient's condition turned out to be stable, I guess the worst thing that could happen to me as a nurse is that I could be called an alarmist by my colleagues. But considering the alternative, I think that checking the patient would be the more prudent decision. Being called an alarmist is not as serious as ignoring my intuition and having the patient die as a result. But what then is the relationship between scientific and nonscientific knowledge? And what role does truth play in these distinctions? I ask.

I can't speak for the others, but I have my own theory, says Dewey. *I am a great admirer and supporter of the sciences. But scientific knowledge is tentative and fallible, and it depends on a background of nonscientific knowledge, such as everyday knowledge,* like St. Francelyn's will still be here tomorrow when you come to work. Though I am not accustomed to Whitehead's jargon, I think I understand his interplay between two modes of experience, the physical and conceptual, and I believe that something like his account is true. *No normal person disbelieves in the existence of the public objects of sense perception. The important point from my standpoint is that the symbols or universals that are used in sense perception are not true or false in any absolute sense. They are more or less useful cognitively for understanding the objects of experience. The more useful the universals are, the truer they are* (Dewey 1969).

Returning to the usefulness of intuition in nursing, I would like to add something, says Whitehead. *The interplay between the two modes of experience, the physical and the conceptual, has one important consequence for the practicing nurse. A nurse always knows more, in*

Dewey's nonscientific sense, than the nurse consciously knows that she knows. Conscious knowledge is limited to the choice of universals that the nurse employs. But direct awareness of the unique individual provides a dim knowledge far beyond that which is highlighted by the universals.[65] Consider for a moment the intuition of the nurses in Dewey's example, that the patient's condition may be getting worse. Hence the nurse who "senses" that something is wrong with her patient is always wise to heed this hunch. When a life is at stake it is wisest to act first and do one's scientific research later.

Are universals always to be evaluated by their cognitive or practical usefulness? I ask. What about spiritual usefulness?

Whitehead responds. Yes indeed, spiritual usefulness is important. *What I would call spiritual usefulness includes both religious experience and aesthetic experience. Both religious experience and aesthetic experience are very helpful for the development of the self* (Whitehead 1967, parts 1 & 4; Whitehead 1960). The difference between the two is that aesthetic experience focuses on a rich but shareable universal, like Beethoven's Fifth Symphony; while religious experience focuses on a Unique Individual, God or the One. In more advanced aesthetic experience it is the complex and shareable universals, usually called works of art, which are the products or objects of conceptual prehension. Perhaps we could say that art is playfulness with sensual universals for the sake of the beauty that can be created. Remember that the conceptual includes the sensual. *These universals may be so complex and rich, especially aesthetically, that it is as if they are shareable individuals.*[66] Consider such works as Beethoven's Fifth Symphony or Michelangelo's *Pieta*. In art or aesthetic experience we do not care whether there is a match between the two modes of experience, the conceptual and the physical. *We are not interested in the existence of an actual unique individual. We enjoy the product of the conceptual pole for its own sake.* Here the word conceptual includes all of the rich aesthetic and sensuous universals.[67]

Whitehead continues. I would suggest that the wise nurse could make extensive use of aesthetics or art in her care for patients. There are those who sometimes worry that art and literature may be used only as a "diversion" by the health care professional, that health care professionals do not recognize the value of art and literature and other aesthetic experiences for understanding and expressing the human condition.[68] *But I believe that aesthetic experience is essential to the spiritual health of the patient, and in my opinion, religious experience may also be very helpful.*[69]

I respond to Whitehead's comments. You will be happy to know that nurses already include art and aesthetics in their care of patients.

Music, painting, literature, dance, and drama, not only allow us to be aware of the depth and intricacy of our feelings but also art is often a shareable universal alleviating a communication problem between nurse and patient. Art by expressing common but complex human condition provides a bridge between persons when other modes of communication break down. I myself have frequently used art to explain a complicated situation to another person when other symbols, such as words, are not as effective. Many children respond better to a story and to puppets than they do to direct conversation. Art can be a means for understanding more complex feelings such as grief and loss, or other complex concepts such as wisdom and ethical and moral dilemmas. Adults often allow themselves to have more complex and positive feelings through music, film, painting, or dance. An aesthetic environment is conducive to contemplative peace. Aesthetics in the preparation and presentation of food nourishes both body and soul. Yet, how often are patients born and how often do they die in environments that are aesthetically ugly or sterile? And how often is food given to a recuperating patient on a tray, all courses together, entrée to drink to dessert, with little thought as to the healing potential of an aesthetically pleasing presentation?

Whitehead adds to my train of thought. *I think the work of art allows the person to achieve a more beautiful unity than is otherwise possible. Prior to art, the subordinate centers of experience within a person may be in partial conflict. The unity achieved by art allows a higher harmony to be achieved within the self.*[70] Some people would call this the self-actualization that occurs within the self as opposed to self-actualization through relations with others. This inner unity achieved through art is what the Pythagoreans were hinting at in their notion that the soul was a Harmony (*Harmonia*).[71] Beauty comes to be within the self by enjoying beautiful objects of experience.[72] Also, the ability of several persons to mutually appreciate beauty within the same object helps them in recognizing one another—"Ah, you also can see what I see!" The result is heightened self-actualization in relation with others.[73]

Have you noticed that something similar can be said about humor? I ask. Art is concerned with complex universals wherein the subordinate universals are in harmony with one another and the whole. But what makes us laugh or what we find humorous is the recognition that within the humorous situation there is a complex of shareable universals that are less than harmonious and predictable. Here humor is similar to art. But where humor is dissimilar to art is that the universals in a humorous complex are surprisingly or sometimes discordantly combined. Even the timing of the sequencing of the universals experienced is essential for good humor. All of these aspects contribute to the experience of the unexpected. For example, the most numerous creature that swims in water is called a "fish." But have you ever caught a "ghoti"? This would be the same creature as the first provided that the "gh" is pronounced as in "enough," the "o" is pronounced as in "women, " and the "ti" is pronounced as in "nation." Anyone for a "ghoti ghreye"?[74]

Hearing no one laugh, I continue anyway. We all know that universals cannot change. It is rather the persons shifting their attention from one universal to another that produce the experience of the unexpected. Note the fun with the spelling of the words in the example I gave. It is even more fun when several persons can laugh together. But this is possible only when the persons attend to the same shareable universals. Unless persons attend to the same shareable universals, the humor will not be seen or appreciated. But when it is, a good laugh does wonders for both body and soul. Where art generally produces harmony within the self, humor results in the catharsis of antecedent disharmony within the self. Producing harmony and discharging disharmony within the self are essential for the health of the person. The spiritually practical function of art is to increase the harmony within the self. The spiritually practical function of humor is to discharge disharmony already existing within the self. But now let's look at the meaning of spirituality itself. I remember that you said earlier, that spiritual usefulness includes both religious experience and aesthetic experience. We have discussed the aesthetic. What about religious experience? I ask Whitehead.

Whitehead responds. Spiritual health is the health of the enduring personality. By enduring personality I mean the highest experient entity within a person. Religious experience, as well as aesthetic experience, heightens spiritual health. But the religious and the aesthetic are not the same, though religion may make use of aesthetics. *Religious experience is often facilitated by the special universals encountered in religious rituals* (Whitehead 1960). But the object of religious experience is the Unique Individual, the One of the mystics. The relation between the one and the One adds another dimension to self-creation or self-actualization in other terminology.

Whitehead continues. *One of the most important hallmarks of religious experience is that it enables the person who experiences religiously or mystically to feel at home in any place or circumstance*, and to feel healthy under any condition (Whitehead 1960). You mentioned earlier about the terminally ill patient who felt healthy even while dying. This is an example of the effect of religious experience. I am reminded also of Socrates sense of "the invulnerability of virtue"—though a good person can be killed, he cannot be harmed. Religious experience is the best antidote possible to all forms of alienation and feelings of isolation. For religious experience is direct intuition of unity of oneself with the One, but a unity that respects the differences between self and Self. You have already covered most of this in your discussions with the mystics. Religious experience, or mystic experience, strengthens the finite self in its process of self-creation. It also provides a kind of guidance, a sense of cosmic significance overarching personal interest.[75]

Aahh! I exclaim. I have learned that there are at least three factors that are necessary for self-creation. These are closely related to the grounds of singularity, the factors that make an individual unique and unduplicatable. But I have also learned that self-creation involves universals as well as the grounds of singularity. As a nurse I must choose among various roles, nursing roles as well as other social roles, such as that of the politician or the mother. These roles are universals, or blends of universals that change with time, but the manner in which I blend the various roles at unique times and places within my life, enhances my uniqueness, and hence is among the grounds of my singularity. The first of these necessary conditions for self-creation is genuine dialogue and relations with other persons. The second is genuine dialogue within the subordinate centers of experience within the self. And the third is genuine dialogue between the one and the One. Have I got this right?

Whitehead nods agreement. But remember, *universals are pure possibilities for determinateness. They are not in themselves actual or determinate. There must be actual entities to actualize the possibilities. Persons and other enduring objects, such as trees, are actual entities. You cannot engage in self creation without making yourself determinate in some way. Hence, it follows that individuals are a blend of universals and singularity. Universals are nothing but possibilities for determinateness. By extension, whenever you engage in self-creation you are blending universals with whatever the grounds of singularity might be in such a way as to produce novelty. But I can think of at least one more condition that is necessary for self-creation and is a ground of the singularity of the individual. This is space and time, actual in the past and potential in the future.*[76]

Is your space time continuum the same as Kant's space-time manifold? I ask.

Yes.[77] Whitehead answers. *But remember your earlier insights about formal and material components with respect to the positioning of the self in space and time. Formal refers to the abstract matrix of space-time positions, and the material component consists of the subjective experience of the individual entity occupying a particular place within the matrix.*[78] For example, consider the nurse at the bedside at 2 pm in your narrative. Her experiences at that time and place occupy a unique position within the single space-time matrix of the universe. But her experiences give content to the event taking place at that time, which included the pronouncement of the death of the patient. *Space-time would mean nothing without the events taking place within it. The mathematical continuum is formal, and by itself it seems to guarantee that no two events are at the same time and place. But the manner in which the present experiencing entity allows the past actual entities to enter into itself adds content or determination to the present entity, which adds to its uniqueness. You also noticed the importance of significant neighboring events for adding to the singularity of the individual experiencing entity.* In your example, the various events are interconnected in such a way as to add to the uniqueness of each: the grieving family, the death of the patients, the need to keep the organs viable.[79]

I have been curious about your theory of symbolic reference (Whitehead 1978, pp. 168–83), which you started to explain it earlier, I respond. I recall that the two components of symbolic reference are experience of past individuals, events, persons, and other enduring objects, and experience of universals. I would like to return to it now and ask you to explain it more thoroughly. I think it is potentially very useful to nursing, and especially in understanding universality and singularity within nursing.

I will be happy to explain it, says Whitehead. *For the successful everyday survival of a person, it is important that the physical, and conceptual poles be successfully synthesized. Remember the physical pole is experience of past individuals and the conceptual pole is experience of universals, both those that were actualized in the past and those that might have been and might be. When the two poles are successfully synthesized then the pink elephant that we see is an actual elephant, and not just an enjoyable and rich product of the aesthetic imagination (or too much alcohol).* But if I am the only one who sees the pink elephant, it is likely that the poles are not successfully synthesized, and I might be wise to seek treatment (Whitehead 1978, pp. 168–83).[80]

Whitehead continues. *The conceptual mode of experience produces potential symbols that allow an experiencing entity to focus on universals and use them as a lens through which to view the uniquely individual object of the physical mode of experience.* Let me give you an example. The pronouncement of the word "patient" is an individual event. But the nurse means by the pronouncement the universal *patient*, which in turn may allow her to make sense or attend to the individual lying in the bed. But the symbolism may go the other way. The nurse may see the individual lying in the bed as symbolizing the universal *patient*. Or she may also see him as symbolizing the universal *person*. You can see that it would be useful for her to do so. However, even if she sees the individual in the bed as symbolizing both of the universals, patient and person, she is still not attending to him in his full uniqueness as an individual. *Though the conceptual mode is useful it also hides much of the uniqueness of the individual. Attending to an individual through a lens of universals allows experience to become conscious. Without universals we could not notice individuals. In fact, shapes, boundaries between one object and another, sounds, and any kind of sensual object, would all be undifferentiated and unprioritized so that experience would be like William James' "big booming buzzing confusion."*[81] *Through the lens of universals we divide the objects of experience into identifiable individuals. But ironically this same lens of universals makes it difficult to be conscious of aspects of the individual outside of the lens. The lens of universals both reveals and conceals at the same time.*[82]

I add to what Whitehead is saying. I recall that some of my patients with schizophrenia are troubled by the inability to discriminate and screen sounds. They tell me the experience is like a jackhammer. Incoming sounds cannot be identified and distinguished from each other. The result is a meaningless cacophony that can produce a terrible headache. I often take for granted, the screening process that allows me just now to attend to your voice while ignoring such interfering sounds as Hegel slurping his beer and Dewey masticating his muffin or the sound of the air conditioning unit in the building. I now know that this screening process is the result of my use of a lens of universals. Even the sounds I hear coming from you I discriminate as words by using lenses of universals. It is my focus on the words symbolized by your sounds that allows me to ignore the other sounds. Some of my friends in the Deaf[83] community tell me that when they were first given hearing aids as children, the result was the meaningless cacophony that the schizophrenic patients report. In order to put up with the hearing aids, they had to learn to use lenses of universals to screen the incoming sounds. Some learned to do this successfully, others simply threw the hearing aids away and embraced a highly developed visual language, American Sign Language.

Whitehead listens attentively and then remarks. You are going deeper into the details of symbolism and conceptual prehension than I often did in my works. *But let me complete the exposition of symbolic reference by returning to the other pole of experience, physical prehension. Physical prehension is direct awareness of an actual entity in the full complexity of its unique individuality. The problem is that the experiencing entity is overwhelmed by the complexity of the object with the result that the object is largely experienced only unconsciously. This intuitive awareness of the actual individual is vague and visceral, but allows the experiencing entity to know the object as undeniably real. Remember the nurses' concern in Dewey's example that something was wrong with the patient. This is not an example of pure physical prehension because the nurses are looking at the individual through the lens of universals, patient. In fact there could be no example of pure physical prehension. All experience is mediated by universals.*[84]

Whitehead continues. The problem faced by the nurses in your example was that they sensed but could not confirm the appropriateness of an additional lens of universals, *wrongness*. Their search was for more specific lenses of universals, such as *gastrointestinal problems, heart problems*, or *flu*, which would allow them to confirm the appropriateness of the universal, *wrongness*, by saying more specifically what was wrong. *Physical prehension makes it impossible for us to be idealists. It assures us that the object exists, but gives us very little usable information about what the object is. But the simplification of the object of experience resulting from viewing it through the lens of universals provided by the conceptual pole allows the awareness of the object to become conscious awareness. Without the high abstraction made possible by conceptual prehension, consciousness would be impossible for human beings.*[85]

Whitehead continues. *But another result of conceptual prehension, of the fact that we view all entities through lenses of universals, rather than in the full complexity of their uniqueness as individuals, is that experience is always partially illusory.*[86] Cognitive error is easy. For example, a person having a first heart attack may confuse the symptoms of epigastric pain, nausea, and vomiting, and tightness in his chest, as indicating simple indigestion accompanied by muscle strain. But the possibility of error cannot be avoided by dropping the lenses of universals, because it is impossible to drop the lenses and remain conscious. The practical way of avoiding error is to be able to use many different lenses of universals. Hence the importance of education, training, and experience for the nurse. All universals are both "right" and "wrong" for the purpose of understanding the actual entities that are the ultimate objects of our experience. They are "right" in the sense that they allow us to focus awareness so as to become conscious of the object. They are "wrong" in the sense that they distort our view of the object by leaving out almost everything that is true of it, while highlighting an aspect of the object that is very one-sided. The wrongness may cause major mistakes, such as the patient misdiagnosing the symptoms of a heart attack. The patient could die if he didn't seek immediate treatment. The mistakes may also be moral and aesthetic, as well as cognitive. Racial prejudice is one example of moral error resulting from using the "wrong" universals. The phantom limb example illustrates another more complicated "wrongness" in the use of universals.

Whitehead continues. Returning to the phantom limb example, it is not just the highest experiencing entity, the enduring personality of the person, that is using the "wrong" universals. Rather, cues associated with the missing limb are fooling subordinate experiencing entities within the person into supposing that the limb still exists, and this judgment is then experienced by the person as a whole. The interesting thing about this particular phenomenon is that the cognitive mistake is first committed, not by the person as a whole, but by some subordinate experiencing entity within the person. One might wish to explore the parallels and differences between this example and the example of the person with Parkinson's disease who makes a mistake concerning the positioning of his feet before attempting to stand. *All conscious experience is symbolic and subject to errors of this kind.* It is sobering to realize that even when we are using the "right" universals, they are "right" only in the sense of allowing for successful experience of the experience of subordinate experiencing entities within and other persons outside. They may also be "right" in the sense of allowing us to act successfully. But *they are not "right" in the sense that they provide us with the final truth about the objects we are experiencing* (Whitehead 1978, pp. 168–83).

Your explanation is helpful, I answer. But if I may, I would like to slightly change the subject for a moment. I am troubled by the difference between the self-creation or self-actualization that results from dialogue among the subordinate experiencing entities in the person and the self-absorption of some of my psychiatric patients. Some of my patients are self-absorbed yet are not self-reflective in the sense required for self-creation. Without the ability for self-reflection such patients have problems perceiving and making choices about their future. Often they see no blending of past with present in such a way as to open up new options for the future. Hence, they are unable to reflect successfully on alternative futures. They are convinced that they have no power to change their situation or to effect their own futures, because they see themselves as victims of the strength and power of others, such as the legal system, their families, the medical community, and so on. If critical thinking involves reflective thinking, then a deficiency in the ability to think critically means that the individual is bound to unreflective unconscious experiences. Hence the opportunity to choose different possible futures is lost. In other words, there is a paucity of options for self-creation. Then there are others who indulge in self-absorption to the extent that they cannot engage in mutually self-creative dialogue with others. They are imprisoned by their subjective experiences. They seem lost within themselves. And there is something else I have noticed.

What is that? asks Whitehead.

I have noticed that the frustration of some of my students attempting to have satisfactory interpersonal relationships with some psychiatric patients is due in part to the one-sidedness of their dialogue with the patients. For example, some patients are so passive that they agree with anything that the student says. Others refuse to engage in dialogue by disagreeing with everything the student says, but offering no justification or explanation. What can you tell me about self-absorption? What light can you shed on extreme compliance or extreme negativism and its barrier to the kind of self-creation that involves genuine dialogue with others?

Let me answer the question about dialogue with others, that is, if Whitehead agrees to answer the question about dialogue within the person, says Hegel.

By all means, says Whitehead. If you don't mind, I will go first.

Fine, Hegel answers. My pilsner glass needs a refill anyway.

Whitehead starts. I haven't addressed this notion of self-absorption in my works, but I can see that it is consistent with my philosophy of the nature of persons. The healthy person enjoys a better or tighter organic unity as a whole than the unhealthy person. By this I mean that the enduring personality provides sufficient unity of direction for the community of experiencing entities within the person so that the individual is definitely *one* person able to marshal the full resources of the subordinate entities within. In a less healthy person there is still an enduring personality, but it is not as successful in coordinating the activities of the subordinate experiencing entities, and hence is less able to do such things as self-reflect or learn from experience. Too much energy is spent in remaining in control to be self-reflective or wise in reaction to changes in the outside environment. Also, there is a tendency to allow the inclinations of various subordinate experiencing entities to direct the experience and actions of the person as a whole. The individual who is incapable of disciplining his sexual urges is an example of this kind of problem, as is the individual who eats imprudently regardless of likely effect on his future health.[87]

I add to Whitehead's explanation. Could it be that there are universals shared by the conscious person and her experient subordinate entities?

Hmmmm. Please continue, says Whitehead.

I take a deep breath and continue. What I have learned is that in order to enter into a sustained and genuine dialogue with another person, the two of us must share universals, that is, something within my past experience must blend with the past experience of the other. I also learned that the two individuals engaged in genuine dialogue must be able to share another set of common universals, a common language. Perhaps the conscious, regnant society within the individual and his subordinate experiencing entities are searching for a common language. Once the common language, or universal is found, a genuine dialogue can begin. Some individuals search all of their lives for such a common language, while others are able to find it with little more than a conscious effort. Could this be an explanation for the differences between self-absorption and self-reflection consistent with your theory? I ask Whitehead. And could chronic depression be partially explained by lack of a common internal "language"?

Hmm! Says Whitehead. I am not sure I can make sense of the notion of an "internal" language.[88] But the notion of an insufficiency in shared universals between the subordinate experiencing entities and the enduring personality, which I grant can be thought of as a kind of "internal" language, is intriguing. I use the notion of "lure" in my philosophical works. *The enduring personality manages to control the subordinate experiencing entities not by acting as an efficient cause, that is, the past compelling the present to change in a certain way, but by presenting a complex of evaluated universals that function as a final cause of the experiences and actions of the subordinate entities. Final causes influence but do not compel,* as you discussed with Plato and Aristotle. The enduring personality can influence through final causes only by means of what you are calling shared universals. *Another way of putting the matter is that a person can be whole and healthy only if there is a common vision shared by the enduring personality and its subordinate experiencing entities. Without a common vision there is disharmony within the self.* And perhaps this could explain depression. The depressed individual is unable to act and unable to engage in more positive self-reflection.[89]

I respond. That might mean that the suicidal individual is one whose enduring personality has despaired of being able to get the cooperation of key subordinate experiencing entities, or one in which the conflict between the subordinate experiencing entities and the enduring personality is unbearable by the latter. The antidepressant medications do not lure, they force or compel. Which means that the enduring personality is attempting to "control" by external factors its own subordinate experiencing entities. The enduring personality has not really reestablished unity within the self. Target subordinate experiencing entities are temporally put down by the chemical.

May I cut in? asks Hegel.

Please do, we respond.

Returning to your worry about your student nurses in their encounters with patients who are either too agreeable or disagreeable, I think I have an explanation for your students' frustration and unhappiness. Genuine dialogue, as the twentieth-century philosopher Martin Buber contended, though I think I deserve some credit for his insights, is essential for the self-development of both participants. *When patients are unable to enter into genuine dialogue, they block the continued self-creation of the nurses. No self is finished. We are all in process of self-creation. Experience of the others' experience of oneself is essential to this process. Honest differences of opinion as in genuine dialogue facilitates this experience of experience of experience. It is not just a matter of what is said, but how I am and how the other is as a speaker, and how each of us perceives the other as a person. It is no wonder your students are frustrated* (Buber 1965; Hegel 1966). Nursing is the profession that has never abandoned the personhood of the patient. Perhaps this is partly the reason that people choose nursing in the first place. When the patient is unable or perhaps unwilling to engage in genuine dialogue it becomes more difficult for both the nurse and the patient to achieve further self-actualization. This is doubly frustrating to the nurse, for she feels an obligation not only to continue her own self-actualization but to be a facilitator of the self-actualization of her patient.

I reply to Hegel. What you have just said gives me new insight into what we in nursing call "therapeutic use of self" on the part of the nurse. The nurse is a facilitator of the self-actualization of her patient. What I am learning is that to achieve therapeutic use of self the nurse cannot hold back on who she is as a person in the manner suggested by some textbooks (Varcarolis 1994, pp. 125–26). But it seems instead that the nurse must enter into genuine dialogue with her patient at whatever level the patient is capable of entering. Perhaps the "holding back" in the textbooks was an awkward way of saying that the nurse must be aware of what the patient is capable of at the moment and must be careful to allow the patient equal participation in the genuine dialogue. A genuine dialogue between nurse and patient does not consist of addressing the patient's behavior. Genuine dialogue is a mutual learning and a co-creative process. Instead of addressing the patient's behavior, which is not part of genuine dialogue, the nurse is as concerned to learn from the patient as to inform the patient. The nurse is the questioning, curious, individual, who wants to learn about herself through the experiences with the patient through learning about the experiences of the patient. For example, what is it like to feel you are not believed by anyone? Or what is it like to feel that others want to do you harm? And why do I not perceive the world in this way? What makes me different from you? What is it like to go to court and have to prove to a judge that your thinking or reasoning is normal? These are all questions that can be answered through genuine dialogue between the nurse and her patient.

I continue. If genuine dialogue is successful, both selves will advance further than would have otherwise been possible, because they will be able to make use of the experiences of the other in their own self-creation. The nurse must be fully honest with patients when they ask about who she is as a person, because that is part of genuine dialogue. Genuine dialogue is more likely to occur if the nurse approaches the patient as an equal, as a fellow human being in the process of self-creation.

Though it is neither necessary nor appropriate to bare all of their secrets, each has past experiences that will be helpful to the other. Genuine dialogue is inconsistent with role playing and the pretense of perfection. Genuineness is needed for healing of the patient and the sustained health of the nurse. It will both help the patient and help to prevent burnout on the part of the nurse. I think that this in turn will be good for the nursing profession, because good nurses will stay in nursing. When there is genuine dialogue, the patient has the opportunity to overcome alienation from his illness and by extension part of himself. Whereas too narrow a focus on the illness of the patient may inadvertently both increase the self-alienation of the patient and widen the gulf between patient and nurse. When the nurse focuses primarily on the illness and the defects of the patient, it implicitly makes the nurse appear to be perfect and the patient defective. In contrast, genuine dialogue acknowledges and uses the strengths of the patient as well as the nurse. Self-creation is co-creative; it requires cooperation between self and self, patient and nurse.

I continue. It is true that the nurse must look for shareable universals between herself and the patient in order to begin genuine dialogue. This is not always possible between any two persons, and hence it will sometimes not be possible in the nurse patient relationship. But in her attempt to enter genuine dialogue with the patient, the nurse will have discovered the universals interesting to the patient. This will be helpful in finding other health providers who might be of more help to the patient. I am reminded of a student nurse who was able to enter into genuine dialogue with a patient, because both were interested in piano. The patient had not been willing to talk with anyone else.

Please, I ask Whitehead, now that I have had an introduction to your theory of experient occasions, I want to know more fully what you mean by them? You write at great length about actual or experient occasions in your major book, *Process and Reality* (Whitehead 1978).

First, says Whitehead, *I agree with Hegel that consciousness is the result of experience of experience, and self-consciousness the result of experience of experience of experience. The formula is rough and general, but serviceable. "Apperception," as both Leibniz and Kant used the term, means "perception of perception," which is the same as experience of experience. And for both philosophers it is the "ap" that adds consciousness to "perception." But this makes the problem of consciousness seem simpler than it is, at least in my opinion. I agree with my colleagues that interpersonal experience of experience is an important factor, but I believe that there is another factor equally important. Experience of experience occurs within the body of a person as well as between person and person.*[90] Let me doodle on my napkin to illustrate my theories (see figure 1).

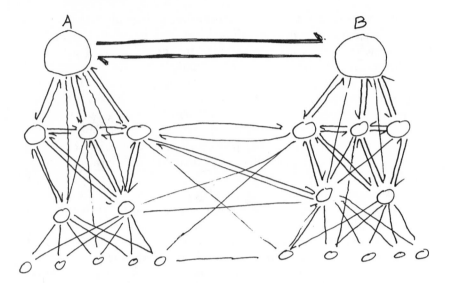

FIGURE 1. Whitehead's Doodling

Whitehead continues to explain his theory of experiencing entities while pointing to the details on the napkin. Let A and B be separate persons. The little circles below the A and B are themselves experiencing subjects. They are not self-conscious, because they are not conscious. But they are experiencing entities nonetheless, many of whom enjoy a kind of preconscious or subconscious awareness of the distinction between self and others, and of their place within the community which is a person. In a living being, these subordinate subjects experience other experiencing subjects. You will notice in the drawing that most experiences are shared in the sense that they are experienced by different higher-level experiencing subjects. What this means is that there are shared points of commonality of experience for different experiencing subjects. That they share something in common is an important point. If there were not points of commonality, if each experient occasion were isolated, there could be no organization throughout the experiences. One occasion would be disconnected from the others, like the bubbles floating from bottom to top in Hegel's pilsner glass. But we know that experiences are organized, that one connects to another in an unfolding network of connections that undergirds the dawning of consciousness.

Now let's take another look at Hegel's pilsner. Notice that the glass contains the beer. Then notice that the beer is liquid. It contains bubbles. The bubbles drift to the top and end in the foam. Taken separately, pilsner glass, beer, liquid, bubbles, and foam, one could ask how do I recognize these multiple entities as a single entity, a pilsner glass of beer? What is the "oneness" that connects these separate individual entities into a single individual entity? Hold that question for a moment. Let's return again to the glass of beer.

Can it be that each particle or subparticle in the beer is a nonexperiencing object? Are they simply objects of our experience? Possibly, but I would challenge that. If they were simply isolated nonexperiencing objects of our experience then how is it that they come together in such a way as to result in beer? If one molecule cannot recognize another molecule as a friendly neighbor with whom to bond, then we could not produce the fine beverage we have here before us. The increasing complexity from one experient occasion to another, from single electrons to complex microscopic communities, implies "memory." Otherwise how would they recognize a friendly neighbor in the first place? *Memory implies history.*

Now let us turn to the human being. Unlike a simple glass of beer the human being is composed of highly complex experient communities, each with memory and each with common shared experiences. Has it not been suggested in your time that viruses like the AIDS virus "seem alive" and even "intelligent"? And haven't you noticed how humans develop certain tolerances to medications after a period of time? How do you explain "intelligent" viruses and the equally "intelligent" reactions of parts of the human body to organisms and medications, if the subordinate entities within the human being are not in themselves experiencing subjects? *It has been a fundamental principal of my philosophy that life is a better concept for understanding all of reality than the notion of the lifeless* (Whitehead 1967a, pp. 75–94).

Now if they are in themselves experiencing subjects, would it not be reasonable to think that an experiencing human being, the enduring personality, is an even more complex experiencing subject, the capstone of all experiencing subjects within the person? If so, then, the enduring personality, the mind of a person, is a judgmental and integrative "mirror" of all the experiencing subjects within the person. The experiencing subjects within are one, yet increased by one. The many experiencing subjects within a person become one experiencing subject, in addition to the many experiencing subjects. The one I refer to is the soul, the mind, the enduring personality. Thus a person is a many become one increased by one. The person is the one. (Whitehead 1978, pp. 99–109).

I think I understand what you are saying. I respond to Whitehead. I remember what Aristotle said about general sensibility. Aristotle said we recognize that various senses are giving us information about the same object through use of "general sensibility." Aristotle wasn't sure how this happened. But now you have provided an answer, if I understand you correctly. The person can recognize form and order in another person or in objects because it mirrors the form and order within himself. Hence form and order must already be familiar.

Whitehead answers, I had something different in mind, although I agree that what you just said is part of the solution. *The little particles are able to recognize friendly neighbors because they possess memory. Memory in this broad sense is the presence of the past in the present. Memory is inconceivable without the presence of the past in the present. Now, extending the notion of the past being present in the present, an experiencing subject, by attending to an object, allows the object to become part of itself. This I call prehension.* It corresponds with intentionality in phenomenology. *When the objects are actual, other persons, enduring objects, experiencing subjects within a person, I call the prehension "physical prehension."* Earlier in our discussion we called this the *physical mode of experience. But when the object is only a possibility, a universal, I call the prehension "conceptual prehension."* Earlier in our discussion we called this *the conceptual mode of experience.* Incidentally, the term I used to refer to universals in most of my works was *"eternal object."*[91]

Is a thought or an idea shared by two people what you might call a conceptual prehension?

Whitehead laughs. Trying to define thoughts or ideas is a very difficult matter. Ideas may be either conceptual or physical depending on whether the object of an experience is a mere possibility or something actual. I don't think these two words are very helpful. Rather, go back to Aristotle's distinction between substances and forms, Aristotle's "this suches." Physical prehension gives us the "thises" and conceptual prehension gives us the "suches."[92] I agree with Aristotle that we combine these two poles of experience, the physical and the conceptual, in experiencing an actual entity such as my teacup here or another person. But it isn't just people that experience "this suches." All actual entities, that is, enduring objects and actual occasions, are experiencing subjects, or are loose combinations of experiencing subjects. *Molecules and atoms are experiencing subjects, but rocks are not. Unlike human beings and other living organisms, rocks are not a many become one increased by one. Rocks lack organic unity. The rock is a nexus. In a nexus the togetherness of the internal entities is not much greater than mere spatial temporal contiguity. In other words, they just happen to be in the same place through the same period of time. But this is not the case with the various parts of a living person.*[93]

All actual entities are experiencing subjects with experience that is bipolar, physical and conceptual. Remember my earlier comments on the difference between these two modes of experience? The physical pole focuses on unique individuals, persons, enduring objects, events. The conceptual pole focuses on universals, on the shareable or repeatable aspects of the unique individuals, persons, enduring objects, and events (Whitehead 1978, part 3). For example, individual potassium and sodium atoms are repelled by each other because each is positively charged and recognizes conceptually the positive charge on the other. And they also share with all other atoms and elementary particles in the present cosmic epoch an aversion to increasing the same charge within themselves by combining with similarly charged others. Interestingly, the nerves make use of this basic antipathy between two patterns among molecules to conduct messages up the axons.[94]

I had a thought to add to what Whitehead was saying. Is it possible that, like the atoms within us, we are attracted to individuals who complement what is within ourselves by providing us what we lack. Is this not similar to the positive ion being attracted by the negative ion? And at the same time we tend to be somewhat repelled by individuals who are too much like ourselves. Is this because we do not want to increase what we already have enough of, if not too much of? Is this similar to the positive ion being repelled by another positive ion?

Whitehead responds. This is possible, but very simple. It also might be misleading if interpreted the wrong way. *The tradition of science over the past several centuries will tempt us to reduce the person to the particles, life to the nonliving. Whereas, my major concern in my philosophy was to correct this tendency. I love science* (Whitehead 1967a). But we should explain the lesser known in terms of the better known, and not the better known by the less known, as R. G. Collingwood said in his *New Leviathan* (Collingwood 1942). *I quite seriously mean to interpret the atom as an experiencing entity rather than experiencing entities in terms of mechanically understood atoms. I carry this all of the way down to the quantum events that are the "stuff" of space and time. These are my actual occasions, and every one of them is an experient occasion.*[95]

Whitehead continues. *The major difference between an elementary particle and a person is not experience, but complexity of experience. It is true that the degree of creativity in a person is immensely higher than that which occurs in the behavior of an elementary particle. This is because the cascading of experience within a person allows for a rich variety in choices, in options for alternative futures. One result is that consciousness exists in persons but not in elementary particles, though both experience. But you are right in not looking at the elementary particle mechanistically, but as an experiencing entity making choices.*[96]

And further, says Whitehead. All experiencing entities are *a many become one increased by one. Even the little elementary particles, each*

individually different from the others, consist of new droplets of experi-
ence in addition to those that have already occurred. In each droplet, the
past is present in the present. And it is the conformity of the present
experience to past experiences that allows for the enduring identity of
the individual elementary particle. Each new occasion in the history of
the individual elementary particle is a many become one increased by
one, because of the presence of the many occasions in the past within the
new occasion in the present, making the occasion in the present a new
one beyond all of the ones that existed before it came to be. Each new
occasion is a unique individual, different from all others, yet sharing
many universals, eternal objects, not only with many occasions in the
history of the individual elementary particle, but with occasions in the
histories of all other elementary particles in the causal past. Creativity,
which I call the Category of the Ultimate in Process and Reality, *is the*
many becoming one and being increased by one. Creativity allows for
the popping into existence of each new occasion. And the conformity of
present to past experience, or the presence of the past in the present,
allows for the endurance of such individuals as elementary particles and
persons.[97]

Whitehead continues. *The transition from the immediately past*
occasion to the newer immediately present occasion is responsible for
the passage of time. In the case of a living person, it is the addition of
newer occasions to those already past that enable the person to endure
through time, to continue to live, and to be the same person in some sig-
nificant sense from day to day. The vehicles of self-creation at the small-
est scale are individual actual occasions in their popping into existence
and in the transition from the newest to a newer. But a person is
immensely larger than single actual occasions. A person is the result of
a cascading of experience of experience in both space and time. Perhaps
now you can see why I was agreeing with your comparison of persons
and elementary particles with respect to attraction and aversion. But
you can see how immensely more complex the matter is than your ini-
tial insight.[98]

I do see that now. I agree that the attraction of one person for
another is a highly more complex matter than the attraction of one elementary particle for another. But I have another question. Remember
that we talked about the attraction and repulsion of ions as being partially responsible for the transmission of messages in nerve cells. Do you
see nerve cells as experiencing subjects? I ask Whitehead.

Yes, I do. *Living cells have sufficiently tight unity to be a many*
become one increased by one. In fact, I do not recognize the possibility
of merely dead or nonexperiencing entities. All actual entities are expe-
riencing subjects, contrary to the popular beliefs of the seventeenth cen-

tury. *I think it is impossible to build anything actual out of dead and nonexperiencing entities as was attempted by seventeenth century philosophers and scientists* (Whitehead 1967a). Remember Descartes' problem with trying to account for interaction between experiencing minds and insentient and mechanical body parts. The difficulty is kind of like that of Wallace in the animated short film, *Wrong Trousers*.[99] The thinking, experiencing Wallace, finds himself inserted into a pair of mechanical trousers over which he has no control. Though Descartes asserts that minds control bodies, he cannot account for how they could possibly do so. Descartes' conception of body pushes him in the direction of a perplexity like that of Wallace with the wrong trousers. *A mechanical body would be the wrong body for a living person. Only a body that is a living society of experiencing entities can be the right body for a person.*

Whitehead continues. But there is an even more fundamental problem than the mind-body problem, which compelled me in my mature philosophical works to rethink all of physical reality in terms of experient occasions.[100] *Experience is required to provide the unity needed for space and time itself. The space-time continuum is a one in a sense that cannot be accounted for mechanically, or atomistically. Space and time not only separate things and events, but they hold them together in the same world. This is the prehensive aspect of space and time, and can be accounted for only by supposing that the events within space and time are prehensive, that is, experiencing. Hence, I came to view even the quantum events of empty space, or the quantum events in those routes of experience that are elementary particles, as experiencing subjects. These are the actual occasions I write so much about in* Process and Reality. *Droplets of experience are the basic stuff of all physical reality, even empty space and time. Hence the formula "experience of experience of experience" applies to all that is actual. Our earlier suggestion that experience of experience produces consciousness and experience of experience of experience produces self-consciousness is too simple. In your words, which I like, immensely more complex hierarchical cascadings of experience are needed for consciousness and finally self-consciousness* (Whitehead 1967a, pp. 69–74).[101]

Now let me think about it for a moment, I said. It seems that Hegel is concentrating on the interpersonal dimension of the problem of consciousness and self-consciousness, and that Whitehead is concentrating on both the interpersonal and the intrapersonal aspects of this problem. What I have learned is that persons both relate to other persons and are complex internally. I have also learned that experience allows the past to be present in the present, and that this is one of the grounds of singularity that makes a person unique. But the present is perpetually becoming past and being replaced by a new present. Each new present event is a unique individual, different from all events that came before. The result is inevitable change or flux. This poses a problem for living persons. How do they succeed in maintaining their identity in the face of the flux?

My thoughts are interrupted by someone approaching the table and speaking to me for the first time. He has a heavy Danish accent. He pulls up a chair to join us and hands me his card. The card identifies the man as Johannes Climactus.[102] But no sooner have I finished reading his card then he abruptly pulls it away from me, tears it up, and hands me another. This time the card reads, Angelus Silesius. I am about to ask him which is his actual name, but he again pulls the card away, tears it up, and hands me a third with an even different name. When the stranger repeats the sequence of retracting and tearing up the card, I become irritated. The stranger notices my irritation and chuckles. By this time I really want to know who he is. So I ask him rather firmly to identify himself. When he presents me with yet another card, I anticipate that he will again remove it from my hand and tear it up. Therefore, I clutch it tightly and pull it away from his reach. This time the card reads, Søren Kierkegaard.[103]

I turn to Kierkegaard. Why do you have so many different names?

Kierkegaard responds. *It is because what I intend to be is more important than what I have been. In listening to the conversation, I think that too much emphasis is being placed on the past. It is true that I recollect my past into my present, and that this is one of the means by which I succeed in maintaining my identity in the face of the flux. But my intention to repeat myself in the future is equally if not more important than my recollection of my past in my present. Granted that I cannot stop the flux, and that I will be different in the future than I am at present, repetition of present into future allows for the subjectivity that makes me a unique person in the truest sense—the truth is subjectivity.*[104]

I am perplexed by part of Kierkegaard's statement. So I ask him a question. Are you using *recollection* as Plato used *recollection?* Is the recollection of the past that you talk about the same as recollection of the Forms in Plato's theory?[105]

What? Answers Kierkegaard, squeezing his Danish pastry tightly enough to crumble it. *Platonic Forms! No! I want nothing to do with systematic philosophy, philosophy that builds systems and attempts to be objective. That which is important to a living person is subjectivity. The problem with systematic philosophy is that it attempts to rise above the subjective in an impossible quest for objectivity. Unlike Platonic recollection, what I call recollection in my* Concluding Unscientific Postscript *is the recollection of my individual past into my individual present.* My view is similar to what I have been hearing Whitehead articulate. *My concern is that the presence of the past in the present that he speaks about is not enough to account for the subjectivity of a living person. I cannot be a person by retreating to my past, but only by leaning into or anticipating my future.*[106]

I am curious, I say to Kierkegaard. If singularity is grounded in subjectivity and in anticipation of the future, and to a lesser extent in the presence of the past in the present, then what is the relationship between universals and individuals?

Kierkegaard laughs hysterically. I try to avoid universals at all costs. I enjoy destroying universals whenever I suspect their existence. I particularly enjoyed tearing up the cards I gave you. From the conversation I have been overhearing I understand why you are interested in universals. But please don't expect any help from me. I suspect that it is much too easy to fall into the trap of uniformity if you don't keep your guard up. For example, I hear you say "patient" in your talks with the other philosophers. "Patient"! Yuck! Hospitals and medical persons are the worst for categorizing people as universals, for treating them as if they were things and diseases, refusing to recognize their unique subjectivity. When in the medical fields are persons ever treated as persons? You dress us alike in those awful hospital gowns, stack us up in rows of beds, in identical rooms, and force us to eat food which is indistinguishable one course from another and one meal from another. And those awful ID bracelets that reduce a person to a mere number. You even give us treatments and medications on the basis of the identification on those bracelets. Even our history is the history of a disease and not a person. In fact, you ask us what our insurance company is before you even ask us our name. And then when I ask about the information included in my chart, I am given the impression that my personal history recorded in the chart does not belong to me, but to my physician and the hospital. And if I want this information, I must fill out forms that presuppose that I am reducible to even more absurd and objectionable universals. So don't talk to me about universals, they are completely inhuman![107]

I am taken somewhat aback by Kierkegaard, and even worry a little bit about his sanity. But I have to admit that he makes some valid and important points. There is definitely a danger in universals. Though they are unavoidable and necessary in my opinion, they are very easily misused by humans. Nurses must be careful not to easily and unreflectively accept universals as appropriate and normal. The stripping of humanity from nurse and patient for a simple but false objectivity is not "the real world," a notion that nursing students are sometimes taught to accept by practicing nurses. What is subjective is most fully real. The objectivity of the past is the fossilized subjectivity of what was originally present. And though the universals are objectively real, they are deficiently real. And unlike the objectively real entities of the past, universals have never been subjectively or fully real. In my search for the grounds of singularity, Kierkegaard's emphasis on subjectivity and the importance of anticipation of the future are important. Although the notions are not necessarily new after my discussions with Whitehead, the emphasis is healthy and corrective and deepens my understanding of key insights.

I feel that my quest is nearing the end. But one more figure approaches our table. It is Edmund Husserl.

Perhaps I can provide some balance between Kierkegaard and Whitehead. I never read Whitehead. But overhearing the discussions I find that I share many insights in common with him. *In my* Phenomenology of Internal Time Consciousness *I develop ideas that are elsewhere labeled the theory of* intentional surplus (Husserl 1964, 1973). Similar ideas can be found in William James, Josiah Royce, and even my sometime student, Martin Heidegger, and of course, in Whitehead. We all agree that *in experience there is a presence of the past in the present, of the present in the present, and of the future in the present. But of course not all in the same sense!* Now that I have worded the insight just this way, I must hasten to include Jean-Paul Sartre in my list of philosophers who agree to the fundamental insight I am attempting to articulate, for my wording is the wording he uses for his three temporal "ecstases." [108]

Husserl continues. *The insight I label* intentional surplus *is that experience is not narrowed to a technical physical present, a punctual now. Rather the now that is experienced retains events that are clockwise already past and even contains events that are clockwise still in the future, not yet present. In the* Phenomenology of Internal Time Consciousness *I notice further that there is a sloping of presentness into pastness in such a fashion that there is no definite boundary between the present and the past. Further, the present leans into the future in such a fashion that there is no definite boundary between the present and the future. But if one considers longer periods of time, the distinction between past, present, and future becomes determinate. For example, a thousand years ago is clearly past, yet a few seconds ago is not. Similarly for the future. Intentional surplus makes it impossible for the boundaries to be clear and distinct, and makes it impossible for the present to be an infinitesimal duration of time.* Notice the similarity between this theory and what Kierkegaard just said about recollection and repetition, or what Whitehead said about memory and anticipation (Husserl 1964).

I ask Husserl. Could you explain what you mean by "phenomenology"?

Husserl responds. Phenomenology can trace its history back to at least Kant. Its fundamental concern is the nature and structure of experience.

I ask Husser!. By experience do you mean experience, experience of experience, and experience of experience of experience?

Husserl responds. Before the discussion of the past few hours, I was inclined to agree with Descartes, that unconscious experience was a contradiction in terms. Because I understood experience as conscious experience, I was inclined to be concerned only with human experience, in Whitehead's and Hegel's terms, experience of experience. But if I accept their phrase, experience of experience, then I must also accept the existence of unconscious experience. In their account, conscious experience can occur only after experience has occurred and is then reflected upon. Hence, without unconscious experience conscious experience would be impossible. Before I heard Whitehead and you discuss hierarchies of cascading experience and subordinate experiencing entities, I was inclined to bracket out any concern with the brain and neurological systems, because I was not inclined to view them as experiencing. But perhaps I was too much imprisoned by eighteenth- and nineteenth-century preconceptions concerning the nature of the body. Frankly I find this new perspective somewhat overwhelming and I would like to be excused to go think it out.

I turn to the group as a whole. Perhaps this is a good place to stop. I would like to reflect on my conversations with all of you. I am hopeful that the result will be a usable philosophy of nursing based on a more adequate understanding of the relationship between universality and singularity. I thank all of you and invite you to read chapter 6, for our philosophy of nursing.

CHAPTER 5

From Jean Watson's Theory of Caring to a Philosophy of Caring

Although we are aware that more than one nurse theorist has developed a theory of caring for nursing, we want to remind the reader that the nurse co-author chose Jean Watson's theory for both personal and philosophical reasons (see chapter 1). We begin this chapter by revisiting the narrative and beginning development of a philosophy of caring. The philosophy of caring will be enfolded in the philosophy of nursing in chapter 6.

Among the many characteristics of nursing illustrated by the narrative, perhaps none is more striking than the nurse's genuine care for the young man in contrast with her need to be objective. The nurse in the narrative is all too aware that the sentiments involved in caring and the objectivity necessary to perform certain procedures skillfully are equally fundamental to good nursing care. The good of the patient requires that nursing care be an adagio between subjectivity and objectivity, nurse and patient.[1] But the nurse also realizes that she needs to disengage herself from her sentiments for the boy for her own sake somewhat, from time to time. The nurse realizes that the intense sentiments and concentration involved in intersubjective caring cannot be sustained for long periods of time without effecting her own health. As a student, the nurse was cautioned by mentors about "boundaries" between herself and her patient. The good nurse knows how to be caring without blurring boundaries between self and other. Have her feelings for this boy and this family obscured those boundaries? Has she let herself become too emotionally entangled?

The nurse in the narrative knows that to care for the boy adequately she has to perform certain tasks skillfully. The performance of these tasks requires a cyclical shift in her awareness from the boy as person to the tasks that need to be done for his healing. Each in turn must either await its place in the shadows of her consciousness or in its full illumination. What the nurse finds impossible is to concentrate with equal intensity on both the boy as person and on the skillful performance of the tasks at the same time. Concentrating on the task requires a temporary diminishment of attention to the boy as a person. The nurse in the narrative wants to be both intersubjective and objective at the same time. Reducing the conflict means seeking a balance between these two modes of experience.

Hence the temporary disengagement from concentration on the person of the patient meets two needs for the nurse in the narrative. It provides the emotional respite she needs to prevent being overwhelmed by her own emotions at a time when she must perform tasks expertly. And the temporary disengagement from intersubjectivity is necessary for the nurse as person. This second aspect is to be discussed later in chapter 6. Some nursing tasks can be performed on "autopilot," but other tasks cannot, no matter what level of expertise is possessed by the nurse. Assessment skills require undivided attention to details. And for the informed novice nurse, learning new skills requires as much concentration as the expert nurse requires for assessment. But the worries of the expert nurse are different from those of the novice. Whereas the novice might be anxious about performing skilled tasks accurately without mistakes, especially if the nurse is aware that a mistake might hurt the patient, the expert nurse does not have the same anxiety. She has performed the tasks so many times that she has learned to perform them on "autopilot." The advantage to performing the tasks on auto pilot is that the nurse can concentrate on the patient as person while at the same time performing the tasks skillfully. In that situation what is in the shadows of the consciousness of the expert nurse is the concentration on the skills. What is illuminated is the patient as person.

But there is a shift in attention from person to skill even in the consciousness of the expert nurse under certain conditions. The shift of the expert nurse's attention from person to task occurs when there is an unforeseen problem. Unforeseen problems could be a change in the vital signs of the patient, a particularly difficult venipuncture, or other such changes. But the nurse, even the expert nurse, cannot give full attention with the same intensity to two objects at the same time. Good nursing requires that she balance both. If the nurse abandons subjectivity, she does so at the risk of becoming too callous. And if she abandons objectivity, she does so at the risk of becoming too sentimental. In either case, she risks harm to the patient.

The narrative shows that centering on the personhood of the boy was both important to the nurse as a person, that is, to her own health and personal growth, as well as for the good of the patient. The problem for the nurse was how to enjoy a deep caring relationship with her patient and yet be sufficiently objective. She needed both of these modes of caring without allowing either to become permanently dominant. Hence, both intersubjectivity and technical skill take their turns in the light and the shadows of the consciousness of the nurse. The nurse in the narrative finds it impossible to concentrate on the two divergent activities intensely at the same time.

When she had been a novice, the nurse had needed to concentrate on developing her skills. And the nurse, even as a novice, was an informed novice. She understood the risks as well as the benefits in what she was attempting to do for the patient. If the nurse were merely performing tasks as prescribed by a manual, it would have been unlikely that she would have appreciated the possible untoward consequences of her actions. To the uninformed novice tasks are more of an adventure than a responsibility. But the informed novice who has had enough education to understand the risks of any nursing procedure, before she even performs the procedure, will want total concentration on learning new skills.

During her novitiate there were times when the nurse had forgotten to give recognition to the personhood of the patient as she fixed her attention on the tasks necessary for the patient to get well. For example, how often have nurses changed IV fluid bags on patients' IV pumps forgetting, in their haste, to acknowledge the person in the bed? This is not an uncommon experience for even the expert nurse under the pressures of time and "patient load."

But the nurse in the narrative is no longer just an informed novice. We know that she is an expert. She has the ability to perform complicated skills on "autopilot." But even now, as an expert nurse, she finds it necessary to shift the focus of her greatest attention away from the boy from time to time, not necessarily for the purpose of developing a skill or for attending to an unforeseen emergency. This time the nurse needed a respite from her feelings of caring. But does the shift away from the boy imply that she has misplaced her caring feelings for him? And does this mean that she is uncaring during this period of "respite" time? The answer is "no." But this will be addressed at greater length in the next chapter through the illumination of universality and singularity. For now it is important to note that self care and care for the other need to be blended harmoniously, they are not really opposites. Self-care and other care need to take their turns in the shadows and highlights of consciousness in a rhythm like that described for subjectivity and objectivity.

But there is a related matter, one that also bothered the nurse in the narrative. Believing that caring is *inter*personal, the nurse in the narrative is puzzled. How it is possible to have caring sentiments for an unconscious person, one who cannot be expected to reciprocate? Even when the boy was alive, he had never been conscious during the time the nurse cared for him. Doesn't *inter*personal imply a relationship or an activity between *two* persons? If so, how can the nurse account for her feelings for an unconscious boy? Could it be that the sentiments of caring for a conscious patient are similar to the sentiments of caring for an unconscious patient, one that the nurse has never known in a conscious state? Are the sentiments of caring for an unconscious human being similar to the feelings of caring for a fine work of art, or any other object for which the subject has a positive interest, as explained earlier in the discussion with Whitehead? Is the caring for even an unconscious patient different from the feelings of care for an inanimate object?

The experience of caring by the nurse in the narrative seems inconsistent with the thesis that caring must be intersubjective, that it requires a relationship between two persons who are not only conscious, but are actively engaged in genuine dialogue and authentic existence. The unconscious patient in the narrative was capable of neither genuine dialogue or authentic existence. Prior to the time of the narrative the boy was unconscious; during the time of the narrative he was deceased. Only the nurse and the family members were capable of authentic existence and genuine dialogue with others. If caring is limited to a reciprocal relationship between two persons, in this case care provider and care receiver, then how do we account for the feelings of the nurse for the boy? Perhaps this problem can be resolved by illuminating the nature of caring itself.

There are several important problems that the narrative illuminates concerning the nature of caring. The first is reflected in a tension between the feelings of the nurse for the boy and the expert performance of skills necessary to help get him well. The second has already been considered, is it possible to have a caring occasion with an unconscious person?

The tension between the feelings and the actions of the nurse in the narrative could be described as a tension between the subjective *sentiments* of caring and the objective *skills* of caring. If so, then this means that the caring of the nurse for the patient involves *two* equally important but interrelated aspects of care—sentiments and skill. The subjective sentiments of caring are describable as the empathetic feelings and other positive emotions that one has for one's fellow human being, that the nurse has for the patient. On the other hand, the objective skills of caring are the tasks that the nurse needs to be able to do skillfully and expertly, regardless of her sentiments toward the patient.

Thus far we have only been talking about sentiments of caring in a positive sense. But sentiments are not always positive. The nurse may have to deal with negative sentiments before positive sentiments of caring are possible. For example, the nurse may personally feel revulsion about having to care for a patient that is known to have harmed someone else. The patient may be known to be a drunk driver who has killed a child, or may be a repeated abuser of his spouse. Or the nurse may feel anger toward a patient who has been self-abusive. In these situations the nurse's sentiments of caring may be stifled by the more powerful negative feelings. The negative feelings may also be an obstacle to the performance of the skills of caring. Yet the nurse is still obligated to care for the patient, regardless of her feelings. Here objectivity is preferable to subjectivity and is healthy and necessary for both nurse and patient.

But there are times when *both* sentiments and skills of caring need to be in the shadows of consciousness for the success of caring. The spotlight of consciousness needs to be focused on something that *distracts* from both of these aspects of caring. In this kind of example, the nurse may have a very positive caring sentiment for the person, but at the same time have a natural repugnance for the foul odors, unseemly wounds, or cancerous ulcers present on his body. In this situation, the nurse can neither afford to be deeply engaged in genuine dialogue with the patient, nor can she be too directly focused on the skilled tasks she is performing. In either case she may be overwhelmed by her own feelings. Both patient and nurse may find superficial chitchat helpful under these conditions. It distracts their attention from the unpleasant realities at hand. When the nurse and the patient are not distracted in such a manner during this time then both become aware of the awfulness of the situation. The patient may become self-conscious and overly apologetic to the nurse for her having to do such a thing. Although there may be times when this would be an entre into helping the patient deal with feelings about his condition, sometimes the patient isn't ready, and the timing may be wrong with respect to the skilled task that needs to be performed.

There are many other situations in which both the sentiments of caring and the skills of caring need to be temporarily in the shadows of the consciousness of the nurse. Superficial conversation is helpful for both nurse and patient when a female nurse has to insert a urinary catheter into a male patient. Genuine dialogue is inappropriate. At the same time the nurse cannot afford to be too focused on the task at hand. But perhaps this example needs no further explanation.

The nurse's sentiments for the patient may actually get in the way of performing other tasks expertly. For example, the nurse who is experiencing the sentiments of caring too intensely may not be able to perform certain necessary procedures that temporarily increase the pain of an already suffering patient. Objectivity during these times, that is, concentrating on the tasks that need to be performed and not on the person of the patient, is healthy for both nurse and patient.

Yet at the same time the nurse's sentiments of caring are part of the motivation for performing the skills of caring expertly. The nurse masters the skills of caring because she genuinely wants to help the patient. Hence the novice nurse despite initial frustration will continue to try until she has developed the skill.

But after mastery of the skills of caring, another kind of problem arises with the sentiments of caring. Sometimes the sense of power that comes from mastery of a technological skill can temporarily captivate the nurse in such a fashion as to eclipse the sentiments of caring. In that situation the nurse's love of technology can so occupy her emotions that there is little room left for the human sentiments of caring. The question is, will she become so captivated by her mastery of the skills that she loses sight of personhood both in herself and in her patient. If she is not aware of the danger of the Sirens' song[2] of technology, she may lose her identity as a person while she increases her identity as skilled technician. Who she is may become narrowly defined by what she does. And the person of the patient may also be submerged in the narrower identity of his disease. Who he is may become defined by what he has. If this happens, both nurse and patient become dehumanized—the nurse as disease chaser, the patient as battleground between technology and disease.

After these personal reflections on the nature of caring we would now like to turn to the theory of Jean Watson for help in illuminating the concept of caring as encountered by the nurse in the narrative. The nurse co-author has chosen to examine the theory of Jean Watson in this chapter in order to shed light on the nurse's conflict in the narrative concerning caring. Watson was the nurse theorist who first enlightened the nurse co-author that a theory of nursing could be based on the thesis that caring is central to nursing (Watson 1979, p. 9). In addition Watson has been a lifelong crusader for nursing's obligation to keep caring in the foreground as essential to good nursing.

When the nurse co-author first read her earlier book, *Nursing: The Philosophy and Science of Caring* (1979), she recognized that Watson's list of carative factors were relevant for understanding caring. But that she could recognize the carative factors as part of caring implies that she already had an understanding of what caring was. Perhaps this pre understanding of caring is what Watson meant when she said that caring is a "given" (Watson 1979, p.10). But if caring is a given, as Watson asserts, then our question is, who or what is the giver and when does caring become given? Though Watson states that caring is a given, her theory does not shed light on the nature of the givenness of caring. Yet what Watson's theory *does* suggest is that we can identify caring through certain conducts and attitudes, conducts and attitudes that she calls the carative factors. Interestingly, in her second book, *Nursing: Human Science and Human Care: A Theory of Nursing* (1985), Watson changed the wording of the carative factors. (Both of these versions of the carative factors are quoted together for comparison later in this chapter.) Though Watson changed the wording of the carative factors from her earlier to her later book, she did not explain her reasons for such a change. It would have been helpful had Watson discussed the rationale for the change in wording, because such an explanation might have better illuminated the elusive nature of caring.

In Watson's first book, she offers the carative factors and the basic assumptions of caring as a foundation for a science of caring. And in her second book Watson adds the notion of transpersonal caring with the actual caring occasion as its exemplar. Recalling that Watson claims that caring is a given and later offers the carative factors as examples of caring, Watson implies that caring can be at least partially revealed through its concomitants or signs. Yet as a given, caring must first be pre-understood by giver, receiver, and observer in order for all three to recognize caring through its concomitants and signs.

While we cannot disagree that caring can be revealed through its concomitants or signs, we do not assume that caring is revealed *fully* through its concomitants or signs. And without a fuller illumination of the nature of caring, nursing is left with the predicament of Tantalus and the overhanging fruit.[3] Like the fruit before Tantalus, the nature of caring is within sight of nursing, but always just out of reach. Hence nursing is left with an unsolved philosophical mystery. On the one hand everyone understands caring, on the other hand, no one can say just what caring is.

As initially gratifying to the nurse co-author as Watson's theory was when she first encountered it, she now recognize that the need for an illumination of caring that is deeper, richer, and more complete. What is essential is answer or at least an illumination of the question "what is the 'given,' in the case of caring, and how did the given become a given?" And who or what is the giver? How is it possible for many people to know what caring is in spite of their inability to adequately expound the nature of caring? As earlier noted, Watson's exposition of caring presupposes that nurses already recognize caring when they encounter it. But it would have been more informative to explain how caring is a given, and to explore the senses in which caring is a given.

Hence, the nature of caring still remains "tantalizingly" close within Watson's theory. And since Watson does not examine the senses in which caring is a given, we will try to do so with the help of what we have learned from the imaginary dialogue with the philosophers.

If caring is a given, as Watson contends, then we return to the question of the source of its givenness. Is the givenness of caring *a priori*? Is it grounded in the sciences? Although we encounter Heidegger briefly in the imaginary dialogues with the philosophers, he has explored the nature of caring in his philosophy. Jean Watson refers to Heidegger's reflections on caring in her work (Watson 1985, pp. 80–81). Does Heidegger's concept of caring explain the nature in which caring is meaningful to nursing (Heidegger 1996, 1, ch. 4)? Or is the nature of caring grounded in some special kind of experience?

As the reader may recall, *a priori* knowledge, according to David Hume, is grounded in relations of ideas. Relations of ideas make such knowledge analytic. And analytic knowledge, concludes David Hume, is trivial or insignificant because such knowledge is not about the world. Only the analytic is *a priori* from David Hume's point of view.

But we know that whatever caring is, it is certainly not insignificant. And caring either is, or ought to be, part of the world. Curiously caring is both in the world and transcends the world.[4] Hence caring *is* and *ought* to be at the same time. That it is an ought to be makes caring in some sense a moral imperative. And Watson herself asserts that caring is a moral imperative (Watson 1988, 1990, 1990a). That caring is *in* the world eliminates the possibility that the knowledge of caring might be *a priori* in Hume's sense, that is, merely analytic *a priori*.

But what about Kant's synthetic *a priori*? Is caring a given because it is synthetic *a priori*? Is the concept of caring *a priori* in the sense in which substance and causality, or space and time, are *a priori*?[5] The answer would have to be "no" for the most part; for caring is not a presupposition of experience in the sense in which space, time, causality, and substance are presuppositions of experience. And yet there is a touch of the *a priori* in the Kantian sense in the case of caring.

For both Hume and Kant, the *a priori* is *knowledge* that is possessed prior to particular experiences. Here it must be remembered that *a priori* and empirical distinguish kinds of *knowledge*—*a priori* knowledge is knowledge prior to experience, and empirical knowledge is knowledge based on experience. Whereas, analytic and synthetic distinguish kinds of *judgments*, propositions, or statements—analytic judgments are true (or false) in virtue of the meanings of their terms, while synthetic judgments require knowledge other than that of language for determination of their truth (or falsity). Kant's philosophy is special in that he allows for synthetic *a priori* judgments and not just for analytic *a priori* judgments. For Kant the synthetic is a kind of judgment. But it is important to note that what Kant means in this case is not a moral judgment. It is a judgment in the sense of a statement or proposition. According to the tenets of logic a proposition is that which is either true or false, and never both.

For example, in a nursing situation, a patient may be given a medication the dosage of which is calibrated on the patient's height and weight. But suppose in an emergency, such as a mass casualty situation, the nurse is unable to take the patient's height and weight because the patient is unconscious and other staff are too busy to assist.

The nurse, based on her experience, judges the patient to be 6′ 3″ and 210 lbs. But later the nurse discovers when she puts the patient on the scale that he is actually 6′ 1.5″ and that he weighs 190 lbs. Now she knows that her original judgment concerning the patient's height and weight was false. This kind of judgment is typical of Kant's synthetic judgments in that its truth or falsity cannot be determined by words alone such as in analytic *a priori* judgments, but only by experience. In analytic *a priori* judgments, such as "bachelors are unmarried," we know the judgments are true in virtue of the meaning of the words in the judgment. But the judgments concerning the patient's height and weight can only be known to be true (or false) on the basis of actual individual experiences, such the nurse's visual assessment or her later weighing of the patient on the scales. Whichever method is used to verify or falsify the judgment, visual assessment or more careful and accurate measurement, the judgments are empirical as well as synthetic. Empirical judgments are synthetic judgments whose truth or falsity can only be determined on the basis of individual experiences, such as determining the weight of the patient by observing or measuring. In the narrative such judgments as the nurse's noting of the time on the clock, or her judgment that the machines were working properly, were synthetic and empirical judgments.

We have established that synthetic judgments are not moral judgments and are not judgments based on the meanings of words alone, but at least some of these judgments can be determined to be true (or false) on the basis of experience. However, there is a question still to be answered. How can any synthetic judgments be *known* to be true *a priori*, that is, prior to any individual experience? Kant's answer is that certain things must be the case in order for there to be any experience at all, and that these things that must be the case, these *presuppositions* of experience, allow us to know *a priori* (prior to all individual experiences) that certain synthetic judgments are true (or false). Interestingly, although Kant says that these presuppositions of experience are necessary for experience, he doesn't explicitly address the question of where they come from. Are they also a given? If so, then he does not explicitly address the question of their givenness. Like Watson's theory of caring, Kant's theory of human experience is tantalizingly incomplete.⁶

Returning to the example of the patient in the emergency situation, and the nurse's judgments about his height and weight, a further illumination of Kant's notion of the synthetic *a priori* is possible. The best examples of Kantian synthetic *a priori* judgments relate to space and time, causality and substance. The nurse can determine empirically the height and weight of the patient. But she already knows prior to observations and measurements, that is, *a priori*, that there will be at least relative permanence of both the weight and height of the patient in the face of the passage of time. The nurse is confident that the patient (substance) will not disappear instantly (time) just because she has stopped observing him. To state this in another way, the nurse is confident that the patient will not shrink to the size of a lady bug in one extreme, or expand to the size of an ocean liner in the opposite extreme. But here the synthetic *a priori* does not assure the nurse that no sudden shrinkage or expansion is possible, it only assures her that if such should occur, it must be for some very good and unusual empirical reasons (causality). There must be a cause of any change. If they are extreme, the nurse might look for something like the device in the movie, *Honey I Shrunk the Kids*, to explain the sudden shrinking of the patient to the size of a ladybug. No such change can occur for no reason at all: this is the synthetic judgment that is known *a priori* (in Kant's perspective).

Hence, the nurse knows that any sudden and dramatic change in weight or height on the part of a patient must be for very serious reasons, such as dehydration. All marked increases or diminishments ought to be investigated carefully, unless they can be attributed to some comedic effect. For even comedy relies on the synthetic *a priori*.

And even small children understand comedy based on the strongly empirical or the synthetic *a priori*. The nurse co-author can remember a time when her son, Tony, was two years old. She had jokingly put her shoe on her head and her hat on her foot and then asked him, "How do you like my new hat and my new shoe?" Tony laughed, indicating that he knew that the hat belonged on her head and the shoe belonged on her foot. Yet when she asked him *why* she couldn't wear the shoe on her head and the hat on her foot, Tony insisted that it was because they simply did not belong there. What Tony was doing by objecting to the placement of the hat and the shoe, was using his strongly empirical knowledge as a test for what was possible.

What the story suggests is the importance of intersubjective validation for making sense of the world. And that general universals (shareables and repeatables) are very important in this respect. Hats belong on heads; shoes belong on feet. Yet at the same time the story indicates the importance of retaining our sensitivity to the uniqueness of individuals and individual experiences. This is not only an example of mother and son sharing a joke in the unusual juxtaposition of hat and foot and shoe and head, but it also indicates the possibility of creating new and unique ways of interpreting the world. Hence universals are necessary for making sense of the world, but attention to uniqueness encourages new and creative ways of thinking.

Returning to the question about caring, is our pre understanding of caring in some sense like Kant's *a priori* knowledge of the truth of some synthetic judgments? The most direct answer is "no," because caring in the nursing or Watsonian sense is not a presupposition of our ability to experience a common or physical world. Though we would be much less happy and much less human, without caring, we would still be able to experience tables and chairs and trees, and be able to tell the difference between these objects and dream objects.

In Kant's Second Critique, *The Critique of Pure Practical Reason* (Kant 1956), and in his *Foundations of the Metaphysics of Morals* (Kant 1980), Kant is concerned with what ought to be and not just with what is. The concept of a person is very important from the perspective of practical reason. Is the givenness of caring due at least in part to the fact that caring is a presupposition of our ability to understand and respect persons as such? It can be argued that caring is a presupposition of a deeper understanding of human nature.

We know that those who lack the pre-understanding of caring in the nursing and Watsonian sense may also be those who are unable to recognize and respect persons as such, either others or themselves. The ability to make choices among a rich variety of possible futures presupposes a sensitivity to self that is possible only with a foundation of caring. Without the ability to recognize self in one's own person and in the other, actions become largely determined by urges of the moment. The moment is the now. Focusing on the now means not being able to learn from the past or anticipate different possible futures. Since caring allows for fuller retention of the past and anticipation of the future, it is in this sense a presupposition of understanding of the self.

It is in the Second Critique that Kant reaches a deeper understanding of the nature of self by reflection on what persons do, their actions. Since the practice of the skills of caring is action, the perspective of the Second Critique is relevant to the notion of caring in the nursing sense. Practical reason is concerned with *what ought to be*, with the rules for action, rather than *what is*. (Remember that theoretical reason is concerned with what is and is relevant to science.) These practical rules for action are summed up by Kant under three kinds of imperatives in the Second Critique. These imperatives are commands that enjoin what ought or ought not be done, rather than judgments about what is true or false. Imperatives are guides to right action, rather truths. All three kinds of imperatives are relevant to caring in the nursing sense.[7]

Hypothetical imperatives are rules or recipes for accomplishing tasks, if it is desired to do so. If you want *a*, you ought not to do *c*, you ought to do *b*. If you want to carry water, you ought not to use a sieve, but you ought to use a pitcher. If you want to take the patient's temperature, you ought not to use a sphygmomenometer, you ought to use a thermometer. And if you want to measure the patient's blood pressure, you ought not to use a thermometer, you ought to use a sphygmomenometer. The hypothetical imperatives are very relevant to the skills of caring, for they are the recipes for performing tasks successfully. Hence, the more knowledgeable a nurse is of hypothetical imperatives, which are the rules of technology, the more skillful her caring of the patient can be. Textbooks and practice are the major sources of the nurse's knowledge of hypothetical imperatives. And in a sense the hypothetical imperatives of nursing are the imperatives of the technology of nursing. However, *all* hypothetical imperatives are potentially of interest to nursing. For the nurse cannot foreknow the limits of the practical knowledge that may be relevant to the skills of caring for an individual patient in unique circumstances. There is no subset of hypothetical imperatives that are exclusively *nursing* hypothetical imperatives. Hence, the practicing nurse must be a renaissance person with the widest possible practical knowledge.

The *assertorical imperative* is the prudential imperative. It is the imperative of enlightened egoism. But we need to caution the reader to avoid misunderstanding. We earlier talked about persons who lacked a pre understanding of caring, and hence lacked an adequate understanding of self, in both their own cases and in the cases of others. Such persons may be said to be *egotists*, but not enlightened *egoists* in the sense Kant means by his account of the assertorical imperative. Kant calls it "assertorical" (meaning a most general matter of fact) because he is impressed by the general fact that all humans desire happiness. Therefore the assertorical imperative reads: "*Because* you desire *happiness*, you ought to do _____ ." The blank is filled in with a long list of things that will add to happiness, such as getting enough exercise, becoming financially secure, cultivating friendships, cultivating a variety of interests including cultivating an interest in other people's welfare. Hence, the enlightened egoist makes a very good neighbor. Surprisingly, the assertorical imperatives are relevant to *both* the skills of caring *and* the sentiments of caring. We use the word "surprisingly" because one might think that caring is merely a moral imperative. Caring is also fun, it is essential to one's personal happiness. The assertorical imperative is the imperative of enlightened self-interest. It is motivated by self-interest and not by morality. Hence, according to the assertorical imperative, the nurse who discovers that caring makes her happier is motivated by self-interest to cultivate her skills and sentiments of caring. This may account in part for why nurses remain in nursing despite poor pay and long hours, and lack of sufficient respect.

In contrast to the hypothetical imperative and the assertorical imperative, the categorial imperative is the moral law. As the reader will recall, the "ought" of the hypothetical imperative is merely technological, it binds only if you want to do something. In contrast the "ought" of the assertorical imperative is a general matter of fact true of all humans. We are all bound by the fact that we desire happiness to do whatever we need to do to acquire happiness. In contrast to these two imperatives, the categorical imperative binds unconditionally. Perhaps one could be a person and not desire happiness. But one could not be a person in the deeper sense and not self-legislate the categorical imperative. For one cannot be a person without being counter causally free (an unconditioned condition), and one cannot be free without self-legislating the categorical imperative. The categorical imperative is essential for being able to say "*I* did it"—"no one and no thing made me do it." I am an unconditioned condition of my actions and all of their consequences. The *categorical imperative* is the moral law. It is a law that all persons ought to self legislate at all times, places, and conditions. It is called "categorical" because it is unconditioned. It is also categorical in the sense of being universal and necessary. But whereas the categories of the understanding are universally and necessarily *true*, the categorical imperative is universally and necessarily *right*.[8] It is always morally wrong (not right) to violate the categorical imperative.

Regarding the concept of caring, Watson asserts that caring is a moral imperative (Watson 1988, 1990, 1990a). In the Kantian sense a moral imperative is a specification of the categorical imperative. So if caring is a moral imperative, then caring should be part of the categorical imperative. If it is part of the categorical imperative, then all people are morally required to care at all times and places, and under all circumstances. And if they are not caring at all times and places, they are violating the moral law.

But if caring is a moral imperative, it is important to know which aspects of caring are morally imperative. A problem arises when we consider the sentiments of caring. For sentiments are seldom under the voluntary control of a person. Individuals are only morally obligated to do what they *can* do. Hence, though we might be morally obligated to work at the cultivation of our ability to have certain feelings, we cannot be morally obligated to *have* particular feelings at a unique individual time and for a unique individual person. Thus, if caring is a moral imperative, it is only the skills of caring that can be morally imperative and not the sentiments of caring.

In the Kantian sense nurses are obligated to perform the skills of caring. They are not obligated to feel the sentiments of caring toward any individual patient. And in the Kantian sense, parents are not obligated to have the sentiments of caring toward any one child, but they are obligated to perform the skills of caring for every child. In like manner, a son or daughter who cares for an elderly parent is not obligated to feel care for that parent, but they are obligated to practice the skills of caring. Interestingly, practicing the skills of caring may often result in happiness, no matter what the sentiments toward the recipient of care. This is because *doing* something out of a sense of moral obligation, while released from a sense of moral obligation to *feel* a certain way, can bring a sense of happiness from knowing that one is fulfilling an obligation as an unconditioned condition, and not just doing what one is emotionally prompted to do (such as out of guilt or pressure of guilt).

In like manner, Kant holds that a person does not possess moral good will unless he or she would continue to perform actions in accordance with the categorical imperative, no matter how they felt. For example, a person may be practicing the skills of caring because of positive feelings, perhaps love, for the recipient of care. But Kant holds that such actions are not morally commendable unless the caregiver would continue to practice the skills of caring in the absence of the feelings, or even in the presence of negative feelings.[9]

Returning to Watson's statement that caring is a moral imperative, without a differentiation between the sentiments of caring and the skills of caring, it might seem that we are morally obligated to have the sentiments of caring for all people in all places and times. But if so, the nurse in the narrative in her retreat into objectivity for temporary respite from her emotions, was behaving immorally. But we know this was not so. Thus, even if caring is a moral imperative in the sense that all persons in all places and times ought to be working on trying to get themselves to feel the sentiments of caring, there is still a problem. The balance between the skills of caring and the sentiments of caring in the case of the nurse in the narrative required that she not devote her time to cultivating sentiments, but get on with what needed to be done. Again one cannot be morally obligated to do the impossible.

But perhaps Kant can still be useful to Watson in the illumination he provides to the concept of caring. The second formulation of the categorical imperative holds that it is wrong to ever treat persons merely as means (an object) and not always also as ends in themselves. This concept of respect for persons as such is kindred to the concept of caring in the nursing sense. For one thing Kant is helpful in seeing why it is temporarily all right to focus on the skills of caring at the price of diminishing the sentiments of caring.

Respect for persons as such obligates the nurse to be caring in all of her transactions with the patient, if not the sentiments of caring, then the skills of caring. This obligation requires that the nurse perform the skills of caring at all times in the manner most respectful to the person of the patient. This kind of respect prevents the nurse from taking short-cuts in techniques that might compromise the patient's safety, even when pressured to do so by time constraints and work load. For example, it requires that the nurse always use the "Five Rights"[10] in administering medications to a patient, because not to do so will compromise the safety of the patient. Another way that the nurse is obligated to respect the patient as a person is never to use acronyms or disease entities or surgical procedures in place of the name of the patient. We are morally obligated in the Kantian sense to refer to Mr. Jones as "a person who has had surgery involving a Coronary Artery Bypass with Graft" and not simply refer to him as "a CABG" (pronounced "cabbage"). In like, manner Ms. Smith doesn't "pee out" her medications within twelve hours, rather the medications are metabolized and excreted through the kidneys.

Returning to the problem of the givenness of caring, Kant would comfort Watson. Kant has the same difficulty with the givenness of morality itself. We have seen that caring is a specification of the categorical imperative, that is, is part of morality. Kant believes that "God, freedom, and immortality," equally inaccessible from the standpoint of theoretical reason and consequently of the sciences, are the presuppositions of morality. By this he can be interpreted as meaning that the givenness of morality is grounded in God, freedom, and immortality. Could the givenness of caring have the same grounds? This would be the case if caring is a specification of the categorical imperative. We will return to this problem in the philosophy of nursing chapter.

And what about Heidegger? Since Watson mentions him, and he has a different view of caring, we will give him a brief examination. Does Heidegger shed light on the givenness of caring? Perhaps a careful look at Heidegger's understanding of caring can be useful. For Heidegger caring is the basic structure of subjectivity (Heidegger 1996, 1, ch. 4). But caring, in the Heideggerian sense, means no more and no less than interest in something. Without interest in something, the something cannot become an object of conscious awareness. Caring, for Heidegger, is simply the precursor of consciousness (Heidegger 1996, 1, ch. 6). Therefore, all experiences of beings in the world are caring experiences in the Heideggerian sense, but the caring is for self and not for others. Science is caring in the Heideggerian sense, because science has an interest in the objects within its domain. But Nazi death camp guards and commandants were also caring in the Heideggerian sense in that they were interested in efficiently executing their prisoners. In fact, in the Heideggerian sense of caring, even the SS was a caring organization!

So when nursing claims to be a caring profession, it is important to make clear the sense of caring that is relevant to nursing. Heidegger is not helpful for the modes of caring consistent with Watson's carative factors, but Heidegger's concept of caring is useful in another sense. Although Jacqueline Fawcett did not use the word "caring" in her view that nursing has domains of interest—person, environment, health, and nursing (Fawcett 1989, pp. 67–74)—the sense of Fawcett's use of the word "interest" is nearly synonymous with Heidegger's sense of caring. In both cases interest is self-interest; Fawcett is trying to self-authenticate nursing, and Heidegger is trying to self-authenticate Dasein (Being-in-the-World).

Yet, Watson refers to Heidegger as helpful for nursing's understanding of human experience (Watson 1985, pp. 80, 92). More specifically, Heidegger is helpful in trying to understand the self. But it is the self in the sense of "me" rather than in the sense of "I" or "we" that is of interest to him. This sense of "me" partially accounts for his interest in poetry. The artist in writing poetry is self-absorbed (Heidegger 1975). And further the artist is trying to simply do something that is aesthetically satisfying to himself, or to understand himself through the writing of the poems, or to understand an individual experience that he has had more clearly. Watson finds Heidegger particularly useful for the manner in which he emphasizes poetry (Watson 1985, pp. 80–81). Yet Watson seems to understand the self-absorption of the poet in her comments on Heidegger. This is evident in the following passage. According to Watson,

> Heidegger referred to the importance of actually undergoing an experience with language, and letting our experiences speak for itself [sic]. He indicated we should let ourselves be transformed by our participation in the process. Morever, poetic expression has the power to touch and move us, to open and transport us. Thus, the poetic quality is related to the experiential meaning and, indeed, deepens the meaning, the felt senses, so that there is increased openness to describe the truth and depth of the experience. (Watson 1985, p. 92)

What is missing from this passage is openness to the other. Poetry is a mode of self-expression, consistent with Heidegger's notion that the authentic existence of the self requires a pulling back from others. Poetry is a means of self reflection and involves self absorption. Heidegger, in *Being and Time* (1, ch. 4), warns against the self being absorbed in the world, in others. Hence, the caring he is advocating in *Being and Time* is self-care. It is egoistic.[11]

But Watson describes the caring occasion that "allows for the presence of the *geist* or spirit of both [the two persons, nurse and individual] . . . [that] expands the limits of openness and has the ability to expand the human capacities." Further Watson says that the caring occasion "is based upon a belief that we learn from one another how to be human by identifying ourselves with others or finding their dilemmas in ourselves" (Watson 1985, p. 59). This learning about ourselves through our relationships with others is inconsistent with what Heidegger had in mind in *Being and Time*. Heidegger believes that we learn about others by projecting our knowledge of ourselves, rather than coming to know about ourselves through our interactions with others. But unlike co-creative genuine dialogue it is a one-way street. For Heidegger, and also Jean-Paul Sartre as well as Sigmund Freud (especially in his theory of intrapsychic conflicts), others are a foil for learning about ourselves (Freud 1960; Sartre 1964). Heidegger's poetry is more concerned with objects, nature, and self, than with interpersonal relations with others.

In the narrative the nurse's caring for the boy did not end with his death. Death was an occasion when caring was needed and it occurred, not only for the boy but for his family. But even on the subject of death, Heidegger's self-absorption is evident. If one were to examine the subject of death in Heidegger's *Being and Time* and then examine Watson's observations and resulting poetry on caring and loss in her second book, a marked difference will be found in the significance of death from the two points of view. On the subject of death Heidegger comments

> Death is the *ownmost* possibility of Da-sein. Being toward it discloses to Da-sein its *ownmost* potentiality-of-being in which it is concerned about the being of Da-sein absolutely. Here the fact can become evident to Da-sein that in the eminent possibility of itself it is torn away from the they, that is, anticipation can always already have torn itself away from the they. The understanding of this "ability," however, first reveals its factical lostness in the everydayness of the they-self.
>
> The ownmost possibility is non-relational. Anticipation lets Da-sein understand that it has to take over solely from itself the potentiality-of-being in which it is concerned absolutely about its ownmost being. Death does not just "belong" in an undifferentiated way to one's own Da-sein, but it *lays claim* on it as something *individual*. The non-relational character of death understood in anticipation individualizes Da-sein down to itself. This individualizing is a way in which the "there" is disclosed for existence. It reveals the fact that any being-together-with what is taken care of and any being-with the others fails when one's ownmost potentiality-of-being is at stake. Da-sein can *authentically* be *itself* only when it makes that possible of its own accord. (Heidegger 1996, p. 243)

What is noticeable in this passage is the independence of self from others, the separation from others even in the face of death. Death is a "me" thing and not a "we" thing for Heidegger. The authentic self dies alone "away from the they."

In Watson's description of caring and loss involving tribal Aboriginal men in Western Australia death, caring, and loss, are experienced as "we" things.

> Laws have been handed down and we abide by law—going back to Moses; they are handed down from generation to generation.
> When I see places my forefathers have been, I imagine myself being there. It tells a story about my ancestors. . . .
> When someone dies in tribe, the closest family relative is to be told first, before the family. It is important that Sister tell the relatives because they won't believe unless it comes from Sister. But important that Sister check with community elders to make sure they inform the correct family.
> After someone dies, only in laws and (aboriginal) community have burial and go to grave. Close family stays together and mourns. Wails, groans, moans, fall prostrate on ground, no clothing; bash self in head and body because they feel to blame. (Watson 1985, pp. 84–85)

Watson's example is laden with interconnectedness between persons, even intergenerational and ancestral connectedness. In contrast with Heidegger view of death, death for the Aborigines is a community event. If caring in the Heideggerian sense is self-centered, rather than other centered, and if caring in the Watsonian sense is fundamentally interpersonal and other centered, can Heidegger illuminate the givenness of caring that is presupposed by nursing? No. For both life and death in the Heideggerian sense are uniquely individual. He is not interested in shared or repeatable universals that connect the death of one person with that of other persons. In contrast, the Australian Aborigines view death ritualistically, with many shared and expected universals; for example, the rules for notification of the death of an individual.

Another possibility about the givenness of caring is that the givenness of caring is the result of scientific inquiry in the traditional sense. Although the combination of "giveness" with "scientific inquiry" is contradictory, let's see how much science can help to illuminate caring. Recalling Aristotle's discussion in chapter 3, science is concerned with what is always or for the most part. This means that science is not just concerned with universals, but universals that tend to be quite general. In the case of caring, are there universals that are quite general that can be identified by scientific inquiry? Watson's title, *Nursing: The Philosophy and Science of Caring*, and her list of the basic assumptions of the science of caring in this book (quoted below), suggest that caring can be known through scientific inquiry, at least to some extent. Although the list of carative factors are an attempt to identify general universals associated with caring, the transactional caring occasion presupposes the unique individuality of not only the event, but the persons involved in the occasion. But it must be granted that there are structures associated with transactional caring occasions that are very general universals, such as being transactional.

The traditional sciences are concerned with the formulation of theories that help in the explanation or understanding of observed facts. When they are successful they are successful descriptively rather than normatively. These sciences can start either with theory or observed facts, but they are obligated to connect the two. The means by which they connect the two are general universals or laws.

In contrast to traditional science, Husserlian phenomenology starts with experience and attempts to identify universal and necessary forms within experience (universals). It is by a process of phenomenological reduction that Husserl attempts to discover the essence or structure of experience. An example of this process, at least of its results, is to be found in Husserl's *Phenomenology of Internal Time Consciousness* (Husserl 1964). The most general universals found there are the structures of time within conscious experience. The present has a spread outness in which it leans into the future while retaining the past. The retention of the past by the present is accompanied by fading on the part of the present, so that it is impossible to determine just where (in time) the present ceases and the past begins. The mix of presentness and pastness changes in favor of pastness as one looks from the standpoint of the present toward the past. In the narrative, the blurring of past, present, and future, is manifested by such experiences on the part of the nurse as consciousness of the clock, the presence of the photographs of the boy alive, the anticipation of the coming of the organ harvesters. The actuality of any one of the nurse's experiences presupposes the mixing of past, present, and future in the manner analyzed in Husserl's work. Hence, in this work, he has identified a most general universal, complex though it is, in human experience, the structure of internal time consciousness.

Watson is also interested in time in her account of transpersonal caring. She has noticed the same mixing of past, present, and future that Husserl noticed.[12] In reference to an actual caring occasion. Watson notes:

> An actual caring occasion is located not only in the simple physical instance of the given moment of time, but the event/experience has internal relations to other objects-subjects in the phenomenal field plus internal subjective relations between the past, present, and imagined future for each person and for the whole. An actual caring occasion can be present in the life of both the nurse and person beyond the physical instance of the given point in time. . . . One cannot clearly distinguish between past and present time even though the present is more subjectively real and the past is more objectively real. The past is prior to, or

in a different mode of being than the present, but it is not clearly distinguishable. Past, present, and future instants merge and fuse. (Watson 1985, p. 60)

What is noted here is that, though the caring occasion is an instance of a unique individual experience, it also exemplifies some most general universals. The general universals of experience are what is of interest to Husserl, at least in the above-cited work, *The Phenomenology of Internal Time Consciousness.* The question is, can the givenness of caring be grounded in these general universals? Husserlian phenomenology might find common structures of caring a fascinationg and appropriate object for study. But once again, caring is a presupposition of such an enterprise and not something that could be given by it.

Both traditional science in general and Husserlian phenomenology are interested in identifying general universals. Science in general is concerned with facts that interpret or support universal and necessary laws. Husserlian phenomenology, in its scientific mode, is concerned with universal and necessary forms (universals) of experience.[13] So neither are interested in unique events or unique individuals as such. Their interest in individuals is as a means for abstracting general universals from the individuals. The uniqueness of individuals is ignored as meaningless noise. In contrast, caring is attentive to the uniqueness of individuals. It is attentive to what is ignored by both traditional science and Husserlian phenomenology.

Since caring in the nursing sense has to do with what ought to be and with making things better in the world, since caring is normative[14] and practical, and since science in the traditional sense is merely descriptive and theoretical, and not normative or practical, then science in the traditional sense cannot be the ground of the givenness of caring for which we have been searching.

But can traditional science make any contribution to the understanding of the nature of caring? It would seem that if science can contribute to the understanding of the nature of caring it is only indirectly. The biological and related sciences can provide information necessary to help the nurse develop and apply the skills of caring. For example, a nurse understands through science that more than one condition can produce a stroke. Treatment of the patient would be different depending on the cause and location of the problem. Hence, though science is indispensable for the knowledge needed for the development and application of the skills of caring, it cannot illuminate the nature of caring itself. Remembering Kant's contribution, science is helpful only for forming new hypothetical imperatives (if one wants to do *a* this can be accomplished by doing *b*). Therefore, science can be helpful only after caring is a given.

Can science describe or observe the intersubjectivity necessary for the sentiments of caring? Intersubjectivity is a very personal experience between two individuals involved in the caring experience. It is especially personal when that experience involves the intense relationship described in Watson's caring occasion. The question remains, how can any kind of inquiry that might be called scientific explain and measure the experience of both persons in this moment of intense intersubjectivity? From the standpoint of the traditional sciences, intersubjectivity like consciousness is a completely opaque concept.

Scientific inquiry would find it difficult to determine specifically which of the conducts or attitudes of an individual were caring. Such an identification requires sensitivity to the uniqueness of the individuals involved in the caring experience, and of the uniqueness of that experience itself. But science is interested in the shareable and repeatable and tries to ignore the elements of singularity that ground uniqueness. Hence, by this reasoning, the identification of caring must be nonscientific.

Yet Watson considers the carative factors as an entrée for the scientific study of caring. If so, then how could the carative factors allow an outside observer to determine that caring has taken place, especially if caring is transpersonal in the sense of Watson's caring occasion? The added difficulty of determining whether a particular carative factor is present at any given time is at least as unamenable to the scientific methods of inquiry as caring itself. Science can only observe behavior. But caring involves more than behavior. Caring involves action.

Perhaps it would be important at this point to explain the differences between action, conduct, and behavior, because we have used these three terms in the discussion of caring. In the conversation with Plato in chapter 3, we discovered the distinction between teleological and efficient causation.

Teleology, the reader is reminded, involves goals or lures that provide the reasons for a person *acting* in a certain way. It is goals or reasons that distinguish actions from simple behavior. On the other hand the concept of efficient causation is involved in the concept of *behavior*. Behavior is the result of *antecedent* conditions. The individual behaves in response to causal stimuli or antecedent conditions that drive the individual to do what is done. Hence, behavior is a reaction to what already is—the result of a push from the past to do something in the present. In contrast, an action aims at the future. It is motivated by a vision of what can be.

The distinction between actions and behaviors on the part of the patient were discussed with Plato in the context of nursing goals for the patient. If the patient met a nursing goal out of fear for the power of the nurse, to please the nurse, or to receive a reward, the patient might be said to be behaving rather than acting since the behavior is the result of the stimulus of fear or some other pre existing condition. But *actions* flow from internalized reasons in such a manner that Kant calls actions unconditioned conditions (freedom). If conduct is reasonable, no causes are sought, and the conduct is viewed as action. The rationale of the action is self-evident. But when conduct is unreasonable, questions are asked about the causes of such conduct. To the extent to which a causal explanation of the conduct is possible, the conduct is behavior and not action. Hence, an outside observer witnessing conduct between nurse and patient that looked like caring, could not know whether the conduct was behavior or action or the degrees of each and changes in the degrees.

But there is a further complication in the distinction between acting and behaving. Even though the patient, in the discussion with Plato concerning nursing goals for the patient, may be acting out of fear and not because of the lure of a better future, the patient is still technically considered to be acting and not simply behaving. This is because the patient is still making a choice, albeit the choice is among the lesser of several evils. There is no good that is being sought except the avoidance of greater evil. The reason for the person acting in this particular way may not be as commendable as the action that is aimed at a good. The confusion between action and behavior is probably what inspires many philosophers to say that no human action is merely behavior. Conduct is a term used for referring to something in between action and behavior.

In an example from the military, nurses in field hospitals under combat conditions are obligated by military regulations to protect their patients by throwing their own bodies on top of the patients to shield them from enemy fire. Hence, in any individual case of a nurse throwing herself on a patient under enemy fire, it can be asked if it is altruism (one of Watson's carative factors), a sense of obligation (either moral or military), foolhardiness, or some other motivation (such as love for the patient), or some combination of the preceding motivations, that prompts the nurse's conduct at any particular moment. In any event the external, observable, component of the conduct, that is the conduct of the nurse, is the same. Science cannot observe the reasons or motivations that distinguish different types of conduct, it can only observe the conduct. Hence the carative factors are not simple observables that can be used to ground a scientific theory of caring. In order to recognize the presence of a carative factor, the observer must first recognize that the conduct is action, and that it is also caring.

Kant makes the distinction between action and behavior in relation to the difference between noumenal and phenomenal reality. The self as noumenally real is, in Kant's language, the unconditioned condition of its actions. Whereas, empirically real (observable) behavior is causally determined. In the example of the patient reaching the nursing goal, Kant would agree with Plato that if the patient and the nurse are in agreement about the positive value of the goal, then the patient is *acting* and we have insight into noumenal reality, which is ultimately or fully real.

In contrast, *behavior*, according to Kant, is appearance rather than ultimate reality. That is to say, viewing any conduct as behavior is viewing it under a convenient but fictional abstraction. For what makes an *action* ultimately real are the unobservable reasons, reasons that allow the action to be an unconditioned condition.

Social science and other "natural" science approaches to human conduct rest on the assumption that persons can be reduced to or understood in terms of their observable behavior. If true, this would be convenient, because observable behavior can be hoped to be amenable to ordinary scientific inquiry. If the conduct is mere behavior, it can be explained causally, which is exactly what the sciences are good at. Regarding Watson's carative factors, there is both a noumenal and a phenomenal aspect to them. The noumenal aspect views conduct as actions, and the phenomenal aspect views conduct as behavior. That which is observed is something that can be interpreted either way, because only the phenomenal aspect is directly observable through sense experience. One can observe a person's figure and coloration through sense perception, but the senses do not allow us to observe the person's reasons for acting. Viewing a person's conduct as conduct is neutral ground between seeing it as action or seeing it as behavior. The senses cannot tell us which it is. But the caring in the carative factors must be noumenal as well as phenomenal. Hence, an outsider cannot be sure that caring is present even though the conduct may be like that of a caring person.

But if it should be of any consolation to Watson and to nursing, Kant would have had a problem with science and the notion of caring too. Since conduct can be viewed either as action or behavior, there is a conflict between action as contra causally free (unconditioned condition) and behavior as causally determined (conditioned condition). Freedom and determinism, in Kant's view, cannot be true of the same world. This motivated him to deny the ultimate reality of the physical world in order to leave room for freedom and action. It follows that the traditional sciences are fundamentally flawed as vehicles for knowledge about ultimate reality (the noumenal world), because the traditional sciences can only know the world that is causally determined (the phenomenal world). Hence, if the reality of action is accepted, that persons act and not simply behave, the physical world (the phenomenal world) must be appearance rather than reality.

So is it possible to know if caring is occurring in a given situation between nurse and patient by attempting to observe both the noumenal and phenomenal levels of reality at the same time? But the question would be "how on earth would one observe the noumenal level?" Certainly not with the senses. For example, is it possible to set up a situation where one nurse is observing what looks like caring conduct on the part of another nurse toward a patient, while a third nurse simply asks the two participants involved in the caring conduct, that is, nurse and patient, if they believe that caring has taken place? Perhaps something like this is being suggested by Watson herself when she recommends an approach for the study of caring that is "qualitative in design" and not traditional in its scientific approach. She says, "My views are most congruent with a phenomenological-existential methodology for study and inquiry" (Watson 1985, p. 76). However, Watson offers no explanation concerning the nature of a "phenomenological-existential methodology."

Does the example above shed any light on the nature of a "phenomenological-existential methodology"? If the nurse, in the example above, were to ask the two participants whether caring took place, how could she know that the responses the participants gave her were not motivated by wanting to please her, by wanting to seem caring whether they were or not, or were made in ignorance of what caring is. Supposing that the nurse observer needed to explain what caring was to the participants, wouldn't she have to do so by talking about conduct in a manner that left it uncertain whether action or behavior was involved? But both the nurse observer and the participants could not make this distinction without already pre-understanding caring.

Perhaps Nicholas Polyani's notion of personal knowledge may be applicable to this problem of distinguishing action from behavior (Polyani, *Personal Knowledge*). In Polyani's view only the participants can have personal knowledge of the inner nature of their conduct so as to determine that it is action rather than behavior. But in order to make this determination about their own conduct, they must have great insight to know that their conduct during the observed event was more motivated by reason than causally determined, and if there was a change in the relative importance of the two factors during the observed event. But even so, they would have to have a pre-understanding of caring to know that they had participated in a caring occasion, even after determining that their conduct was action rather than behavior. This makes the job of the nurse observer very difficult. She must determine the level of insight on the part of the participants. For only if their level of insight was high would they be able to determine whether their conduct was behavior or action, and to what degrees, at any given moment.

So in order to have a scientific study of caring, whether the study be scientific in the traditional or human senses, there are certain requirements that must be met. The nurse and patient involved in the caring occasion must have insight into their own conduct during the entire caring event. Both must be sensitive to when caring conduct is action or behavior and to what degree. This requires that they are both participants at the same time in the caring event and self-observers in the caring event, because insight requires self-observation—experience of experience of experience in Hegel and Whitehead's senses. In addition, nurse and patient participants in the caring event and the nurse observer must have similar views about the nature of caring. All three must pre-understand caring in the same fashion. In addition to the other requirements the caring event must occur on cue when nurse and patient participants and nurse observer are all there at the same time. There can be no spontaneity in this caring event. Perhaps the skills of caring may be studied in this fashion. But what about the sentiments of caring? Can a caring occasion happen on cue with all of the prerequisites needed for a study in place? These are some of the difficulties that stand in the way of a science of caring.

As if the above difficulties are not enough, there is yet an additional difficulty. In order for the outside observer to be able to trust the participants' answers to questions concerning their experience of caring occasion, the outside observer must be assured that the participants understand and be able to distinguish between the skills of caring, the sentiments of caring, and a very special event Watson refers to as the caring occasion. But the nurse observer can know this only by having herself entered into a caring occasion with both of the participants at some time in the past or the present. Hence, observing the external conduct associated with a carative factor won't work, unless the observer has personal knowledge of the participants through having previously enjoyed a caring occasion with the participants. Having caring occasions with others will not suffice, because this will not give her knowledge of these particular participants.

If the traditional sciences are only partially helpful to caring by allowing us to increase our repertory of hypothetical imperatives relevant to the skills of caring, perhaps we need to turn to the human sciences as a possibility for understanding the givenness and nature of caring. But the key questions here are whether there *are* human sciences, and if there are, whether the givenness of caring can be illuminated by human science. We have discovered that the givenness of caring cannot be based on science in the traditional sense, natural science. But whether or not there are human sciences is still debatable. Human science would study human conduct as action, while traditional science studies human conduct as behavior. But actions per se are unobservable. Is it possible for the human scientist to reconstruct the reasons for the persons whose conduct he or she is attempting to understand as actions. Jürgen Habermas in his book *Communicative Action* is trying to lay the philosophical foundations for this type of science.

But as yet there do not seem to be disciplines that are human sciences. One could argue that psychiatry is such. But on examination psychiatry views human conduct as behavior caused by chemical imbalances, environment, birth trauma, early childhood traumas, or perhaps genetic defects. The legal system, to the contrary, tends to see conduct as action, and hence as punishable. For only if a person is responsible is he or she punishable. Hence, many courtroom battles between prosecution and defense are in fact fought over whether conduct is to be viewed as action or behavior.

But supposing that there are human sciences, even a human science could not provide its own evidence or data. It would theorize about, or attempt to explain, data from nonscientific sources, such as the senses, or perhaps some special kind of intuition. Science is impossible except in the context of nonscientific knowledge. Science needs something to theorize about which it cannot produce for itself. For example, nurses for a long time have been aware that newborn infants have pain. Yet physicians argued for an equally long time that the neurological systems of neonates were insufficiently developed for them to feel pain. Nancy Hester, nurse researcher, devised a study for distinguishing the cries of pain from other types of cries of infants, such as cries of boredom, hunger, uncomfortableness, the need for human touch, and fright. This allowed her to confirm what the nurses intuitively sensed and refute what the doctors theoretically claimed: newborn infants do experience pain. The nonscientific knowledge behind Nancy Hester's study was the intuitive and personal knowledge of practicing nurses working with newborn infants. But Nancy Hester's study was traditional science in that it looked at the infants' conduct as behavior.[15]

If, as Watson proposes, "Transpersonal human care and caring transactions are those scientific, professional, ethical, yet esthetic, creative and personalized giving-receiving behaviors and responses between two people (nurse and other) that allow for contact between the subjective world of the experiencing persons (through physical, mental, or spiritual routes or some combination thereof" (Watson 1985, p. 58), then how is science to observe that those behaviors and responses have occurred?

But what about transpersonal human care and caring transactions as noted in the quotation above? If transpersonal caring is part of the caring occasion as Watson indicates (Watson 1985, p. 59) and the caring occasion "has the ability to expand human capacities" (Watson 1985, p. 59), and if the caring occasion is an "ideal of intersubjectivity," which "increases the range of certain events that could occur in space and time at the moment as well as in the future, " then how can science, even human science, with its descriptive inquiry be of help in illuminating the nature of caring in nursing?

We are left with the possibility that caring is also known through a very special kind of experience. This possibility will be considered and argued for at length in the philosophy of nursing chapter along with some of the corollaries of there being a special kind of experience. We end the discussion of science and caring with the conclusion that caring is a given for science, not something that science can produce or explain. Whatever the ground of the givenness of caring it is something other than the sciences, even the human sciences. Granted that the last point will need to be developed at much further length, but not in this book.[16]

After having discussed Watson's concept of caring at some length, with many suggestions of our own, we think it only fair to allow the reader to review Watson's thinking in her own words. Hence, we have taken the liberty of several long quotes over the next few pages, with very little exposition.

Watson approaches caring through basic assumptions of caring, through listing ten carative factors of caring, through examination of the caring occasion, and indirectly through attention to aesthetics and time. We will focus on these topics exclusively.

In her earlier work Watson introduced caring by listing "basic assumptions for the science of caring in nursing" (Watson 1979, pp. 8–9), and then in terms of ten carative factors. The basic assumptions, in Jean Watson's words, are as follows:

1. Caring can be effectively demonstrated and practiced only interpersonally.

2. Caring consists of carative factors that result in the satisfaction of certain human needs.

3. Effective caring promotes health and individual or family growth.

4. Caring responses accept a person not only as he or she is now but as what he or she may become.

5. A caring environment is one that offers the development of potential while allowing the person to choose the best action for himself or herself at a given point in time.

6. Caring is more "healthogenic" than is curing. The practice of caring integrates biophysical knowledge with knowledge of human behavior to generate or promote health and to provide ministrations to those who are ill. A science of caring is therefore complementary to the science of curing.

7. The practice of caring is central to nursing. (Watson 1979, pp. 8–9)

Watson's basic assumptions provide a broad umbrella under which to understand caring and from which to generate her ten carative factors. In turn the ten carative "factors . . . form a structure for studying and understanding nursing as the science of caring" (Watson 1979, p. 9). They are as follows:

1. The formation of a humanistic-altruistic system of values

2. The instillation of faith-hope

3. The cultivation of sensitivity to oneself and to others

4. The development of a help-trust relationship

5. The promotion and acceptance of the expression of positive and negative feelings

6. The systematic use of the scientific problem-solving method for decision making

7. The promotion of interpersonal teaching-learning

8. The provision for a supportive, protective, and (or) corrective mental, physical, sociocultural, and spiritual environment

9. Assistance with the gratification of human needs

10. The allowance for existential-phenomenological forces (Watson 1979, pp. 9–10)

In her second major book, Watson describes the caring occasion as an occurrence of transpersonal caring. She tells us that

transpersonal refers to an intersubjective human-to-human relationship in which the person of the nurse affects and is affected by the person of the other. Both are fully present in the moment and feel a union with the other. They share a phenomenal field which becomes part of the life history of both and are coparticipants in becoming in the now and the future. Such an ideal of caring entails an ideal of intersubjectivity, in which both persons are involved. (Watson 1985, p. 58n)

In this description of the caring occasion Watson leaves no doubt that caring is a reciprocal relationship between two conscious individuals, at least in the caring occasion. But elsewhere in the same second book, Watson comments that "human care requires the nurse to possess specific intentions, a will, values, and a commitment to an ideal of inter-subjective human-to-human care transaction that is directed toward the preservation of personhood and humanity of both nurse and patient" (Watson 1985, p. 75). Clearly in this second quotation, Watson is putting the responsibility squarely on the shoulders of the nurse to preserve the personhood and humanity of both nurse and patient. This allows her to say that it is possible to have a caring relationship with an unconscious patient (Watson 1985, p. 75). But she also says that "the interventions in this theory [her theory] are related to the human care process with full participation of the nurse/person with the patient/person" (Watson 1985, p. 74), which would make it seem impossible to have a caring relationship with an unconscious patient.

In her second book Watson also revises her ten carative factors. For the convenience of the reader in comparing the revised with the original, the revised is placed in italics:

1. The formation of a humanistic-altruistic system of values
1. *Humanistic-altruistic system of values*

2. The instillation of faith-hope
2. *Faith-hope*

3. The cultivation of sensitivity to oneself and to others
3. *Sensitivity to self and others*

4. The development of a help-trust relationship
4. *Helping-trusting, human care relationship*

5. The promotion and acceptance of the expression of positive and negative feelings
5. *Expressing positive and negative feelings*

6. The systematic use of the scientific problem-solving method for decision making
6. *Creative problem-solving caring process*

7. The promotion of interpersonal teaching-learning
7. *Transpersonal teaching-learning*

8. The provision for a supportive, protective, and (or) corrective mental, physical, sociocultural, and spiritual environment
8. *Supportive, protective, and/or corrective mental, physical, societal, and spiritual environment*

9. Assistance with the gratification of human needs
9. *Human needs assistance*

10. The allowance for existential-phenomenological forces
10. *Existential-phenomenological-spiritual forces* (Watson 1979, pp. 9–10; Watson 1985, 75)

Watson hasn't explained why the wording was changed between her 1979 work and her 1985 work. What is notable is that she dropped the *action* verbs in her later list. At first glance this does not seem to be a positive step because of the already noticed relationship between caring and action. But this seems to be neutral with respect to the distinction between the sentiments and the skills of caring.

Perhaps in an attempt to get a better understanding of the givenness of caring, it would be useful to reconsider Watson's insistence on the importance of the caring occasion for the growth of both nurse and patient. A fundamental aspect of the caring occasion would seem to be sensitivity to the uniqueness and actual histories of each person.

> The moment of the caring occasion becomes part of the past life history of both persons and presents both with new opportunities. Such an ideal of intersubjectivity between the nurse and the patient is based upon a belief that we learn from one another how to be human by identifying ourselves with others or finding their dilemmas in ourselves. (Watson 1985, p. 59)

Is there a tension here between Watson's stated preference for a "phenomenological analysis of experience" that "brackets out the existential element" and focuses on shared universals, and the attentiveness of the caring occasion for the uniqueness of the other person? Is Watson in danger of tilting toward universal forms and ignoring the uniqueness of individuals, albeit the "'essences'" or "'ideal types' exemplified by the experiences"? (Watson 1985, p. 80).

If the nurse in the narrative were to turn to Jean Watson's theory for help with her two basic problems concerning caring in nursing, what might she expect given the basic assumptions and the ten carative factors? First, she would agree with Watson about the centrality of caring to nursing (Basic Assumption 7). But she would immediately have trouble with the assumption that caring must be interpersonal (Basic Assumption 1). For what troubled the nurse in the narrative was that caring occurred in spite of the lack of an interpersonal relationship in the ordinary sense of that phrase. In Watson's theory it is impossible to have such a relationship with a comatose patient. But perhaps the term "ordinary sense" of interpersonal relations is too narrow. Watson's has used the terms "interpersonal," "transpersonal," and "intersubjective," fairly much interchangeably. If Watson is using these in the existentialist senses, and there is reason to interpret her this way (Watson 1985, p. 54):("the nurse is a co-participant in a process of which the ideal of caring is intersubjectivity"), then caring is limited to relations between conscious persons. On the other hand, Watson does not use the word "conscious." Is this intentional?

Basic Assumption 4, that "caring responses accept a person not only as what he or she is now but as what he or she may become" is puzzling for explaining the nurse's feelings for the patient in the narrative. It is obvious that the nurse accepted the young man as he "was now." What is not so obvious is that the finality of death can be folded under the rubric of "becoming something else." Yet, before she lists the ten carative factors, that is, in her introduction, Watson states that the caring process can help a person "attain . . . health or die a peaceful death" (Watson 1979, p. 7). This is more useful for understanding the narrative than the language of the carative factor. Perhaps it would be useful and comforting to the nurse in the narrative if Watson were to include language among her basic assumptions or carative factors concerning the nurse's role in helping the patient and family accept a natural and peaceful death.

In the narrative, the nurse's caring for the family comes under Basic Assumption 3, "effective caring promotes health and individual or family growth." The nurse is promoting the health and growth of the family by helping them through a crisis in their lives. The family in turn are enabled to achieve closure concerning their son's accidental death, because they were confident that everything was being done to cure him that could have been done. Their confidence was the result of the demonstration of proficiency by the nurse. Although the nurse could promote the health of the family in the narrative, she could not promote the health of the dead boy. However, she could indirectly help promote the health of the recipients of the boy's organs. By maintaining the machines that nourished the young man's organs she could assure that the organs were as healthy as possible.

The nurse in the narrative would find the dualism between caring and curing in Basic Assumption 6 to be at least puzzling.[17] She might feel that her work in attempting to cure the boy was undervalued, and perhaps even dishonored, by associating nursing only with caring and not also with curing (Watson 1979, p. 8). The nurse was certainly not a physician, yet she spent long hours helping to cure the boy before he died. But if curing is not considered part of nursing, then what was the nurse doing? It was not nursing, it was not medicine. Perhaps she is in a kind of professional limbo between nursing and medicine. Yet before the boy died, she felt it was her duty as a good nurse, and it was certainly her desire, to do her best to cure the boy of the problems that were making his death likely. And she certainly would have done so if it had been possible. And she would not have been willing to hand over all aspects of curing to medicine "whole cloth." For the caring performed by the nurse in the narrative included curing until the time the patient died. This strongly implies that caring and curing are not just complementary, but that good caring includes curing when possible and appropriate. But caring is capable of continuing when curing is impossible.

Is caring understood simply by what it does, how it changes the nurse or the patient in the caring occasion? Or, is caring to be defined operationally in terms of caring behaviors? (The distinction between behavior and action would suggest otherwise.) Is caring a "given" as Watson's claims it is (Watson 1979, p.10)? Is it knowable mainly only through metaphor as Watson suggests? Is the essence of nursing, caring, to remain "invisible and unrecognized"? Is it to remain "covert, intangible, tacit, [and] 'soft'"? Watson was asking for a new language to "express these aspects of caring. But is this new language to be restricted to metaphor, or will it be possible to illuminate caring more directly and fully?" (Watson, 1987, p. 11).

Some of Watson's work may be seen as a search for a more adequate language of caring. She may be seen as implying this through her interest in art, aesthetics, mysticism, spirituality, and poetry. But many puzzles remain unresolved.

Yet when we read her initial and subsequent works more carefully and thoroughly in preparation for this book, we were surprised to notice that the individual descriptions of such things as the "carative factors" detracted from rather than supported the impression of the book as a whole. This left us puzzled about the origin of our initial awareness of the nature of caring and consequently the nature of nursing. Is caring such that its meaning is lost in the attempts to explain or define it? Does nursing need to look for language that expounds the meaning of caring while conveying a sense of its beauty and of its central importance? How is something as fundamental to nursing as caring illuminated? Can it be illuminated only by what it does? If so then listing the carative factors might be justified as an appropriate first step in the illumination of the central concept. And yet the carative factors were less than a full illumination or exposition of the concept of caring.

In Watson's attempts to understand caring, we have encountered many dichotomies, such as that between curing and caring, an unresolved uncertainty about the relationship between caring and clinical competencies, and a number of unanswered questions, not the least of which is the possibility of having caring sentiments for an unconscious or deceased person. We believe that an illumination of caring requires a return to universals and individuals, and the distinction between universality and singularity within the individual. This we will address in the next chapter.

CHAPTER 6

Philosophy of Nursing

Universality and singularity have given us a clearer understanding of what nursing is and what makes nursing unique. In this sense, universality and singularity have illuminated nursing. Universality and singularity have allowed us to achieve new insights that illuminate the concept of nursing in depth. Nursing is interested in that which is repeatable and shareable, the universals. Yet nursing is interested in the uniqueness of persons and events—especially events that change the lives of persons.

Though persons and events are unique, persons and events are a combination of universality and singularity. Hence a very important uniqueness about nursing is the way in which nurses balance the complexity of the shareables with the unexpected uniqueness of persons and events.

In fact, what we, the co-authors, have choose to call a "nursing event" is a unique occasion, nonrepeatable and nonshareable, having a specific address in time and space, between two unique persons, patient and nurse, brought together by the universals of health and illness.

But the way that nurses acquire, develop, and use technological skills is a combination again of universality and singularity. There are standards (universals) in the development and the use of technology (universals), yet each nurse and each occasion is unique in the application of the technology to unique persons. The practicing nurse assesses a unique situation and improvises as necessary, perhaps combining several skills to achieve one objective. Hence, creativity in nursing is a combination of universality and singularity.

Assessing a unique individual patient in a unique situation requires great skill and great knowledge on the part of the nurse. He must be sensitive to a changing situation, comfortable with complexity and sometimes even chaos, and have the wisdom and the delicacy to balance the ever changing mix of universals and individuals.

But how is this wisdom obtained? Nursing wisdom is obtained from several different sources. The nurse uses science, physical and human, technology, nonscientific knowledge, intuition, and past nursing experience, both individual and collective. Though we have already examined many of these sources of wisdom, we have yet to address the complexities of intuition as it occurs in nursing. Nursing knowledge combines universality and singularity, and hence we need to examine the grounds of singularity more fully. In addition we also need to look at the nursing event once again, for further illumination of the concept of nursing. But the nursing event requires that we look at the nature of persons as communities of experiencing entities. That persons are communities of experiencing entities means that nursing views the body as within the self and not the self as within the body. In order to understand both the person as a whole and his or her subordinate experiencing entities, it is necessary to revisit the distinction between behavior, conduct, and action, and why it is essential to view each nursing event as an opportunity for the patient to make the transition from behavior to action. These topics were addressed partially in earlier chapters, but will be developed more fully in this chapter.

EXPOSITION OF NURSING BASED ON
UNIVERSALITY AND SINGULARITY

The reader will notice that the title of this section is "an exposition of nursing." We have intentionally avoided the use of the phrase "definition of nursing." We have chosen to expound rather than define nursing, because the writing of this book has strengthened our conviction that no simple definition of nursing is possible. The reason that no simple definition of nursing is possible lies in the elusiveness of the concept of nursing and the complexity of nursing itself. Nursing is complex because the practicing nurse is concerned with persons in all of their complexity.

Persons are a combination of shareable universals and yet are unique. But adding to the complexity of persons, the imaginary discussions with the philosophers called our attention to the fact that persons also straddle more than one world—Plato's intelligible and sensible worlds, Kant's noumenal and phenomenal worlds, Whitehead's Everlastingness and the temporal world, the world of the mystic's One and the everyday world.

Since nursing chooses to remain focused on persons, nursing chooses to straddle more than one world. Nursing requires that the individual nurse be as nearly a renaissance person as possible, in order to understand and appreciate the uniqueness of each individual person and event.

Persons combine universality and singularity. On the one hand there is a long list, if not an infinitely long list, of universals that are true of any individual person. But on the other hand the uniqueness of each individual person is guaranteed by multiple grounds of singularity (discussed later in this chapter). Although practicing nurses are interested in what is shareable by persons, and in fact nursing research is often directed toward discovering the shareables (qualitative and quantitative) in persons and nursing events, nurses respect the uniqueness of persons and the uniqueness of the events that are parts of the lives of persons. Appreciating the uniqueness of events, the nurse engaged in a nursing event with a patient is aware of how each event is connected to the openness or closedness of future possibilities for the patient and also for the nurse. And though nursing employs universals to develop skills and uses technology important to the health of the individual person, nursing never allows itself to stray too far away from its home, lured by the glitter and power of technology. Nursing's home is beside unique persons, and nursing draws its vitality from unique persons and events.

Perhaps there is a parallel to be found here in Grimm's fairy tale of Hansel and Gretel. Like Hansel and Gretel who let themselves be temporarily lured away from their home by the appeal of confectionary delights, nurses too can be temporarily lured away from home by the appeal of the power of technology. Following the confectionary delights, Hansel and Gretel almost ended up in the witch's oven. If nursing strays too far from its home beside persons, it too may disappear. But the story of Hansel and Gretel had a happy ending. They escaped the witch and the lure of the confectionary delights and found their way home again. But they took pieces of the confectionary delights home with them (Grimm and Grimm 1812, p. 22). Nursing also needs to follow the example of Hansel and Gretel. Nursing saves itself from destruction by returning home to the patient, but with the "confections" of technology that are useful for the good care and can be shared with the patient. Nursing retains its vitality by returning home. Nursing corrects its fascination with new technologies needed for the skills of caring (universality) with its focus on the unique individual person and event (singularity). Good nursing requires balancing these two factors, universality and singularity, in the nurse, in the patient, and in the nursing event.

The coming together of two unique persons with their unique pasts, patient and nurse, in a unique nursing event with its unique past, is at least partially the result of the general universals, health and illness. It is the presence or absence of these two universals that prompts the occurrence of the nursing event. The skills and knowledge that the nurse brings to the nursing event is a complex mixture of universals drawn from the sciences, everyday nonscientific knowledge, and the past experiences of both himself and other nurses. The way that the nurse sees through the veil of universals to grasp the uniqueness of the person of the patient and the uniqueness of the nursing event is through intuition.

KINDS OF INTUITION RELEVANT TO NURSING

The notion of intuition is ambiguous because there are several different kinds of intuition. The discussions in this book up to now have encountered a variety of kinds of intuition or direct awareness. Sometimes we have used the term "intuition," and sometimes we have used the term "direct awareness." These two terms "intuition" and "direct awareness" have been used interchangeably in this book. In this we conform to the practice of Plato, Descartes, and Whitehead, who have also used these terms interchangeably. But is perhaps time to pause now and take inventory of the senses or meanings of *intuition*.

First, there is intuition of everyday objects. Intuition of everyday objects gives persons assurance of the existence of these everyday objects. Intuition of everyday objects prevents persons from being idealists in their view of sense perception. Descartes was an idealist in this sense. Because Descartes did not recognize this first type of intuition, he had to prove the existence of the physical world including his own body—he was afraid the physical world including his body might merely be an idea in his mind. So it is important to have intuition of everyday objects. In this kind of intuition the imposition of universals is necessary, because, though we can intuit that there are undeniably real objects before us, it is only after we have imposed universals on the objects that we can see that there are two of them, and that one is a tree and the other is a chair.

Another kind of everyday intuition, similar to the first, is the kind of intuition that let's us know that the everyday object before us is another person. It is important for us as persons to be able to distinguish another person from such objects as chairs or trees, because it would be a waste of time to try to have an interpersonal relationship with a chair, and it would probably be quite difficult to have one with a tree.

And in another kind of everyday intuition we see through the mask of universals to the uniqueness of the individual. Related to this kind of intuition is what is often called "hunch" in nursing—for example, a hunch that a patient's condition is improving or getting worse without the mediation of such universals as vital signs. But these kinds of intuition are vague and visceral. Hence, it is wise, if time and circumstances allow, to seek the support of universals before taking action. But it is equally wise not to ignore this kind of intuition. For by this means, we know more than we know that we know. The function of the universals is to allow us to more clearly know what we know.

Before we examine the final kind of intuition, understanding of the first three kinds of intuition is of special importance to nursing. Because the first three along with the fourth help to define the uniqueness of nursing. Hence it is worthwhile to stop and take another look at these kinds of intuition. What is at stake that is very important to nursing is the notion of what a person is. One's notion of the nature of persons effects the manner in which one treats or relates to persons.

Hidden in the explanations of the first three forms of intuition is a basic understanding of the relationship between the self and the self, and the self and the world and other selves. Perhaps the easiest way to uncover what is hidden is by comparing Descartes' view of self, objects, and other persons, with our views on these same subjects.

In the first type of intuition the reader will recall that it is an intuition of everyday objects. Without this kind of intuition persons cannot be sure that everyday objects, perceived by the senses, actually exist. They might be just ideas in the mind. Descartes' idealism consisted of accepting this as a real possibility, that everyday objects might only be ideas in the mind. If so, then the body, an everyday object, might also just be an idea in the mind. When Descartes says that the idea of the body is in the mind does this have the same meaning as when we say that the body is in the self?

The answer is definitely not. For Descartes the mind would continue to exist regardless of the reality of the body. All that is in the mind is the *idea* of the body, and not the body itself. Hence, for Descartes the body is a kind of mechanical vessel that the mind occupies for a temporary period of time. The body may be broken and in need of repair like any machine. But treatment or mistreatment of the body really should not have that much effect on the mind, for the mind is independent of the body in Descartes' view. In his view, Descartes is really just a mind with no more moral obligations toward his body, than toward a machine. The body is simply something to use and keep in reasonable repair for pragmatic reasons.

And what about knowledge of the existence of other selves on Descartes' view? Descartes looks around and sees other machines (vessels) similar to his own body, which make noises and move about as though there were also inhabited by minds. But he cannot prove that the other bodies have minds. For all he can know they are simply clever automata (robots). All he can do is see what their bodies do, he cannot experience their experience. This is because he denies the possibility of the second and third types of intuition listed above. Empathy and caring, even for himself, are inconsistent with his basic philosophy.

This view has been the dominant view of traditional science. Objectifying the body and separating it into parts is compatible with this view—as is viewing the parts as isolated, so that what happens to one part has little effect on the whole or on other parts. Side effects of treatment or medication are anomalies from this point of view, and are treated by isolating the effected parts through additional treatments or medications. This can result in an infinite regress. The ultimate solution is either replacing the affected parts or simply abandoning the body altogether as unfixable and obsolete. However, the rejection of newly transplanted body parts is also hard to explain from this point of view, because, if the body were simply a machine, why would neighboring parts be concerned enough with each other to be bothered by the presence of a stranger? As merely mechanical parts they are incapable of concern. Hence, the problem of organ rejection has to be due to something merely mechanical like a chemical trigger.

Our view, on the other hand, sees the body as present in the self (the mind) in quite a different sense than Descartes held that the idea of the body was in the mind. For the experience of the experiencing entities is taken up into the experience of the self. Hence, the body is present in the self, not as idea only, but in its full actuality. In its actuality the body is not a machine but is a very highly organized society of interacting experiencing entities—with the interaction being due to the presence of each within the experience of the others. Thus, if one part dies, the others mourn the loss. At the same time they tend to be unfriendly to foreigners or strangers, until they become acquainted. What effects anyone experiencing entity within the person effects the whole, including all other experiencing entities.

Hence, instead of viewing a transplant as a transplant, it might be more effective to introduce the new experiencing entities to those in the community they are joining, and the members of the community to them. This suggests a different approach than the present approach of simply attacking the defenses of the community and forcing both new members and the older members of the community to tolerate each other by destroying the ability of all of the members to protect themselves. We find the view that a person is a community of experiencing entities to be a much more suitable basis for a philosophy of nursing than the traditional scientific materialism, which views the body as merely mechanical.[1] This helps understand why persuasion is more effective than force when dealing with the community of experiencing entities that is a person. Experiencing entities are motivated by reasons, by beauty, by a sense of harmony, by the good. To get their cooperation the nurse needs to provide them with a vision. Hence, destroying the body's immune system, if it needs to be done, should be done prudently with respect for the living community that is sacrificed for the good of the whole.

There is yet another kind of intuition, different from those above, which is connected with religious and mystic experience. While everyday intuition has the finite as its object, this different kind of intuition has the Infinite as its object, or at least a symbol or avatar of the Infinite as its object. The kind of intuition that allows us to sense the reality of an Infinite One beyond the me and the you (the I and the Thou), but inclusive of the me and the you (I-Thou), is the ground of religious or mystic experience. Religious or mystic experience is of the One.

In chapter 3 we learned from the mystics that there are two pathways of intuition to the One. The first pathway is traveled through service to other finite individuals in the manner described by St. Francis and in the manner that is a part of nursing. Nursing's service to others involves caring and the importance of interpersonal relations. This in turn reminds both nurses and their patients of their place in the community of persons and the presence of this community in a larger One, and, in turn, the presence of the One in the community and its individuals.

The other pathway to direct awareness of the One involves something other than the care of persons. This path is exemplified by Meister Eckhart. This second kind of mystic is more concerned with the relationship between self and the One, a relationship unmediated by other persons. That which catalyzes the mystic experience in this second case is contemplation of the Infinite. (See the discussions with the mystics in chapter 3.)

Contemplation of the One helps the nurse find meaning in present action and reassurance about the ultimate rightness of things. Contemplation of the One can also help the nurse rise above a current situation regardless of the patient. Such contemplation helps restore her strength in the face of trying circumstances. For example, contemplation of the One may enable the nurse to have sentiments of caring toward a misanthropic patient who has been rude and mean. In these circumstances, when the patient has been rude and mean to the nurse, but the nurse must still care for the patient, the nurse might recall that "whatsoever you do to the least of these you do unto me."

But though we have suggested that the second pathway to intuition of the One may be helpful to nurses in difficult circumstances, it is the first pathway to intuition of the One that is more directly associated with caring in nursing, because it is the pathway of service to others. Caring intensifies consciousness by facilitating a greater unity among the diversity of experiencing entities within the persons, both nurse and patient. Having established inner beauty, they are in a position to appreciate beauty in relations with others and with the One. Though caring cannot guarantee the I-Thou experience, there can be no I-Thou relationship without caring.

It follows that there is a kind of *circle of caring* from subordinate experiencing entities within a person, to the person as one, to interpersonal relations between persons, to the relationship between the community of persons and the Infinite One, to the return of heaven into earth (discussed with the phases of the universe toward the end of this chapter) that supports and recognizes the value to the whole of the simplest experiencing entities within individual persons. Integral to the circle of caring is the I-Thou relationships in all of their varying kinds and degrees. There are more kinds and degrees of this relationship in our philosophy than were recognized by Martin Buber. Self to self relationships within the person are I-Thou relationships. Self to self relations with other persons are I-Thou relationships. Self to One relations are I-Thou relationships. Perhaps the following symbols are useful: i-i (subordinate experiencing entities to one another), we-I (subordinate experiencing entities to the self as a whole), I-we (self as a whole to its subordinate experiencing entities), I-*Thou* (interpersonal), We-*One* (community of finite persons to the Infinite One), One-*I* (the return of heaven into earth).

Individuals at all levels from subordinate experiencing entities, to persons, to the One, combine universality and singularity. Each is a unique individual whose uniqueness is guaranteed by singularity, but shares many universals with other individuals. Though each individual is one, its oneness requires a diverse many in which each of the many are unique and distinct one from another. As Whitehead says, there is no one without many and no many without one (Whitehead 1978, part 1).

THE SIGNIFICANCE OF THE NURSING EVENT

We have chosen to call the encounter between nurse and patient a "nursing event." Each event is time limited. Each event has a beginning, a middle, and an end. Each event is unique and nonrepeatable.

Every nursing event is a caring event. And every nursing event is an opportunity for caring in its deepest sense. The nursing event opens up opportunities for self to understand and appreciate self and for self to commune with other selves, and for self to participate in the greater Self. Thus, the nursing event is an opportunity for co creation at three levels—within the self, between selves, and between self and Self.[2]

A nursing event involves nurse and patient, health and illness, and a mix of skills of caring and sentiments of caring. Like all events the nursing event occurs in a determinate time and place. Though it has a definite beginning, middle, and end, its antecedents were occurring long before its beginning, and its resonances will endure long after its end.

The nursing event has significance beyond the present situation. It has within itself the opportunity for growth of both patient and nurse toward self-actualization. Yet the same event could have consequences that are disastrous or tragic. For example, an application of a clean or sterile dressing on a patient's wound has significance beyond the nursing event by preventing future infection and promoting healing of the wound. If the skill is not properly performed, serious infection, gangrene, or septicemia, might occur, leading to serious consequences, if not death.

But while the careful application of the skills of caring are important in a nursing event, there is significance beyond the simple changing of a dressing. In any nursing event, the manner in which the nurse relates to the person of the patient[3] while performing the skills of caring can affect the continued self-creativity of both patient and nurse. If the nurse were to focus on the dressing of the wound in a manner that denies the personhood of the patient and treats his arm as if it were a mechanical object, then the nurse communicates to the patient that neither he nor his arm are different from inanimate objects.

From the above example, it is important to note that the nursing event is *never neutral* with respect to the co-creativity of the two persons, patient and nurse. By never neutral we mean not static. Time is passing; the persons are changing. Co-creativity can be either positive or negative. In the example of treating a patient as an inanimate object, the co-creativity is negative. By dehumanizing the patient the nurse also dehumanizes herself. And by dehumanizing the patient's arm, the nurse has contributed to a further deterioration of the self to self community within the patient. Unless the patient comes into the nursing event already attuned to his subordinate experiencing entities, and can ignore the nurse's attitude, the conduct of the nurse in this case is likely to create alienation between the patient and his subordinate experiencing entities. He is encouraged by the nurse's attitude to view or reinforce the view of his own body as an imperfect, alienated, inanimate object rather than a community of experiencing entities.

It is possible and perhaps likely that the nurse treats his own community of subordinate experiencing entities in the same manner that he is treating the patient. If so, then the nurse who treats the patient as object, treats himself as object. He is impairing the harmony between himself and his own subordinate experiencing entities. And if it is true that opportunities for co-creation are being denied by the nurse's attitude and actions toward the patient, then the patient is made less able to help the nurse correct his own error. Both patient and nurse are less able to be mutually helpful. Healing involves the effort of the entire community of experiencing entities within a person. Therefore, no action on the nurse's part is neutral. If the patient's subordinate experiencing entities continue to be treated as mechanical objects, they may object in the form of pain, discomfort, and many types of illness. These may be pleas on their part for recognition and comfort. If so this is a new and helpful way of looking at these frequently occurring conditions in nursing events.

But on the other hand the nurse who is aware of the importance of harmony within herself is also aware of the importance of harmony within her patient. Nursing's role in the restoration and maintenance of the health of the patient is not to isolate parts of the person, but to reconcile the parts with the community as a whole in a unity of effort to facilitate the healing process. Hence, the panic among the subordinate experiencing entities created by the invasion of the sharp edge of a surgeon's knife, or the harsh chemicals of prescribed medications, can be calmed by the nurse's gentle touch so that healing can take place.

We have written about the self-to-self relationship within the person (the i to i). We are about to describe more in depth what has already been introduced in the paragraph before the present section. How does this self-to-self communication occur? What happens when understanding of self is obstructed?

Self-to-self appreciation and understanding presuppose that the self is a harmonious community "speaking" the same language. It is perhaps difficult to think of self-to-self appreciation and understanding among the subordinate experiencing entities of a person as involving a language. We often think of only the overall self as having a language. But not all language is spoken language. The subordinate experiencing entities communicate in different types of languages, not necessarily more primitive than the spoken language of the overall self. Chemical languages may be more complex than spoken languages. The challenge for the overall self, aware that the language of the subordinate experiencing entities is different, is to find universals that allow translation from the one language into the other. To understand the language of the subordinate entities, the overall self must occasionally become self-absorbed or self-contemplative (self-meditative), turn attention inward rather than outward.

Self-to-self communication, like self-to-other communication, is not always going to be successful. But when successful the result is harmony and peace. When it is not, there is a sense of uneasiness, of anxious disharmony.

When there is harmony and successful communication, the conscious self is able to meet the needs of the subordinate experiencing entities in a way that brings harmony, peace, and unity. For example, thirst or hunger are experiences of the overall self. In response, the overall self seeks food or drink. But when there is a miscommunication of the overall self with its subordinate experiencing entities, the opposite can occur.

Loneliness and the need for touch or consolation may be misunderstood as hunger or thirst. The overall self may attempt to satisfy these needs in such a way that the individual overeats or overdrinks. But if the need is for human touch, then no matter how much food and water are consumed, the subordinate experiencing entities are left dissatisfied. Hunger and thirst are not the only ways that the need for human touch can be misunderstood by the overall self. Sometimes the need for touch is misunderstood as a need for sexual contact. If nonsexual touch is what is needed by the subordinate experiencing entities, then the sexual contact will also leave dissatisfaction.

Still one further consideration involving "touching" makes any simple explanation incomplete. There are a number of varieties of human touch. In addition to physical touch, of which there are many subvarieties, there is spiritual touch, intellectual touch, and intersubjective emotional touch.

Physical touch may seem easy to define. But from the standpoint of the theory of a person as a community of experiencing entities, physical touch may well involve all of the other major varieties of touch. Physical touch can be soothing or hurtful, and many shades in between. Physical touch is sometimes able to open up avenues of communication within self and between selves, without the use of spoken language. But physical touch can also be cruel, painful, or acerbic to the subordinate experiencing entities and to the self as a whole under certain conditions. Although touch is a universal, its full significance depends on the uniqueness of the individual persons and the uniqueness of the individual event along with all of the relevant universals.

Spiritual touch involves opening self to other and allowing the other to become part of oneself though yet still apart from and different from oneself. Spiritual touch involves the whole person with emphasis on uniqueness and singularity—though universals do remain important. Universals are the facilitators of spiritual touch, because they focus attention on the other. But the result of spiritual touch is a kind of union respectful of differences between the two persons. Spiritual touch involves a deeper and different kind of intimacy than physical touch. (Could this be what Jean Watson meant by "transpersonal caring occasion"?)

Intellectual touch is enjoyed by two persons who enjoy common universals, for example, philosophy or nursing. Intellectual touch is enjoyed by the members of phage groups in the sciences as well as nursing. A phage group shares common assumptions and methodologies, with the members communicating frequently with each other, and supporting each other in their common intellectual endeavors. This type of touch is possible via computer on the Internet, and by traditional correspondence. Communication by telephone begins to blur the boundaries between intellectual and spiritual touch. Voice symbolizes an individual in his or her uniqueness, even at great distances, allowing spiritual touch in spite of the distance. In the case of intellectual touch the tilt is toward universals away from the uniqueness of individuals. But at the same time unique individuals can be reassured by intellectual touch that they belong to a community that shares universals.

Sometimes the need for spiritual touch on the part of the subordinate experiencing entities is different from the kind of touch, physical or intellectual, needed by the overall self. While the subordinate experiencing entities may very well need and want spiritual touch, the overall self may want and need intersubjective or physical touch. If the need for spiritual touch by the subordinate experiencing entities is misinterpreted by the overall self, the overall self may misinterpret the needs of the subordinate entities in a variety of different ways. For example, a hunger for spiritual touch on the part of subordinate experiencing entities may be seen by the overall self as a hunger for material possessions. Collecting material goods will have no limit and produce no ultimate satisfaction, if there is misinterpretation of the real needs of the subordinate experiencing entities. Such misinterpretation can result in exhaustion of finances as well as despair among the subordinate experiencing entities. Yet when the overall self and the subordinate experiencing entities are in tune with each other, then there is harmony within the person. Such harmony within the person creates an openness that allows for the same kind of harmony with another person. The unity with the other person may then be like the unity within the self.

Perhaps it is useful here to remember the distinction between conduct that is behavior and conduct that is action. (This distinction was introduced in chapter 5, and is developed more fully later in this chapter.) When we first introduced these distinctions, we were thinking of the overall self, of the person as a whole. But genuine dialogue *within the self*, between the overall self and its subordinate experiencing entities, calls attention to another and initially surprising application of this distinction. Genuine dialogue within the self transforms urges, which are causes of behavior, into reasons for action. Behavior that is a response to urges results in the overall self feeling anxious, empty, dissatisfied, unfulfilled, and sometimes guilty. There is lack of the kind of freedom that allows a person to be an unconditioned conditioned. But conduct that has been converted to action by genuine dialogue within the self results in the opposite feelings—peace, fulfillment, satisfaction, and self-satisfaction. And even when there has been miscommunication between the overall self and its subordinate experiencing entities on some particular occasion, the overall history of genuine dialogue makes it possible for the self to learn from its mistakes, without the above feelings of guilt and frustration. We suggest that learning from mistakes and the co-creative process of self with self is an important, and up until now overlooked but vital, factor in self-actualization.

As mentioned before, no nursing event is merely neutral, because each time that a nurse performs a skill of caring, he is communicating with the patient. The nurse cannot simply perform a task on a patient and expect that even though he is not engaged with the patient as a person, he is doing no harm. If the nurse is aware of the importance of any nursing event for the co-creation of both patient and nurse, then both patient and nurse have opportunities for self-actualization.

If the nurse is harried and forgets to acknowledge the importance of the event to the patient and to himself and in his haste he is inattentive to the patient as person, he unwittingly imparts a blaring message to the patient by his silent neglect. The nurse communicates the same message if he engages in social conversation with coworkers to the exclusion of the patient while the nurse performs a skill. The message the nurse is imparting is that the patient is an object as passive as Resusci-Annie.[4] Or the nurse is imparting the message that the patient is not a member of the community of persons. In some institutions under some conditions patients come to expect this kind of conduct from a nurse and accept it as *pro forma*. Both patient and nurse under these circumstances allow the opportunity for growth within the event to slip away unnoticed. But no event is neutral; if they do not grow, they experience dehumanization.

The nursing event, having significance beyond the present, requires a great responsibility for the nurse. Unless the nurse is aware of this responsibility, there may be unintended consequences. Recalling that the nurse and patient come together in the nursing event, because of the universals of health and illness, even the most benign encounters with the health care system reminds the patient of a fear that the patient could be dependent on others because of illness.

The thought of dependency on others for those who value independence and self-reliance is a cause of anxiety. If the nurse is aware of the possible impact on the patient of the attitudes that she expresses in her own conduct, she will not inadvertently give the patient a message that the patient's dependence, however temporary and necessary, is unacceptable. Treating patients as if they are useless objects and not part of the community of persons, by ignoring them and treating them as if they are not fully present, fuels the worst fears of the patient regarding illness and dependency. The message, though conveyed covertly is powerful. It is hidden within the nurse's attitude toward certain skills. The least important tasks are delegated to less educated and less skilled coworkers. However, the "least important tasks" are often especially sensitive to the personhood of patients and to their self-image as independent contributing persons. If nursing isn't careful to examine the hierarchy given to the skills of caring, the wrong message may be conveyed to the patient.

For example, bed baths, assisting with ambulation, changing soiled linen, and assisting with feeding fall into this category of "least important tasks." By noticing that the nurse is not interested in doing these tasks, the patient is left with the impression that these tasks are not valued. The patient begins to perceive these basic human nurturing acts and events as distasteful, unimportant, and a nuisance. And further, the patient who has need of the nurse's assistance in these matters begins to perceive self as distasteful, unimportant, and a nuisance. These are the events that are at the very heart of dependency and are occasioning the greatest fears on the part of the patient. But these events offer the greatest opportunities for self-actualization of both nurse and patient because these are the events that require close physical contact with the patient, and a partnership in the most sensitive situation for the patient, that of dependency. The sensitive nurse recognizes the importance of these events because the closeness between the persons that occurs in these events provides the nurse with the opportunity to soothe and calm the patient's fears.

When the nurse wants to encourage self-awareness and unity on the part of the person of the patient, the nurse knows that when the patient is most vulnerable the patient is also most open to new insights about self. Frequently the vulnerability and dependence is shameful to the patient, especially a patient who values self-sufficiency and independence. It is not unusual for patients to apologize to the nurse for their lack of independence and automatically assume that their dependency is an annoyance to the nurse. When the nurse delegates these responsibilities to less skilled coworkers, the nurse sends a message to the patient that the patient's fears are valid, that the patient's state of dependency is indeed a bother. This cannot be corrected by later addressing the patient's dependency needs intellectually, and by verbally assuring the patient that it is appropriate to be dependent on others at certain times, for the nurse's actions have already given the patient the opposite message.

But when the nurse is fully aware of the significance of these events, there is opportunity for growth on the part of both patient and nurse. The bed bath may be a great opportunity for the nurse, in genuine dialogue with the patient, to talk about the natural part that dependency plays in the healing process, or to help the patient become aware that any illness is an opportunity to take time for self-reflection. It may also be an opportunity to revisit the vision he has for his future given the changes he may need to make due to the nature of his illness. In this manner the patient is enabled to use his illness to reassess the meaning of his life in the light of his illness. The opportunity for awareness created by the illness has been noticed by at least one other nurse author (Martinez 1993).

Recalling that a person is a community of experiencing entities, the bed bath is an opportunity for the nurse to gently introduce or reintroduce the patient to the subordinate experiencing entities within himself. When the patient is bathing himself, the nurse can call his attention to how soothing it feels to his subordinate experiencing entities when the temperature of the water is just right, when his touch is just right, when his attitude toward them is friendly and appreciative. The nurse can also help the patient recognize the difference between his gentle touch to himself and a harsher touch, and how the subordinate experiencing entities experience each, and how he feels as a whole in response to their experience.

The bed bath and some other nursing activities require that the nurse touch the patient for longer periods of time and more intimately than in other nursing activities. For example, the touch required in feeding patients, assisting them to dress, helping them with range of motion exercises or in assisting them to walk are far more intimate than the touch necessary to take a patient's blood pressure. But all of these types of touch are yet more intimate than care mediated by machines. All of these occasions are opportunities for reintroducing self to self, for transpersonal caring, and for satisfying the need for physical, intellectual, and spiritual touch, as discussed earlier.

It is clear that the nurse cannot overestimate the value of just the right touch at just the right moment for the patient. For many patients, touching has been taken solely to mean an entrée to sexual intimacy or perhaps physical abuse. The nurse's touch in the nursing event can help these individuals understand the differences between touch as a pleasurable human-to-human experience valued as an end in itself and the touch that is a means to sexual intimacy or abuse. The intimacy between persons in these examples of nursing events requires the greatest of skill on the part of the nurse, and requires harmonious participation on the part of the nurse's subordinate experiencing entities. In the ideal situation the patient and the nurse will respond as a unified community of experiencing entities. This event may help restore unity that may be lacking within the community of experiencing entities that is the patient. If the patient is sensitive to touch, perhaps because of past experiences, the nurse needs to expertly and delicately balance the gentle rhythm between the skills of caring and the sentiments of caring. It follows that, because of the very nature of these events, they are some of the greatest opportunities for growth on the part of both patient and nurse.

Self-discovery involves among other things the patient's sensitivity to his own subordinate experiencing entities. This sensitivity on the part of the patient to his own community of experiencing entities involves an appreciation for the synchrony and beauty of the community of experiencing entities engaged in continually rebalancing the harmony within the community. Any nursing event is a cherished opportunity for the nurse to reintroduce self to self, that is the person within the patient to himself, thus encouraging unity of self on the patient's part. Therapeutic touch can be understood as the nurse's use of her community of experiencing entities to soothe the community of experiencing entities within the patient, recognizing and soothing different subcommunities in turn as the nurse's hands glide gently above specific areas of the patient. The nurse can also help the patient be sensitive to his subordinate experiencing entities by including relaxation techniques or providing the patient with an environment conducive to meditation.

Another way the nurse in the nursing event is in a unique position to help the patient become more aware of the synchrony within himself is by helping him recognize that the harmony within himself is not static, but that synchrony is a pattern among the changes over time that is melodic and rhythmically beautiful. In the life of any individual person there are deformations (changes) and periodicities (cycles among the changes). Periodicities are the consequences of changes between opposites.[5] Systole and diastole in the circulatory system and the sleep wake cycle in the neurological system are two examples of harmonious periodicities. The nurse helps the patient recognize that the synchrony within himself is part of the synchrony within the universe.

It has become clearer that the nursing event is a microcosmos that affects the entire macrocosmos. Returning to the patient who fears illness and dependency because it separates him from full membership in the community of persons, the nursing event is an opportunity to reassure a frightened patient that he will not be abandoned, and that the patient is useful and contributing to the community as a whole no matter what the state of the patient's dependency. It is an opportunity for the nurse to enlighten the patient about how the community that is the patient rallies to preserve and enhance the vitality of the remaining members of the community. Both patient and nurse can enjoy the marvel of the community that is a person as it adapts to new situations. Persons are communities of experiencing entities. And persons are members of the larger community of persons. Because of the interrelations in the larger community of persons, when the nurse is mindful of the importance of the nursing event to an individual patient and nurse, the nurse is also aware of the importance of the event for the community of persons as a whole.

Thus, when the nurse has successfully helped the patient allay fears of illness and dependency, the nurse has helped to change the attitude of all other members of the community of persons to health and illness. This contrasts to the traditional health care system that treats parts as if they are isolated from the whole, and ignores the fact that causing one person to be anxious about illness or dependency increases the anxiety of the entire community. Traditional health care places disproportionate emphasis on self-reliance and overemphasis on perfection of body parts. In turn this view has sent a reverberating message throughout the community of persons that getting sick is scary, that a sick body must be fixed or even abandoned altogether. The future on such a view is frightening. In contrast this philosophy of nursing is proposing that no one is abandoned, that everyone is part of the community of persons, that there is harmonious synchrony in the rhythms within the person, and that the harmony within each person is part of the harmony of the cosmos. All contribute to the harmony of the cosmos and are in turn enjoying its community.

Thus far we have discussed nursing events that offer opportunities for personal growth in both nurse and patient—when both nurse and patient are conscious. But in chapters 2 and 5 a question was left unanswered about whether a nurse can be caring for an unconscious patient. Viewing persons as communities of experiencing entities helps understand the caring sentiments of many nurses for unconscious, and even recently deceased, patients. Though the young man in the narrative who was the patient was unconscious, there was still awareness on the part of the subordinate experiencing entities within him. These subordinate experiencing entities were experiencing the nurse through her care for the patient, and could be perceived as responding to the care that she was giving the boy. From the point of view of the insights that have been developed in this work, the times in the narrative when the boy was almost regaining consciousness, can be viewed as times when his subordinate experiencing entities were trying to awaken him. Though the subordinate experiencing entities were never successful in reawakening the boy, they were responsive to the nurse's touch and to her voice. Though the boy remained unconscious, experience was still occurring within him. A kind of I-Thou relationship between the nurse and the community of still experiencing entities within the unconscious body of the boy was taking place.

Although the nurse could sense this I-Thou relationship, she was was puzzled by it and could not explain it, especially not from the mechanistic view of persons. Although a conscious I-Thou relationship is recognized by many—Jean Watson, Martin Buber, and G. W. F. Hegel, among others—none could help resolve the puzzle of the nurse about the nurse's sentiments for an unconscious patient. It is only in the metaphysics of Whitehead and in our liberal interpretation of his philosophy that we get an understanding of what was happening in the nurse's experience of the unconscious patient. Here we find our theory that a person is a community of experiencing entities more helpful than Whitehead's theory that a person is a structured society.

Many practicing nurses have experienced family members trying to reawaken their dying comatose loved ones. In these instances, the family members seem to intuitively sense the appropriateness of talking to the patient. But these sessions can seem odd and uncomfortable to the scientifically minded health care staff. Activities like these may be viewed as superstitious, but tolerable because they can do no harm to the patient, and seem to comfort the family.

But the sensitive nurse keeps the question open about whether this type of activity might be effective, or perhaps consoling and reassuring both to the family and to the dying patient. Sometimes patients awaken and report having heard the entreaties of the family for them to come back. Some have reported that it took all of their strength to *get back*, to reawaken, and that they are not sure that they would have reawakened without the family calling to them. From the perspective of this philosophy of nursing "all of the strength" required to reawaken refers to the needed cooperation of the subordinate experiencing entities.

Of course those who do not reawaken cannot corroborate the helpfulness of this kind of activity. But from the perspective of this philosophy, it is reasonable to suppose that this activity is consoling to the subordinate experiencing entities of a dying patient, and perhaps even to the subordinate experiencing entities for a time after the overall self is no longer living. This is partially corroborated by the intuition of many sensitive nurses. Returning to the dying comatose patient and the family entreating him to awaken, the damage to the community of experiencing entities may be too great for recovery. In this case, the caring nurse may help allow for a peaceful death on the part of the community of subordinate experiencing entities by reminding them, that though there is real tragedy in the immediate end of their world, the touch and solace of another human being reminds them of their place in a larger community and can kindle their hope that there is also an ultimate rightness in things.

There are occasions when all life support has been removed including feeding tubes and water in order to let the patient die, when physicians and family have concluded that any further effort to save life is *futile*. Sometimes under these circumstances the family remains with the patient until the legal pronouncement of death. But many times the family is not present. The physician is also long gone, usually having left before the family left. It is at these times that the only person who remains with the patient is the nurse.

But when there *are* other persons present, it is often another patient, perhaps the roommate of the dying patient. At these times it is the nurse who provides comfort to the anxious roommate while still caring for the dying patient. And it is the nurse who will later provide comfort and solace to that same roommate after the death of his roommate has taken place.

Any nurse knows that caring for the comatose patient who is dying is not the same experience as caring for the body of a dead patient—even when the dead patient is the same patient the nurse cared for while he was still alive. While the comatose patient is dying many practicing nurses will pause, soothe them, stroke their forehead, wipe their face and arms with a damp cloth when their fever is high, and speak a few comforting words to them. The nurse senses a response from these patients, even though they are comatose.

But even after the patient has been pronounced dead, and the nurse is wrapping the patient's body in a shroud, many of the subordinate experiencing entities that are the body of the patient continue to live for a time. Death does not come all at once to all members of the community that is a person. Hence, it is appropriate to continue to treat the remains of the person with respect. There may continue to be contact between the nurse's subordinate experiencing entities and those still living within the body of the patient. But the responses fade with time as mortality decimates the population of experiencing entities within the body of the deceased patient. When not understood this experience can be weird and unsettling.[6]

In light of the view that persons are communities of experiencing entities, these experiences of practicing nurses make more sense. Most of the subordinate experiencing entities are still living and responsive in the comatose dying patient. But many of them are still living and responsive in the deceased patient. Death is not the departure of the enduring personality from the body, but a transition in the disintegration of the community of experiencing entities beyond which there is no practical hope that the enduring personality can be reconstituted and awaken (at least not in this present world, and not without the reconstitution of the entire community of experiencing entities that is the body). But the community does not perish instantly, but by degrees over hours and days. This explains the intuition of the nurse for the appropriateness of her soothing activities toward the patient. It also explains the failure for there to be an absolute difference between the dead and the dying patient. Again, the reaching out of subordinate experiencing entities within oneself to those within the body of a deceased person can be weird and unsettling for those who view persons mechanistically.

The intuition many persons experience when they are coming down with illness or disease may be explained by the internal communications between subordinate experiencing entities and their attempts to alert the overall self to the need to take better care. In response the sensitive overall self responds by drinking more juices, getting more rest, and avoiding strenuous activities for a time. The traditional view cannot explain this feeling and often must wait for breakdown or tissue damage in order to diagnose the problem. But persons often sense that there is a problem long before science can detect it. Sometimes these hunches are corroborated by full-blown illness, and sometimes they are not.

This can be viewed in at least two ways. Traditional science would say that the hunches (intuitions) are untrustworthy because the correlations between feeling that one is getting sick and actually being sick may not be statistically significant. But from the perspective of a person as a community of experiencing entities, these hunches are viewed as veridical intuitions of the experiences of subordinate experiencing entities within the person. The prudent person follows the lead of the hunches and takes precautions that prevent breakdown, thereby ruining the statistical results of the scientist.

But in situations when a hunch of physical illness is followed by an actual and serious illness within the body, many subordinate experiencing entities have experiences of weirdness and upset similar to those of the nurse who was caring for the body of the dead patient described earlier. The subordinate experiencing entities reach out to their neighbors, but the experiencing entities in the body of a deceased person respond oddly. They are often distressed or absent. This helps to explain how the dying patient knows that she is dying. The overall self is sensing the mourning of the remaining subordinate experiencing entities for their fallen comrades and the impending fall of the community as a whole. Yet this same self may feel at peace when there is also direct awareness of the presence of the One.

But when the hunch is not followed by full-blown illness, this is apt to be because the subordinate experiencing entities have solved the problem before the illness is full-blown. They have successfully convinced the overall self to take precautions and get extra rest so that they can deal with the problems internal to their community without having to expend unnecessary energies elsewhere. They have succeeded in isolating and destroying the intruding disease before the disease entities have gotten to the threshold level detectable by the usual scientific techniques.

And perhaps one of the ways the subordinate experiencing entities detect hostile invaders of their community, is that the invaders do not speak the same language as the experiencing entities within the person—chemically, or electromagnetically. Here we encounter universals in the form of language. The invader does not share the correct universals with the home experiencing entities. Still another difference is that the past that is present in the present of the members of the home community is quite different than the past that is present in the experience of the invaders. There is a common history shared by the subordinate experiencing entities of the person that is not shared with the invaders. Hence the problem is not just wrong universals but uniquely different pasts. If so, this also helps understand the phenomenon of the rejection of transplanted organs discussed earlier in this chapter. The transplanted organ may have a different chemical language and certainly does not share the same common past.

When we remember that there are 50 trillion individual cells in the human body, which is a very much larger number than the 6 billion individual humans presently living on earth, it is amazing that such a large community is able to act as a whole, as a single person. And when we consider that each cell is an equally complex community of subordinate experiencing entities, we begin to get a glimpse of how very amazing we are as living persons. This is why the Greeks called persons *microcosms*. This is, if anything, an understatement. Persons are more complex internally than is the entire observable universe external to a person (not counting other persons).

Though it may be convenient to think of the parts of the body as isolated and mechanical, they are really *experiencing* entities. Their sensitivity to one another is sufficient so that it is impossible to effect one part without effecting all other parts to some degree. In this view there is no such thing as a side effect of a treatment or medication—because any change in a part is naturally going to effect all other parts and the whole. Side effects are not really side effects, but unintended and unforeseen effects. The interrelatedness of the experiencing entities within the human body guarantees that there will always be "side effects," and further that the "side effects" will be more numerous and far reaching than the intended effect. Hence, whenever a medication or treatment is about to be used, it is never neutral. So it is well to pause and consider whether the immediate problem is serious enough to warrant the risk of the unknown additional effects.

The nursing event is a highly complex unique situation that incorporates many universals. But there is often conflict between the uniqueness and some of the universals within the event that creates dilemmas for the nurse. The nurse in the narrative was responsible for the care of the patient and also for the care of the machines that kept his organs alive. The nurse in the narrative found herself orchestrating a balance between the needs of the patient as a person and the needs of the machines that were to keep his organs alive for transplant. We are reminded of similar occasions when nurses have had to choose between mechanical safety and gentle dignity in their care for a patient.

Technology has advanced to the point where machines are capable of sustaining bodily functions under conditions where the patient would have been long dead without the machines. But to be able to sustain the patient's life adequately, these life-sustaining machines have become so numerous that they are like a dense grove of trees surrounding the patient's bed, so dense that human touch between nurse and patient is impossible, or at least very difficult.

One example that comes to mind is that of an unconscious patient with a very serious cardiac condition, a condition in which any additional strain, such as that involved in even passive movement by the nurse, may precipitate fatal cardiac arrest. If the patient's condition remains this critical for an extensive period of time, dilemmas arise for the nurse in caring for the patient. These dilemmas can be of at least two kinds involving the skills of caring and the sentiments of caring.

One consequence of a tenuous but lengthy condition, such as the one described above, is that the linens under the patient cannot be changed adequately, because this involves moving the patient. For a limited period of time, changing the linens is not much of a problem. But as the condition continues to be stabilized but stabilized so delicately that the patient's condition still remains critical over an extended period of time, there are increasing problems. Caring for one condition may cause a worsening of another condition. The patient's life is so tenuous that any movement, even the most gentle and passive movement such as the log-roll method used by nurses to change bed linens, may result in irreversible cardiac arrest and death. It is not long before these patients are having to endure an unclean and undignified situation, lying in their own secretions and often in their own excrement.

Nurses who are caring and sensitive are in conflict. If they should leave the patient in this condition, then they run the risk of opportunistic pneumonia or bedsores, incidental infections that can also kill the patient. Machines can help because they can aerate his lungs and vary mattress pressure so as to lessen the chance of bedsores. But machines cannot guarantee that these conditions won't occur. Since the nurse cannot see the condition of the patient adequately without moving the patient, the nurse is limited in the number of avenues open for acquiring knowledge about the patient. But even if the machines could guarantee that pneumonia or bedsores wouldn't occur, there is the very real problem of the patient's dignity and the problem of the lack of human touch, which is more helpful in healing or providing for a dignified death than any machine. The laying on of hands, the gentle touch of the nurse, can either strengthen the resolve of the subordinate experiencing entities to fight for the survival of the community or give them comfort they need to die a dignified death.

What may be preventing the nurse from simply dismissing the problem and walking away may be her intuition of the discomfort of the subordinate experiencing entities within the patient. They are receiving no solace from the surrounding machines. The machines are lifeless. The machines are unresponsive. The experiencing entities within the machines bear no experiential relations to the machines as a whole. The machines lack organic unity. Hence, the experiencing entities that are the body of the patient may be more than uncomfortable; they may be in panic. This is what the nurse may be sensing—pleas on the part of these experiencing entities. But again the nurse is aware that offering solace may hasten the death of the patient. She is afraid that her caring for the patient under these conditions might actually kill him. Yet she cannot afford to do nothing to correct the situation. Other members of the health care team—physicians and other nurses—may sympathize with the nurse's dilemma. But they too have no definitive answer and defer the decision to the nurse.

There is the remaining possibility that the subordinate experiencing entities within the dying patient are awaiting the solace that the nurse has to offer so that they can surrender their battle in dignity.

So the question remains, does the nurse change the linens, or not?

THE GIVENNESS OF CARING:
RETURN OF HEAVEN INTO EARTH

The notion of the return of heaven into earth is important as a basis for understanding the nature of the givenness of caring. The return of heaven into earth is also helpful for illuminating the nature of religious experience, and the experience of the mystics. The return of heaven into earth is mentioned briefly by Whitehead in part 5 of *Process and Reality*. There Whitehead posits *four phases of the universe* or "four creative phases in which the universe accomplishes its actuality" (Whitehead 1978, p. 350). We find these phases of creative advance of the universe very suggestive and have elaborated them far beyond Whitehead's original text. Among other matters, Whitehead did not have the advantage of the more recent Big Bang cosmologies, which we synthesize with the four phases to create our own cosmology. A brief exposition of the four creative phases of the universe sheds more light on the nature and given-ness of caring.

First of all, though the word "phase" implies temporal succession, this is misleading in the case of the "four phases" of the universe. The relationship between the four phases is "all at once" rather than spread out in time. Each phase presupposes the other three, and one of the four phases, the first, is eternal rather than temporal. All of the other phases are everlasting—from time without beginning to time without end. Each of these four phases have always already been. No one of them could be temporally first. One of Whitehead's aliases for the first phase, the eternal phase, is the "Primordial Nature of God."

The first phase is "first" only logically or conceptually, not tempo-rally. The first phase is the value ranking of pure possibilities. It "occurs" independently of the other phases of the universe only in the sense that nothing that is or occurs in the other phases of the universe influences the value ranking of pure possibilities in the first phase. For this reason, and because the first phase is concerned with the very essence of importance or prize worthiness, it is appropriate to follow Whitehead in calling this first phase the "Primordial Nature of God."

In many respects the first phase of the universe is not dissimilar to Plato's intelligible world of Forms. But whereas Plato thought that his Forms were eminently real (more real than visible individuals), and capable of separate existence, we hold that the first phase of the universe is deficiently real (dependent for its reality on the other phases of the universe). Whitehead's phrase, quoted above, that "the universe accom-plishes its actuality" implies that the universe is always in the process of creating itself. The exception is the primordial nature of God, which is eternal, and is used by the other phases in their self-formation as a lure. But because the first phase is deficiently real the primordial nature of God is incapable of acting as an efficient cause. The first phase depends on the other three phases for its deficient reality. Without them it would not be.

The primordial nature of God: "the phase of conceptual origina-tion, deficient in actuality, but infinite in its adjustment of valuation" (Whitehead 1978, p. 350). As "deficient in actuality" the primordial nature of God is pure form (universal). Plato's theory of an intelligible world of eternal value-ranked Forms, with Beauty itself, Goodness itself, and Wisdom itself at the top of the hierarchy of positive pure possibili-ties gives us a glimpse of the nature of this first phase of the universe. But because this phase is deficiently real, it can only account for the intellectual recognition of what ought to be done to be caring. To be actually caring is possible only for the complex actual entities that are persons. Love is more fundamental than eternal law. When Jean Watson removed the action verbs from the list of her original list of carative factors, the result was that the carative factors became deficiently real universals, in need of persons for their actualization. This would be caring at this first phase level.

The second phase of the universe is the temporal world, the world of finite individuals, such as the nurse and the patient. The second phase is our everyday world. This is the "phase of physical origination, with its multiplicity of actualities. In this phase full actuality[7] is attained; but there is deficiency in the solidarity of individuals with each other" (Whitehead 1978, p. 350). Without the higher phases of the universe one is born, lives, and dies, feeling alone and without meaning.

In nursing, the individual nurse and the individual patient, if limited to the second phase, would be incapable of fully adequate interpersonal relations. They would remain partially isolated from each other. To the extent to which this was so, the sentiments of caring would become difficult. Only some of the *skills* of caring could be performed in terms of roles governed by universals.

It is in the second phase that evils or deficiencies such as "lack of adequate unison of becoming," and "the fading of the past" are found. At least relative to the second phase of the universe, the fading of the past results in time being "the ultimate evil" (Whitehead 1978, p. 340). Time destroys all that is valuable including our own memories of our own past as well our memories of other persons and things.[8]

The presence of the past in the present is one of the important grounds of singularity (see section on the grounds of singularity below and Whitehead in chapter 4). Hence the fading of the past undercuts the uniqueness of living individuals and the memory of unique events. Without the influences of the third and fourth phases and the value adjusted forms of the first phase, nothing would be significant or important. Without the influences of the third and fourth phases that will introduce everlastingness, adequate solidarity, and the value-adjusted forms of the first phase that provide eternal standards, nothing in the temporal world would be significant or important for any length of time.

Without the third and fourth phases, satisfaction is shallow and fleeting, nothing satisfies, at least not for any length of time. For example, though a nurse may receive awards, recognition, prestigious appointments, which temporarily bring a sense of victory or accomplishment in the second phase of the universe, the temporal world, the sense of accomplishment quickly fades and is replaced by a feeling of emptiness. For in the temporal world, awards are quickly forgotten.

But different from the fleeting satisfactions that come from rewards and accolades in the second phase, many nurses remember the deeper and more enduring satisfaction that comes from direct care of patients.

They recognize that this satisfaction is different from the satisfaction that comes from accolades. This kind of deeper and more enduring satisfaction is what makes or produces the longing to return to the heart of nursing, being with the patient in a nursing event. Though the act of caring happens in the second phase of the universe, it cannot be grounded here. It is grounded in the higher phases of the universe.

Without higher phases of creative advance than the second phase of the universe, there would be no ground for caring, as will be argued. Nursing would be concerned with nothing more significant than such activities as matching acuity levels of the patients with the competencies of the nurses, matching bed counts with numbers of nurses, or the shifting of nurses and patients to satisfy administrative requirements. These factors multiply the evil of time because they guarantee that the past will fade. It is easier to forget individual patients and events when they are mere numbers on a page, or mere items in diagnostic categories.

In contrast, caring helps combat the evil of time by refocusing attention on the value of the individual person and the individual event. Caring is accompanied by an intuition of *importance*[9] that combats the fading of the past, and provides a much deeper and enduring kind of satisfaction. It is the caring in the third and fourth phases of the universe that grounds "the objective immortality of the past."

Caring prevents the fading of the past. Caring allows for "adequate unison of becoming"—it allows persons to be fully connected to each other in the same present. Caring allows the I-Thou relationship to be adequate and complete. Caring guarantees that no one is alone. And only with caring are adequate interpersonal relations possible. Further, the third and fourth phases allow the openness of the future within the second phase to be a source of adventure rather than something to be feared. Genuine caring occurs in the second phase, but is grounded in all of the other phases of the universe.[10]

Though the caring practiced by the nurse can have no effect on *the primordial nature* of God, because the primordial nature of God is pure form (universal); nonetheless, the caring practiced by the nurse plays a significant role in the *creation* of the consequent nature of God (God as actual and Individual). It is to this nature of God, the consequent nature of God, that the practicing nurse makes a significant contribution through caring. The contribution is *significant* because caring is essential to the consequent nature of God. "God is love" *means* "God is caring." But the opportunities for caring are minimal in everlastingness—everything is already too good. By contrast the opportunities for caring are rich and varied within the temporal world. Hence, caring in the nursing event has significance beyond the moment for the two finite individuals involved in the caring occasion. The significance of caring transcends the temporal world. It is here that we find part of the ground of the givenness of caring.

The third phase of the universe "is the phase of perfected actuality, in which the many are one everlastingly, without the qualification of any loss either of individual identity or completeness of unity. In everlastingness, immediacy is reconciled with objective immortality" (Whitehead 1978, pp. 350–51). This is the phase of everlastingness—*the consequent nature of God*. But this "perfected actuality" (an incautious and somewhat inaccurate phrase on Whitehead's part) undercuts God's opportunity for caring within everlastingness. God needs the caring moments in the temporal world.

The consequent nature of God is conscious, and the consequent nature of God changes as a result of the enjoyment of the novelty provided by the second phase temporal world. However, we would add to Whitehead's statements in part 5 of *Process and Reality*, that it is as true to say that the consequent nature of God is a community of infinitely many everlasting individuals, as it is to say that the consequent nature of God is a single Individual. It is as true to say that God is many as that God is one.

As the finite person is one person and yet a unified society of many subordinate experiencing entities, the consequent nature of God can be viewed as either one Individual or a unified community of infinitely many everlasting individuals. We speculate that each of the persons who function as subordinate experiencing entities within the consequent nature of God had a beginning in the past, and in fact within the second phase of the universe. These individuals are everlasting only with respect to the future. In either case, the case of finite persons within the temporal world, or God as actual as the third phase of creative advance, "the many become one and are increased by one" (Whitehead 1978, p. 21).This leads to additional speculation on our part that the destiny of persons within the temporal world is to become subordinate experiencing entities within the consequent nature of God. In addition, we suspect that this will increase rather than diminish our freedom and identity as unique individuals.

The third phase of creative advance is the phase of the universe in which the evils of the second phase are overcome. This is the phase in which the disparate temporal worlds find unity and "apotheosis" (Whitehead 1978, p. 348). We speculate that our observable universe, which is a local neighborhood in the present cosmic epoch, is destined for apotheosis in the relatively distant future. From time without beginning the apotheoses of cosmic epochs in the second phase of creative advance have provided sustenance for the third phase of creative advance. God is as dependent on the world as the world is dependent on God.

The significance of the third phase for caring and nursing lies in the special value that is placed on caring. Universality and singularity are both essential to caring. The universal of caring is of special significance to the consequent nature of God, but without unique individual *acts* of caring, the universal of caring would be empty. Therefore, *any* individual act of caring is of special interest to God. These acts of caring need not be so momentous as the caring occasion as described by Watson, although this is ideal. These acts of caring can be simple acts of kindness, such as pausing to give drink to a thirsty patient, or adjusting his pillow. Though the word caring itself is not used by Whitehead, we find caring to be exemplified in the following passage, which describes God's role in the world:

> God's role is not the combat of productive force with productive force, of destructive force with destructive force; it lies in the patient operation of the overpowering rationality of his conceptual harmonization. He does not create the world, He saves it: or, more accurately, he is the poet of the world, with tender patience leading it by his vision of truth, beauty, and goodness. (Whitehead 1978, p. 346)

Acts of caring transcend ordinary time. The unity enjoyed by two persons in the act of caring involves the higher and more adequate unity that exists in the consequent nature of God.

Though nurses are harried and pressured by time and insufficient numbers to do the kind of caring that patients as persons require, when caring takes place at all, even the smallest moments of time achieve a special objective immortality in the divine experience. God ignores the evils within the world, at least those that cannot be taken up within a larger good. But the goodness of caring guarantees that the individual acts of caring will be "saved" by being taken up into the consequent nature of God. No act of caring is ignored.

> The wisdom of subjective aim [God's wisdom] prehends every actuality [in the second phase] for what it can be in such a perfected system [heaven or everlastingness]—its sufferings, its sorrows, its failures, its triumphs, its immediacies of joy—woven by rightness of feeling into the harmony of the universal feeling [God's feeling], which is always immediate, always many, always one, always with novel advance, moving onward and never perishing. The revolts of destructive evil, purely self-regarding [motivated by private interest in disregard of universal importance], are dismissed into their triviality of merely individual facts [vanity]; and yet the good they did achieve in individual joy, individual sorrow, in the introduction of needed contrast, is yet saved by its relation to the completed whole. The image—and it is but an image—the image under which this operative growth of God's nature is best conceived, is that of a tender care that nothing be lost.

The consequent nature of God is his judgment on the world. He saves the world as it passes into the immediacy of his own life. It is the judgment of a tenderness which loses nothing that can be saved. It is also the judgment of a wisdom which uses what in the temporal world is mere wreckage. (Whitehead 1978, p. 346)

The fourth phase of the universe can be called "the return of heaven into earth." It is in the fourth phase that we find the ground of the givenness of caring in its fullest meaning. It is in the fourth phase that the finite whisper of caring returns as a resounding heavenly chorus. And it is also the fourth phase that accounts for religious experience and the mystic's vision. It is in the fourth phase that we are made aware of the presence of the gentle companion in each caring occasion, that makes it impossible to feel alone, that assures us of the ultimate rightness of things in spite of immediate evil. Whitehead's language is subtle and complex:

In the fourth phase, the creative advance completes itself. For the perfected actuality passes back into the temporal world, and qualifies this world so that each temporal actuality includes it as an immediate fact of relevant experience. For the kingdom of heaven is with us today. The action of the fourth phase is the love of God for the world. It is the particular providence [individual act] for the particular occasions [individual event]. *What is done in the world is transformed into a reality in heaven, and the reality in heaven passes back into the world. By reason of this reciprocal relation, the love in the world passes into the love in heaven, and floods back again into the world. In this sense, God is the great companion—the fellow sufferer who understands.*[11]

We find here [in the fourth phase] the final application of the doctrine of objective immortality. Throughout the perishing occasions in the life of each temporal Creature, the inward source of distaste or of refreshment, the judge arising out of the very nature of things, redeemer or goddess of mischief, is the transformation of Itself, everlasting in the Being of God. In this way, the insistent craving is justified—the insistent craving that zest for existence be refreshed by the ever-present, unfading importance of our immediate actions, which perish and yet live for evermore. (Whitehead 1978, p. 351)

This passage makes it clear why caring is important and that no act of caring is trivial. Caring is involved in all four phases of the universe. Hence, the caring nurse influences and is influenced by the consequent nature of God through the fourth phase of the universe.

In the first phase of the universe caring is an abstract universal. Although Whitehead does not enumerate the contents of the primordial nature of God, he does refer us to Plato's world of Forms in explanation of what he has in mind: "But eternal objects, as in God's primordial nature, constitute the Platonic world of ideas" (Whitehead 1978, p. 46). Passages such as this hint that Whitehead might not object to considering the one, the true, the good, and the beautiful, as fundamental to the primordial nature of God. This would make caring as part of the primordial nature of God an abstract universal related to the Form of the Good. As such, caring in the primordial nature of God provides guidelines for acts of caring in the second phase of the universe, the temporal world. As such caring in the primordial nature of God is an archetypal template unaffected by anything that happens, including acts of caring in the second phase. It is eternal.

Neither Plato nor Whitehead talk about caring in this manner. Not in Plato's Forms, not in Whitehead's primordial nature of God, is caring directly addressed. But, our personal view is that caring is fundamental to the Good or to value-adjusted possibilities. Failure to mention it is an oversight on the part of both philosophers. But nursing is able to correct this oversight and place caring in its proper position. While it is agreed that caring affects the consequent nature of God, it can be argued that caring is part of the primordial nature of God.

But it is in the second phase, the temporal world, that acts of caring between finite individuals are of special significance. They allow for the occurrence of divine caring in the third phase—everlastingness. This in turn returns back, in the fourth phase, into the second phase, the temporal world, and allows for caring between finite individuals to be much more than would be possible in a mere temporal world. Thus, the sentiments of caring are grounded in the fourth phase, the return of heaven into earth. It can be concluded that every caring action between a nurse and a patient that involves both the skills and the sentiments of caring is an occasion of co-creation involving nurse, involving patient, and also involving the consequent nature of God, and has as its guide the primordial nature of God. Because of its very goodness this event combines special objective immortality with immediacy in the divine experience, and this immediacy is returned to the finite care giver via the fourth phase of creative advance. Here we believe we have found the ground of the "givenness of caring" about which Watson writes.

DISEASED SPIRITUALITY AND
MISPLACED INDIVIDUALITY

Thus far we have been relating nursing to healthy spirituality. But lest the reader be confused by some of the contemporary radical groups who profess religious dogma and loyalty to temporal religious leaders, it is worthwhile to make distinctions between the healthy spirituality of nursing and the diseased spirituality of these groups with their "messianic" leaders.

The kind of spirituality that comes from the return of heaven into earth, that is associated with caring, is quite different from the so-called spirituality associated with groups of persons that surrender their individual identities to that of their temporal leader or the group. Though such groups use terminology similar to that of the section on the Return of Heaven into Earth, such as "heaven," "the universe," "the One," "brotherhood," "sisterhood," "God," and "the good of the Whole," among other terms, the meaning of these terms as used by these groups is quite different from their meaning in the above section on caring and the four phases of the universe.

The kind of spirituality involved in the nursing event is inclusive of all persons, and respectful of the unique individuality of each. In contrast to the attitudes of those in closed communities, caring, which is the heart of nursing, requires openness, acceptance, and support of diversity. It does not condemn diversity or isolate persons from other persons outside of its own community.

Caring in the nursing sense not only values diversity, it requires diversity, because diversity is necessary for genuine dialogue and the openness to the future that is required by co creativity. The rubric of creativity, "the many become one and are increased by one" requires that the diversity of each of the ones that are the many be preserved for the sake of the richness of the unity of the new one. That is, a diminishment of the diversity among the many ones diminishes the possibilities for the new one.

When groups "swallow up" individuals and destroy or deny their diversity, the many become one but are decreased by more than one, for each of the many is diminished, and the new one is diminished. Genuine dialogue is denigrated into mutual delusion.

In these groups closed to outside dialogue, self-to-self dialogue within the person is difficult if not impossible, because self-to-self dialogue within the person involves honesty and self-reflection that can enhance the uniqueness of the individual and the diversity within the group. In healthy internal self-to-self relations one recognizes one's own subordinate experiencing entities. Healthy internal self-to-self relations increase the freedom and diversity of each individual. But in diseased spirituality, the body is seen as a vessel alien from the self and a burden to the self. It is not recognized as a community of subordinate experiencing entities. The power of the temporal leader requires that the followers see their bodies in this manner. For healthier self-to-self relations within the person of each member would prevent them from accepting many of the suggestions of the leader. When self-to-self relations are healthy, self-mutilation is viewed with abhorrence. Group suicide becomes impossible.

The self-to-One relationship in the closed groups is also impaired, because the self-to-One relationship is mediated by the temporal leader. Using the insights from the four phases of the universe, the return of heaven into earth is an individual experience which requires no group, no leader, no dogma, and no obedience to the dogma or a group leader. In groups in which spirituality has gone wrong, the leader, obedience to the leader, the dogma and unquestioned adherence to it, all get in the way of direct awareness of the One, of the return of heaven into earth.

The appropriation of the positive value of the work of the group members by the temporal leader again creates a block between the individual person and the One. The symbols of the group, such as common dress, common habits, common dogma, common ritual, and common icons, diminish the uniqueness of the individuals of the group. Recalling Whitehead's evils of the temporal world, the relationships between leader, followers, and symbols, enhances the fading of the past. The fading of the past is increased by the substitution of myth for actual history.[12] The past is taken away. Relations to the larger world are blocked by the symbols. The result, as is ultimately the case with temporal accolades and rewards, is lack of fulfillment.

As freewill is surrendered to the leader, the conduct of the individual members is denigrated from action to behavior rewarded or punished by the temporal leader. Since the connection to the eternal and the everlasting is not present, the temporal leader must continually remind and reinforce obedience and loyalty to his will. Action presupposes diversity, but especially that the self is an unconditioned condition. What the group demands is subordination of the will of the individual group member to the will of the temporal group leader. Such subordination is inconsistent with the individual being an unconditioned condition—it is inconsistent with action and self determination.

Nursing presupposes that both nurse and patient are persons in a higher sense than is possible within a closed group with its diseased spirituality.

BEHAVIOR, CONDUCT, ACTION, AND SELF-CREATION

The unity of the person is enhanced by self-discovery. Self-discovery expands one's freedom to act. Recalling the differences between behavior, conduct, and action (expounded in chapter 5), when persons are acting, the action is understood as wise and hence it is reason enough for the action. There is no cause of action, as is the case in conduct recognized as behavior. Wise and successful actions provide their own rewards and their own reasons.

Behavior on the other hand is causally determined, or is conduct viewed as if it were causally determined. Though the techniques of behaviorism appear to offer a quick solution, they do so at the cost of the diminishment of freedom, action, and personhood. For unless the transition from behavior to action takes place in the patient, both patient and nurse are diminished as persons, because genuine dialogue cannot take place under those conditions. In addition, the behavioral changes cannot be expected to endure beyond the time the nurse is applying negative and positive reinforcements. Remove the cause and the effect will cease to be.

But sometimes the patients' conduct indicates that they are unable or having difficulty acting from reason. As a result they may be violating their own rights as persons by self-mutilation or the rights of others as persons by abuse. Under the conditions when the consciousness of the patient is unable to effectively focus his or her community of subordinate experiencing entities into a common vision, reasoning may be ineffective. In these circumstances, the techniques of the behaviorist may be appropriate and practical when they are viewed as temporary measures and not ends in themselves. However, if these techniques become permanent treatments, with little hope of genuine dialogue between nurse and patient, then the diminishment of the personhood of both nurse and patient is too high a price to pay. It is inhumane to expect nurses to work under conditions where patients are discharged from acute care settings as soon as they become well enough to act only to be replaced by another set of patients who need to be behaviorally conditioned. It is inhumane because it is self-alienating and self-diminishing. Hence it is important that nurses working under these conditions be rotated into healthier environments, where they can engage in genuine dialogue with patients, for both their sake and the sake of their patients. It is also important to improve the health of these environments by minimizing the use of behaviorist techniques. Behaviorist techniques need to be replaced by treatments that help patients transform conduct into action.

But sometimes external control of the conduct of persons, when used wisely, may free patients to start the transition from conduct to action. For example, a child with a medical diagnosis of attention deficit hyperactivity disorder (ADHD) is unable without great difficulty to control the impulse to move. The concentration required to control movement is of necessity self-absorbing. But the self-absorption required to control behavior is not the same as Heidegger's self-absorption, where self-absorption leads to more enlightened action. In the ADHD child, concentrating on impulse control or the control of behavior in response to urges leaves little or no room for action. But with the help of medication and behaviorist techniques the problem of impulse control is diminished, leaving the child the energy and focus needed for learning and developing relationships with others. This in turn opens up an avenue for the child to be able to mature to the level of personhood, of freedom expressed in action. The switch from behavior to action frees both the nurse and the patient. It opens the possibility for transpersonal caring and co creation.

As long as the patient is behaving and not acting, both nurse and patient have limited freedom. The behavior modifier (the nurse) assumes responsibility for the behavior of the patient; because, it is assumed that, if the rewards were great enough, or the punishment severe enough, the patient would behave properly. Hence, if the patient does not behave properly the behavior-modifying nurse is responsible. She didn't do what she should have done. Examples illustrating the assumption that the responsibility for controlling behavior lies on the nurse and other health providers, and not the patient, are to be found in the many reports in the news laying the blame on the health care agent for releasing a patient from a psychiatric facility too soon, rather than holding the patient accountable for the action. This implies that the health care agent is responsible for the patient's behavior—that the patient was not "behaviorally modified" enough before being released.

Hence, it is necessary for both patient and nurse to advance beyond the relationship involved in behaviorist techniques as soon as possible, because it limits both of their abilities to continue to develop as persons. No nurse would be wise to accept this kind of relationship with a patient unless there is no alternative and unless the relationship is temporary. No wise nurse will accept this role as permanent, but only as a means for enabling the patient to make the transition to action.

THE GROUNDS OF SINGULARITY

What are persons? How are they unique? What do they have in common with some other persons, what do they share in common with all other persons?

Reflecting on the discussions with the philosophers, the notion of persons remains elusive. But what we have learned though the development of this philosophy is that individual persons are a combination of universals and singularity. Universals are that which can be shared or repeated with other persons and objects. Personhood is a universal. Personhood is shareable and personhood is repeatable. But as a universal personhood is deficiently real (merely a pure possibility), that is, personhood has no actuality without individual persons. In fact, it is difficult to think about personhood without thinking about individual persons. If personhood is a shareable universal, then personhood is not the ground of singularity that distinguishes any one person from all other persons. What is it then that guarantees the irreducible uniqueness of each person?

Singularity, though it is that which makes individual persons unique, might also seem in a sense to be a universal. Since all persons, and more generally all individuals, including events, are unique, and since singularity is the ground of uniqueness of individuals, singularity is shared by all individuals. Ironically, this would appear to make singularity among the most general of all universals. Yet singularity is the opposite of universality. Hence, to suppose that the word "singularity" solves the problem of the uniqueness of individuals is a mistake. For the word would tempt us to view singularity as simply one more universal, which it is not. Is this why it is impossible to find that which is unique in an individual by stripping away every possible universal? This would work only if singularity were one more universal—the very last one remaining after all others have been stripped away.

The fact that after all universals have been stripped away, nothing is left, is not evidence that individuals are reducible to universals. Rather it is evidence that no individual can exist without universals in addition to singularity. This does not imply that universals are sufficient for the actuality of an individual, but rather that they are necessary.

So if stripping away every universal to expose the uniqueness of an individual is not an adequate means of revealing the uniqueness, then what is the relation between singularity and unique persons? Perhaps it is the way in which universals are actualized in one person in contrast to the way in which they are actualized in any other person, that is the combination of universals, that makes each individual unique—and not particular universals that makes an individual unique.

This may be a beginning of the understanding of singularity, but the problem of singularity is much more complex. The problem of the ground of singularity is not solvable in terms of universals. It is insufficient to think of a person, or other individuals such as events or ordinary enduring objects, as simply unique arrangements of universals.

We are reminded of the time in nursing's recent past when an effort was made to find the uniqueness of nursing by stripping away everything that was shared (universals) with other professions in the quest for something that was uniquely nursing's. It is no less surprising that when nursing stripped away everything that was shared or shareable, there was nothing left. Just as stripping away universals to expose the uniqueness in persons doesn't work, it is not surprising that it didn't work for nursing either. Nursing's uniqueness, lies in part, in the way the universals are combined. It does not consist in a set of universals that belong to it exclusively.

The reader will notice that we have just referred to nursing as a one, that is, as an individual. Persons are individuals. Communities of persons are individuals. Events are also individuals. Traditions are individuals. In fact is it impossible to think of anything that is actual that is not an individual. It is equally difficult then to find something that is not an individual. This makes the search for universality as elusive as the search for singularity. Hence, the goal of traditional science to strip all elements of uniqueness from the individual is equally impossible as the attempt to find pure universals without their usual contexts in unique individuality.

Extending this discovery a bit further, universals are never found except in individuals (or as possibilities for individuals) and individuals are never found without universals. Aristotle noticed this in his theory of form (universals) and matter (the ground of the uniqueness of individuals). Kant also noticed that universals and individuals require each other. Kant tells us that form (universals) without matter (unique individuality) is empty (unreal), and that matter (unique individuality) without form (universals) is blind (unknowable). Whitehead also noticed this in his account of actual entities (individuals) and eternal objects (universals). For Whitehead any attempt to reduce individuals to universals commits the Fallacy of Misplaced Concreteness (Whitehead 1967a, ch. 5). This is because a mere universal, no matter how complex, is deficiently real. Mere universals bake no cakes.

Having just targeted the word "singularity," and having noticed the lure of language to turn it into a universal, and having also recognized that any other word that we could choose would face equal difficulties, we will keep the word "singularity" to refer to that which makes individuals unique, that which guarantees their uniqueness.[13]

What are the grounds of singularity that have been uncovered in the process of the earlier chapters of this book? There seem to be at least seven grounds of singularity. Because of their elusiveness and their importance in general and to nursing in particular, because of nursing's concern with unique individuals and events, attention has been paid to uncovering these grounds in the imaginary discussions with the philosophers. Several of these grounds of singularity blend together, and in fact, all seven are present in each individual person or event.

1. One ground of singularity noticed by Kant and other philosophers is the formal ground of space-time viewed as a continuum or manifold. No two actual entities enjoy the same address within the space-time manifold. This fact alone guarantees the uniqueness of an individual vis-à-vis all other individuals within the universe, both indi-

vidual events and enduring individuals such as persons. In the narrative, the nursing event had a unique place in space and time. It occurred in an individual room in an individual hospital on an individual afternoon. The unique lives of the persons involved intersected in that room during that period of time. Though there were a number of general universals present, as well as those quite common in nursing experiences, so that this was not an untypical nursing event, the event nonetheless was uniquely individual.

2. In addition to having a unique address, each actual individual, especially persons and their subordinate experiencing entities, makes decisions in a process of self creation which deepens uniqueness. But what does it mean to make a decision? In chapter 5, (and also in the section above) Kant was helpful in drawing a distinction between behavior and action. The kind of decision making that is important to singularity is the kind of decision making that is important to action. Actions are unconditioned conditions of their consequences, though of course there are always limits to the freedom of finite experiencing entities. Such an entity chooses among the possibilities open to itself a complex and consistent subset (from the much larger original set of possibilities) that it embodies in itself. For example, the nurse in the narrative could not make a decision to bring the boy back to life, because she lacked the power to do so, but she could decide to balance the skills of caring and the sentiments of caring in such a fashion as to get through the afternoon. The consistent subset of possibilities, though technically a universal, is so complex that it is highly unlikely to be embodied in a second individual event, in the past, in the present, or in the future.

It is probably more difficult to think of subordinate experiencing entities making free choices than to think of persons as a whole making such decisions. But subordinate experiencing entities do make free choices, and must do so for the sake of the changing and enduring stability of the community that is a person. For example, it is the subordinate experiencing entities which take notice when postsynaptic neuroreceptors are being blocked, perhaps by medication. They conclude that it is desirable for the safety of the community to increase the number of receptors to counterbalance the blockage, and act on this conclusion. The overall result is the development of tolerance to a medication that is an annoyance to the physician and the patient, but makes sense from the point of view of the subordinate experiencing entities.

3. The content of the actual world is different for each individual— no two actual entities grow out of the same actual world. Since each new individual synthesizes pure possibilities with the actual entities drawn from its past in its own act of self-creation, the fact that the past is different for each individual guarantees the uniqueness of each. The con-

tent of the actual world is an additional ground of singularity. The actual world is a unique individual grounding the uniqueness of the event that grows out of it. But actual worlds overlap. The actual world of a more recent event contains the actual worlds of its predecessors.

4. But in addition to the general difference between the actual world of any one actual entity in comparison with any other, there is a difference in the significant or "lighthouse" events that provide the context for a present actual entity. For example, the present of all persons alive on earth, November 22, 1963, included the assassination of John Fitzgerald Kennedy, then president of the United States. This was a "lighthouse" event for the experient occasions in the lives of almost every living person in America, and many persons on earth on that day. Camelot was dead! In the narrative, for the family, the lighthouse event was the accident that led to the death of their son. The family members will probably always remember what they were doing when they got the phone call, as they will be able to remember their last words with the young man. Without the lighthouse event they could not have recalled the details of that particular day.

5. There is an element of nonrationality in the decision-making process of a new actual entity that makes it impossible to predict the full uniqueness that will result from its act of self-creation. This nonrationality must not be confused with the causal determinism associated with behavior. It is associated with action. Actions must be performed in many instances without sufficient reason. Sufficient reason would leave a person with only one choice. But in most situations there are a number of choices that are equally rational. But at the same time it is necessary for an individual to make a decision. Hence the decision must be made for other than rational reasons. Viewed positively, this ground of singularity is a source of novelty, of newness, of freshness that imbues life with adventure. Viewed negatively, it is a source of chaos and indeterminacy.

In the example of the nurse, in the earlier part of this chapter, and the intensive care patient who is not able to be moved without threat to his life, there was more than one decision that was equally reasonable— to change or not to change the linens. We left the question open to the reader to decide what to do under those conditions, in order that the reader have the opportunity for self-creation. Either choice the reader might make would be morally and professionally permissible.

Dilemmas illustrate this particular ground of singularity. Ethical dilemmas are momentous because of the seriousness of the decision that must be made combined with the lack of sufficient reason for either choice.

6. In addition to the nonrationality in the self-creativity of the finite individual, there is the nonrationality[14] and uniqueness of the infinite but

enduring Individual—everlastingness in the four phases of the universe. Uniqueness and novelty are grounded in the infinite as well as the finite. We sense cosmic importance transcending personal interest, and are lured by cosmic importance to act in a manner harmonious with the basic rightness in the world.

Religious or mystic experience provides us with nonscientific knowledge that we each play a role in the unfolding or self-creation of the unique and infinite One. This insight enhances our individuality rather than diminishes it. Our intrinsic value is increased by the fact that our lives are also extrinsically valuable. This differs from grounds number 3 and 4. Here the ground of singularity is "the return of heaven into earth"[15] rather than the presence of the past in the present or the present in the present.

7. Paradoxically, the realm of universals, which are the opposite of singularity, provides an additional ground for singularity. Being more than infinite in number these pure possibilities for definiteness on the part of actual entities can be woven together in combinations so unusual as to heighten the singularity derived from the other grounds. They also constitute a reservoir of possibilities that has not been exhausted and will not be exhausted, though time be without beginning or end, and though the universe be actually infinite. But whether this is an additional ground beyond the preceding two is arguable. Nonrationality is a notion that results from the sheer immensity of pure possibility combined with the necessity of choosing among possibilities *without sufficient reason*.

NURSING THROUGH THE METAPHOR OF THE ADAGIO

Perhaps no other metaphor can better capture the beauty, the rhythm, and the harmony integral within a nursing event, than the metaphor of an adagio. An adagio is a ballet, a ballet of two individual dancers each in perfect balance with the other. The performers are brought together by a shared love of the dance and by a mutual sense of adventure.

But though they come together as diverse individuals, they understand that to create something new and unique, they must combine their artistry while retaining their unique individuality. If their performance is to be beautiful, the beauty of the performance is to be found in the synchrony and harmony of the two individual dancers performing as one. Each performer in an adagio must be attuned to the language of the other such that the slightest improvisation of one is met by its counterpart in the other.

Practice over time transforms the uniqueness of the individual performers into a new and unique "one." The vitality of the new "one" in turn, draws its breath and its life from the vitality and uniqueness of the individual dancers.

As they practice together, the individual dancers learn from one another. The possibilities that are created by this engagement surpass any that could have been imagined alone.

If the dancers have perfected their art, the performance is beauty itself. The audience is caught up in the event, an event that is in itself unique and nonrepeatable. This unique and nonrepeatable event becomes part of the history of each dancer and also part of the history of each of the members of the audience.

CHAPTER 7

Conclusion

At the outset of this book, we were searching for an adequate way of expressing what we understood about the nature of nursing. What we did understand is that nursing uses knowledge from a variety of sources, with traditional and human sciences being among the sources; and that nursing is interested in individual persons. Since traditional science, and other ways of knowing, are concerned with what is shareable and repeatable, the uniqueness of the individuals that nursing is interested in seemed incompatible with science and many other modes of knowledge. If the sciences can only illuminate what is shareable, and nursing works with unique individuals, how are the shareables of science made relevant or applicable to the unique individuals? What we initially learned in the imaginary discussions with the philosophers is that the shareable and repeatable is known in philosophy as universals, and that which guarantees the uniqueness of individuals is what philosophers call singularity.

Although we were acquainted with the concepts and the terminology of universality and individuality, it was apparent that before we could use them as a lens to adequately illuminate nursing, we needed to improve our understanding of universality and singularity.

The approach to understanding universality and singularity, and universals and individuals, was through imaginary conversations with philosophers, from Plato to the twentieth century, in an imaginary setting, St. Francelyn's Hospital. We chose this format, imaginary conversations, because it gave us freedom to ask questions of the philosophers without becoming overly involved in debates about different possible interpretations of each philosopher. The device of imaginary conversations also allowed us to treat the philosophers as contemporaries and make them more human. The primary goal, in chapters 3 and 4, was to illuminate nursing rather than advance scholarly understanding of the history of philosophy. We chose interpretations of each philosopher that we thought were reasonably accurate, but that were especially useful for illuminating nursing.

But in the process of illuminating nursing, we made a pleasant serendipitous discovery. Nursing provides a different and valuable perspective for reinterpreting the history of philosophy. Hence, the illumination of nursing and philosophy is two-way or reciprocal. An example of nursing illuminating philosophy is the new respect nursing provides for Plato's Theory of Forms, especially the Form of the Good, which has taken a beating from twentieth-century philosophers.[1] Similarly, nursing finds value in the deontological ethics of Kant, which contemporary philosophers do not always appreciate.[2]

But the fundamental lesson that we learned from these conversations with the philosophers is that all individuals—persons, events, and other entities—are a combination of universality and singularity. Each person has much in common with other persons. The common shared factors are universals. We also learned that the ways in which persons are definite from moment to moment are repeatable. Again, repeatables are universals. Yet every individual—persons, events, and other entities—is unique. In contrast to universals, individuals are *not* repeatable or shareable. And through the conversations with the philosophers, we learned that the uniqueness of the individual is guaranteed by several different grounds of singularity (summarized in chapter 6).

The grounds of singularity turned out to be the uniqueness of the place of each event within the formal structure of the space-time manifold, the presence of the content of the past in the present, the uniqueness of the lighthouse events from the perspective of any individual point of view, the decision-making process of the present individual, the availability to the present individual of a multiplicity of pure possibilities from which to choose, the lack of sufficient reason for choice (nonrationality), and the nonrationality of the consequent nature of God (which means there aren't sufficient reasons for everlastingness, nor for any particular stage in its creative advance).

Among the grounds of singularity, we learned that respecting the uniqueness of a person, both nurse and patient, required that special emphasis be placed on the individuals decision-making processes. Both nurse and patient have to be free, unconditioned conditions, in order that conduct be action and not just behavior. Though the nurse sometimes needs to use behaviorist techniques to help certain patients develop more control of their urges or impulses, we learned that progress in therapy requires that the patient be enabled to make the transition from behavior to action. The freedom presupposed by action is incompatible with behaviorist techniques.

The uniqueness of a person also depends on the uniqueness of the person's past. Therefore any record keeping is important to the endurance of a patient and to the patient's freedom to act and make choices. What is written in a patient's chart *about* the patient is only partially complete. The patient himself must write in his chart about his experiences and contribute to the decisions that effect him. This raises questions about the current health care practice of keeping patient records from the patients, of holding that these records belong to the institution and not the patient. This practice depersonalizes the patient in a manner that is unjustifiable, if not morally offensive.

But returning to the issue of the mutual illumination of nursing and philosophy, a problem at the beginning of this book was to provide an illustration of the complexity of nursing that would be understandable and accessible to non-nurses, especially the philosophers in the dialogues and to readers outside of nursing. There needed to be an introduction to the uniqueness of the nursing event that circumvented the prejudice of language for universals. This prompted the placement of the narrative in chapter 2, which drew upon the thirty-five years of nursing experience of the nurse member of our team.

The narrative described an afternoon in the life of a nurse caring for a boy who had just died, but whose body was being maintained on life-support systems for the sake of transplanting his organs. The narrative's function was to provide a paradigmatic nursing event that focused discussion and inquiry throughout the book. It was a paradigm because it not only included many of the phenomena encountered by many nurses at some time in their nursing practice, but it also illustrated some of the more momentous issues that make nursing special—especially the life and death issues.[3]

But the narrative format had an additional advantage. The narrative also provides each reader with a common experience of nursing against which to judge the development of our philosophy of nursing throughout this book. And finally, we use the narrative to support our belief that nursing practice itself has enough richness to generate many nursing theories as well as a philosophy of nursing. In addition the narrative gives meaning and vitality to philosophical concepts of general interest to philosophers.[4]

Once we had more adequately developed the meaning of universality and singularity, we were able to use the lens of universality and singularity to illuminate nursing in most, if not all, of its aspects. At the beginning of chapters 3 and 4, our intention was simply to illuminate universality and singularity, and then later use the lens to illuminate nursing.

But during the discussions with the philosophers, nursing examples became a way to illuminate the complex philosophical concepts. Ironically, we wanted to understand nursing through the lens of universality and singularity, but in order to understand universality and singularity we had to use the lens of nursing practice in order to clear away the fog of distinctions generated by traditional philosophy. As a consequence the illumination of nursing was interwoven with the illumination of universality and singularity. An additional consequence is that our philosophy of nursing was under construction at least as early as chapter 3, and in retrospect is implicit in chapter 2, the narrative. Hence, we do not encourage readers to skip to chapter 6, hoping for a shorter version of our philosophy of nursing.

During this journey with universality and singularity, we learned that the sciences, traditional and human, could not succeed in fully enlightening us about what is unique in individuals. In fact, the sciences have a tendency to obscure that which is unique in individuals.[5] But the sciences could be helpful, however, in illuminating what is shareable or common among individuals. In nursing practice, if what makes a person unique is not understood and appreciated, there is too often a tilt toward universals at the expense of the individual. The simple application of recipes garnered from the sciences results in a diminishment of the personhood of both nurse and patient. An example of this is the use of "algorithms" to make decisions about the care of a unique individual at a unique moment in time.[6] It makes the practice of nursing mechanical, sometimes hurtful, and removes the fun and adventure.

Even the scientists, though they can understand what they share in common with others by means of their science, cannot use their science to grasp what is unique about their own selves. That led us to the question of how anyone manages to get through the lenses of universals to the uniqueness of individuals. There had to be another way than the method of scientific inquiry. Hence, we turned to the mystics.

The mystics assured us that there were other ways of knowing than science. By describing their knowing through direct awareness or intuition, they made us realize that the joy, if not the beatitude, that comes from direct awareness of the One reveals an aspect of reality not grasped by the sciences. The emotion of joy peaked our interest because of what we already knew about caring. It further peaked our interest when the mystics informed us that service to others was a major route to direct awareness of the One. Again the connection with caring was apparent. The next question then was whether direct awareness and intuition could help us grasp the uniqueness of persons and events.

But even intuition turned out to be complex. It was necessary to examine the different varieties of intuition before we could go on. We discovered distinctions between everyday intuition of ordinary objects, everyday intuition of other persons, and direct awareness of the One. In fact all of the varieties of human intuition turned out to be relevant to understanding nursing events.

Remembering what the mystics said about the connection between service to others and the joy of direct intuition of the One, what emerged was a reaffirmation of what Watson earlier proposed—that the nature or heart of nursing is caring. Yet even caring was complex. Watson did not use the lens of universality and singularity to develop the concept of caring. But had Watson used the lens of universality and singularity, she would have discovered what we did, that there are two aspects of caring equally important to nursing—the skills of caring and the sentiments of caring.

But without the benefit of the lens of universality and singularity, Watson tends to emphasize the sentiments of caring while diminishing the importance of the skills of caring as central to caring. But we differ from Watson. We hold that the skills of caring and the sentiments of caring are equally important. In diminishing the importance of the skills of caring, Watson overlooks the complexities of the tension between the skills and the sentiments of caring in any unique nursing event. In any unique nursing event the skills of caring and the sentiments of caring need to be combined to provide a pathway to the everlastingness of caring and the return of heaven into earth.

We next discovered that the skills of caring involve the sentiments of caring in a dance understandable through the metaphor of the adagio (see the end of chapter 6). Each, the skills and the sentiments, are holographically interrelated, and each takes its turn in the umbra and the penumbra of the consciousness of the nurse within the nursing event. Without the lens of universality and singularity Watson missed this tension and interrelatedness between the sentiments and the skills of caring in the nursing event. It is the artistry of the nurse that balances the sentiments and the skills of caring within the nursing event.

But to perform any skill of caring the nurse must combine two things: sentiments of caring with a minimum threshold of ability to perform the technique. We say "minimal" and not "mastery" to avoid the misunderstanding that the novice learning a skill cannot be caring because she has not yet mastered the techniques of the skill, or that the expert nurse, because she has mastery of the skills, will always be performing the skills in a caring way. We learned in the examination of caring, that as long as both novice and expert remember that the skills of caring are practiced, not as an end in themselves, but in service to a whole person, they cannot help but perform the task in a caring manner. Remembering that the skills of caring are in service to persons will help guard against nursing's being lured away from its home, personal care of the individual patient, in order to join the circus of exciting new technology.[7]

Recapitulating—if the technique of the skills of caring is performed mechanically, it is not performed as a skill of caring. To be a skill of caring the technique must not only be performed successfully, it must be performed caringly—that is, the sentiments of caring must be present.

However, this is not to imply that the patients themselves are always the object of the sentiments of caring. In the case of the skills of caring it is the rightness and goodness of the action that is one important object of the sentiments of caring. The allows the nurse, and indeed enjoins the nurse, to perform the skills of caring, in spite of reprehensible behavior or character on the part of the patient that causes the nurse difficulty having caring sentiments for the patient. But the patient remains the most obvious object of the sentiments of caring.

Individual nurses may worry about whether they are sufficiently caring, because they are unable to always feel the sentiments of caring. But worrying about such a matter is in itself an indication of caring. It is the nurse that does not worry that is of concern, for it is the sentiments of caring that distinguishes the true nurse from the mere technician.

Both of these aspects of caring, the skills of caring and the sentiments of caring, involve universals and individuals, but the tilt is toward universals in the case of the skills of caring. While in the case of the sentiments of caring, the tilt is toward individuality—for the sentiments are between two unique individuals in a unique situation, though the sentiments per se are universals.

In order to better understand nursing and caring, we found it necessary to further develop the concept of what we call the nursing event. In the nursing event, which is a unique individual, two other unique individuals, nurse and patient, are brought together by the universals, health and illness. Every nursing event involves caring.

We were also curious about what might be meant by the givenness of caring, discussed by Watson. But we were especially curious about the ground of the givenness of caring. It seemed quite unsatisfactory to simply say, as Watson did, that caring was a given. If caring is a given, where is it given, when is it given, and who is the giver? What impressed us in the course of the journey in this book is the mystery in the ground of the givenness of caring. In the detective work needed for at least partially resolving this mystery, we found ourselves deep into philosophical cosmology and theology as encountered in Whitehead's four phases of the universe. This inquiry lead us to the realization that the abiding value of caring, and the deep satisfaction that caring provides, may be the result of a phenomenon Whitehead's calls "the return of heaven into earth." Perhaps it is here that the ground of the givenness of caring is to be finally found. Caring brings everlasting satisfaction because it involves co-creativity not just between nurse and patient, but between nurse, patient, and the consequent nature of God. Therefore, the simplest occasion of caring on earth is returned to the carer as a resounding heavenly choir.

And perhaps the most profound discovery of all that we made in our pilgrimage with universality and singularity, universals and individuals, as illuminating nursing, is a new and different perspective for viewing the living person differing from that of traditional science. Our discovery, based on Whitehead's understanding of persons, is that a person is not a mind in a body, as Descartes and his followers thought, but a person is a community of experiencing entities. In this new perspective the body is within the self, and the self is within a greater Self.[8] Furthermore, this same encapsulating structure of experience is repeated throughout the entire universe from the smallest quantum event to God as everlasting. What is more, this new perspective has far-reaching implications for nursing in all of its aspects.

This new and better view of the nature of a person at last frees nursing from the view of traditional science that persons, at least their bodies, are reducible to the universals that are the focus of chemistry, biology, and physics. From this traditional point of view a person is simply an arrangement of atoms changing as a result of chemical processes and other antecedent conditions.

Seeing persons as communities of experiencing entities is compatible with nursing's insight that persons are more than the sum of their body parts, and that persons are not causally determined by genetics, chemistry, environment, or anything else. The notion that persons are a community of experiencing entities means that nothing is value-neutral. If something affects any part, it affects all. Viewing persons as communities of experiencing entities brings a whole new meaning to the notion of the side effects of medications and treatments.

Instead of the side effects of treatment and medication being regarded as nuisances, in this new view, multiple consequences of any intervention are *expected*. Nothing that affects one part can fail to affect all other parts and the whole. This means that nursing's role is to help soothe the disturbed subordinate experiencing entities and help restore the harmony of the whole. Given the more than astronomical complexity of the community of experiencing entities that is a single living person, the belief that anyone can ever know all of the consequences of a treatment or medication on a unique person is dubitable, if not absurd.

The new view of a person as a community of experiencing entities changes the notion of medical or nursing specialties. Instead of specialties these are areas of concentration within the whole. The notion of a specialty in the traditional sense is incompatible with the view that a person has organic unity as a whole. The primary care provider in the new view is the patient himself or herself with assistance from a generalist who is sensitive to the person as a community of experiencing entities. The best primary care providers are the patients themselves in communion with their subordinate experiencing entities. Nursing's role is to enable this to happen.

This new way of thinking separates nursing from any other health care profession. While others are content with treating their part of a person, the nurse enjoys the adventure and the joy of caring for the person as a whole in all of his or her uniqueness and complexity. The nurse is the most capable heath care provider for enabling patients to be their own primary care providers. What we have learned is that the benefit for the nurse participating in this venture with the patient is the fulfillment of her own personhood in an act of co-creation with the patient.

NOTES

CHAPTER 1. INTRODUCTION

1. Merriam Webster's *Collegiate Dictionary*, 10th ed. From Britannica CD ROM 2 (1995).

2. Though a few changes were made to protect confidentiality, and dramatic license was taken to fill in gaps, the event described in the narrative actually happened.

3. If this seems odd, it is because it is a particularly weak approach to grounding singularity.

4. E.g., John Caputo, *Radical Hermeneutics* (Caputo 1987).

5. Even proper nouns, which are intended to label unique individuals, are repeatable formula. Take the name "Mary": As a repeatable formula, the name is a universal. It is eternal and unchanging. It is the same regardless of which individual it is intended to label. But any such individual will be progressing from birth to death, while her name remains unchanged. Is Mary at age two months the same individual as Mary at 103 years? Hence, there is tension and rich interrelatedness between "Mary" and Mary, the word and the individual.

6. "Individual nurse" can mean an individual nurse or an individual group of nurses.

7. "Individual patient," unless otherwise specified, can mean a single person, or an entity which is also individual, such as a community, a family, or a group.

8. We use the term "patient" throughout this book to mean "the recipient of nursing care."

9. Whether the individual is an event, or an enduring entity, such as a person or a mountain.

10. Paradoxically, individuality is a universal—though an odd or peculiar universal. The problem is that individuality is too general to function as an ordinary universal. An entity must be an individual before it is capable of being determinate in any of the more ordinary ways. Actuality and individuality mutually presuppose each other. Universals are possibilities for determinateness on the part of actual entities which are necessarily individuals.

11. Our goal is not to argue for the correctness of our interpretation of the philosophers, but to show the usefulness of our interpretation for nursing and the philosophy of nursing. However, we have made every effort to be correct—relying directly on the primary material. What we have not done is survey the lengthy history of debates over interpretations of the philosophers. This would

make the present work unmanageably long and detract from its usefulness for nursing. Interested readers might consult works such as Frederick Copleston, *The History of Philosophy*, in its many volumes.

CHAPTER 2. NARRATIVE

1. Hilary Putnam, University of Colorado at Denver, Fall 1996, drew the distinction between science and nonscientific knowledge. He teaches a course at Harvard on Nonscientific Knowledge. In this he follows the pragmatist tradition of John Dewey.

2. Temporality is a universal shared by all individuals. But this universal should not be confused with the time of the world (the universe), which is an empty individual filled with all of the actual individuals of the past. Hence, the concept of time is ambiguous: it means both temporality (a universal) and the individual time of the world (an "empty" individual).

3. That time as a whole is an individual that contains all of the individual "times" is analogous to the relationship between the One and each one (see chapter 3) as regarded by the mystics. Interestingly, Sir Isaac Newton, perhaps for similar reasons, called space and time the sensorium of God (*Principia*, Scholium) (see chapter 4).

4. It is an empty, uniquely individual, form, and as such tests the limits of any simple form matter distinction. (Cf. Kant.)

5. Compare with material on the consequent nature of God in chapter 6.

6. Here we encounter a series of nested universals from the more abstract and general "bringing of a pizza" to the much more specific universal "bringing of a pizza in the context of organ harvesting." Cf. Whitehead (1967a), Abstraction.

CHAPTER 3. UNIVERSALITY AND SINGULARITY IN NURSING PRACTICE AS ILLUMINATED BY IMAGINARY DISCUSSIONS WITH GREEK, MEDIEVAL, AND EARLY MODERN PHILOSOPHERS

1. Aristotle: "Science is concerned with what is always or for the most part." He draws the expected conclusion, that there is no science of the individual. R. G. Collingwood in his *Idea of History*, objects, maintaining that history is a science in spite of its concern with individual events and persons (Collingwood 1956, pp. 249–56). But Collingwood is voicing a minority position on the connection between science and individuals, and even Collingwood admits that the historian uses universals in order to know individuals.

2. Since these imaginary discussions are posited to take place between a nurse and the philosophers, we shift to the first person singular throughout these discussions. We imagine the "I" to be the nurse co-author, Janice Brencick.

3. Plato (1963). Special use was made of the *Phaedo, Meno, Republic* (bks 6, 7, 10), and the *Timaeus*. These are in general, the middle period dia-

logues where the theory of Forms is discussed in its more speculative versions. But whether Plato was a "Platonist" is a question that cannot be definitively answered because of Plato's care to distance himself from the views of the protagonists in his dialogues. We assume he was, at least on some major points, a "Platonist"; that is, that he *separated* the Forms (as Aristotle tells us in several passages in the *Metaphysics:* 987b1ff., 1078b30, 1086b1–5), and that he *value-ranked* them (in the words of Whitehead in *Process and Reality*, part 5). The value-ranking is the result of putting the Form of the Good at the top, as in the account of the Divided Line, *Rep.,* book 6.

4. We will use the convention of italicizing the more direct paraphrases of philosopher's ideas. Material not italicized is less direct and more interpretive. The doctrine of recollection is introduced in several different dialogues, among them the *Meno, Phaedo,* and *Phaedrus.*

5. Cf. the notion of the philosopher king in the *Republic.* Knowledge comes from recollection of the Forms, never from taking a vote.

6. Emanation is a Neoplatonic notion (all lower forms of being spring into existence out of imitation of the One or the Good). But the account of the Divided Line in Plato's *Republic*, 507b2–511e, is easily interpreted as suggesting that the Form of the Good is responsible for the being of the other Forms, as well as the being of the mathematicals below the Forms, and indirectly through the lower Forms and the mathematicals of visible individuals in the visible world. Whether Plato himself believed in a "great chain of being" has been debated and will continue to be debated.

7. Aristotle tells us that Plato *separated* the Forms in three different passages in his, Aristotle's, *Metaphysics.* The *Phaedrus* with its myth of the tripartite soul, travelling between the world of Forms and the sensible world, confirms Aristotle's interpretation of Plato. The Forms are real independently of the sensible world and independently of *psyche* (soul) and *nous* (mind). In Plato's view, the mind is part of the soul—the highest part.

8. Key dialogues for these insights are the *Phaedrus* with its myth of *eros* and the tripartite soul, and the *Phaedo* for a few pages after 102a.

9. Again, the key dialogues for these insights are the *Phaedrus* with its myth of eros and the tripartite soul, and the *Phaedo* for a few pages after 102a.

10. This is clearly so for the Neoplatonic interpreters of Plato, Plotinus and others, and it is arguably so for Plato. Beauty itself may be seen as a high Form immediately "under" the Form of the Good. Or, alternatively, Beauty itself, Goodness itself, Truth itself, Unity itself, Being itself may be seen as mutually entailing or containing one another. As such, these five syncategorematic concepts become very important to medieval theology. Here the point is that to the extent something is good it is beautiful, and conversely.

11. The reasoning here is similar to that regarding Beauty itself and the Form of the Good. Justice is another high Form "entailed" by the Form of the Good as it entails the Form of the Good. For the Platonist, a just act enhances the being or reality of the person acting. An unjust act diminishes the being of the person.

12. This is not the case. We are not seeking a science of the individual. But there is no point in arguing the matter with Plato.

13. Plato, *Phaedrus*. In this dialogue Plato argues that it is better to love Beauty itself than beauty in a sensible individual.

14. For Aristotle, the senses provide us with direct access to universals, his forms.

15. Socrates the human is a paradigmatic example of substance (*ousia*) in Aristotle's philosophy. This is to say that Socrates, a sensible individual, is fully real. In contrast, forms or universals are real only to the extent to which they ingress into individuals, such as Socrates. Cf. *Categories*, chs. 1–5.

16. *Met.* 1039b20 ff. This passage is explicitly concerned with the impossibility of defining an individual. But since an individual cannot be defined, there can be no knowledge of what is always or for the most part true of an individual.

17. *Post. An.* 71a1–73b. Here Aristotle presents his position that not all scientific knowledge is demonstrable, though this is true of science in the strict sense. Science in the strict sense would be knowledge of what is always, since it would be knowledge of what is demonstrable. But Aristotle finds it reasonable to allow science to include "what is for the most part" as well as "what is always."

18. The one possible exception is Aristotle's Unmoved Mover (*Metaphysics*, book Lambda). Otherwise, forms, universals, are shareable or repeatable aspects of individuals.

19. One very clear example is the shape (*morphe*) of a pottery vase in the section on the four causes (*aitia*) in *Physics*, book 2.

20. On these matters Aristotle is in general agreement with Plato. For mathematics see books Mu and Nu of Aristotle's *Metaphysics*. The account of the Prime Movers in book Lambda is also relevant. They move in their circular orbits because of their love for the Unmoved Mover, not because the Unmoved Mover is acting as an efficient cause, compelling them to move.

21. This theory of forms as universals permeates Aristotle's works. Cf. *Physics*, 1 and 2.

22. The language, "repeatable" and "shareable," we have adopted from Alfred North Whitehead. *Kathalos*, universal, is that which can be repeated or shared and yet be the same. Aristotle worries in ch. 13, of book Zeta of his *Metaphysics*, whether *morphe* (form) is always *kathalos* (universal).

23. Socrates is a "this such," an individual human being.

24. *Metaphysics*, book Zeta, ch. 13.

25. The only exception that Aristotle makes is the Unmoved Mover.

26. The discussion in the *Categories* differs from that of book Zeta of the *Metaphysics*. Aristotle labels the substance forms (both species and genera) substance in a secondary sense in the *Categories*. In book Zeta he seems to be arguing that the proximate species is substance in a primary sense, and that the genus (e.g., animal) is not substance in any sense.

27. *Metaphysics*, bk Zeta, ch. 13.

28. *Matter* in Aristotle's sense (*hyle*) must not be confused with the so-called *matter* of twentieth-century physics (the particles out of which atomic elements are constituted). For example, a hydrogen atom is a this such, it combines a repeatable form with unique individuality. The form (one electron combined

with one proton) is shared by each individual hydrogen atom with all other hydrogen atoms. The puzzle is what makes any one hydrogen atom different from all other hydrogen atoms. Aristotle's less than satisfactory answer was that it was its matter (*hyle*) that made it different.

29. Cf. Aristotle, *Categories*.

30. This is a creative clarification of some of Aristotle's questioning about essences in *Metaphysics*, Zeta.

31. Aristotle tentatively foreshadows John Locke's distinction between "real" and "nominal" essences. A nominal essence is good enough for human practical purposes. But the usefulness of a nominal essence should not be mistaken as evidence that the nominal essence is the "full," "true," or "real" essence.

32. *Metaphysics*, Zeta.

33. *Metaphysics*, Zeta.

34. *Nichomachean Ethics*, book 10.

35. *De Anima (On the Soul)*, 430a20–25 and other passages in book 3 on the active intellect. *Physics*, book 4. *Nichomachean Ethics*, book 10.

36. *De Anima (On the Soul)*, 430a20–25.

37. *Metaphysics*, book Lambda, contains Aristotle's longest treatise on the Unmoved Mover. But there are additional passages in *On the Soul* and also in the *Physics*, that directly or indirectly allude to the Unmoved Mover.

38. Any collection of the fragments of the presocratics will do. Philip Wheelright, *The Presocratics,* is available (Wheelright 1986).

39. *Met.*, book Lambda.

40. The unity is too tight for the occurrence of discursive thinking. Plotinus would argue for an eternal realm of ideas, each reflecting the others eternally, without the possibility of change. The multiplicity of eternity is one step down from the perfect unity of Being.

41. *Met.*, book Lambda: only the species is everlasting, individuals are mortal.

42. *Met.*, book Zeta, toward the end. This is a creative interpretation of passages in this text.

43. Cf. *On Generation and Corruption* and book Lambda of the *Metaphysics*.

44. *De Anima* 425a22–30. That this is not a sixth sense follows from *De Anima* 424b20 ff.

45. The shudder quotes are essential; for the universe is not a universal, it is a unique individual.

46. Hildegard of Bingen, *Scivias*, translated by B. Hozeski (Sante Fe: Bear & Company, 1986). Hildegard was a medieval mystic.

47. E. Z. Brunn and G. Epiney-Burgard, *Women Mystics in Medieval Europe* (New York: Paragon House, 1989), pp. 3–36.

48. Florence Nightingale: It is nature that heals, not the caregiver.

49. Both Spinoza and Plotinus present this view of reality in their works. Spinoza in his *Ethics* and Plotinus in the *Enneads*.

50. William James, *The Varieties of Religious Experience* (New York: The New American Library, 1958), pp. 292–94. E. Underhill, *Mysticism: A Study in*

the Nature of Development of Man's Spiritual Consciousness, 12th ed. rev. (London: Lowe & Brydone, 1967), pp. 81–94.

51. The language that the "Truth" of religion is a "grand illusion" was used by W. T. Stace in his 1948, *Atlantic Monthly* (July 15th), article, "Man against Darkness."

52. O. Sacks, *Migraine*, revised and expanded (Berkeley: University of California Press, 1992), p. 299ff.

53. This is not intentionally paradoxical, rather the finite individuals are free to choose the degree and kind of their oneness with the One. And no matter the degree of their oneness with the One they retain their distinct individuality.

If one must choose a status for the One, individual or universal, the One is a very special and unique Individual. But the word "individual" is insufficiently mysterious to convey the nature of the One or God, and there are problems with the indefinite article "a." The word "individual" implies a simplicity and a this worldliness that is inconsistent with God or the One. The word "individual" invites an anthropomorphism that is rejected by every philosophical theologian from Xenophanes of Colophon, sixth century BCE, to the present. (God is not an old man with a white beard!) Hence, it is important to say that God or the One "is individual," not "is *an* individual."

On the issue of whether the One is determinate, whether universals are shared by the One with the ones, it is probably as true to say yes as to say no. The problem is that the life of the One must be different from the life of finite persons, as the consciousness of the One is different from that of finite individuals. Hence, the unwillingness of some medieval theologians, such as Maimonides (in his *Guide for the Perplexed*) to allow that God even has attributes. Maimonides' problems were several: extreme monism seemed to be inconsistent with allowing even this kind of diversity into the Divine nature (saying that God has attributes such as omniscience). But he also had a problem with language, which was shared by Aquinas: How can terms applied to finite beings have the same meaning when applied to God? Consequently, both Maimonides and Aquinas endorse "the negative way," that it is only possible to say what God is not. And Maimonides insists that no statement made about God in a human language can be literally true (God doesn't have wings!).

54. A. N. Whitehead, *Religion in the Making.* Religious experience enables a person to feel at home in any circumstance.

55. Heraclitus, DK 118: "A dry soul is wisest and best," and DK 89: "The waking have one world in common, whereas each sleeper turns away to a private world of his own."

56. G. Harkness, *Mysticism: Its Meaning and Message* (New York: Abingdon Press, 1973), pp. 153–57.

57. Descartes, *Rules for the Direction of the Understanding.*

58. S. Toulmin, *Cosmopolis*: Relates the story of the Jesuits keeping the heart of the assassinated King Henry IV of France (Henry Navarre), in a jar at La Fleche, where Descartes went to school. Young Henry of Navarre was the "JFK" of his day, a young, glamorous king who many people hoped would make peace between the Catholics and the Protestants. But when he was assassinated in an open carriage in 1610, all hope for peace was destroyed. The

Thirty Years War that followed was one of the greatest bloodbaths in all of European history. The Treaty of Westphalia in 1648, ending the war, was only seven years after the publication of the first edition of Descartes' *Meditations*. These events had a tremendous impact on Descartes. His unwillingness to make unfounded knowledge claims was perhaps one result, his extreme distrust of emotions was another result. It can be conjectured that the Jesuits kept the heart, which symbolized passion, in order to remind themselves of the need to balance faith with reason in order to control the passions. This part of the lesson was not understood by Descartes. He thought only reason was trustworthy.

59. Descartes expressed this hope in his *Meditations on First Philosophy*. If he came back in the twentieth century, he would admit his hope had not been fulfilled, and would probably admit that it never can be; that is, physics can never be science in the sense that Descartes gave to the word "science." The problem is that the theories of physics are tentative and fallible; whereas science, on Descartes' account, requires indubitability.

60. Meditation I.

61. Descartes foreshadowed John Locke's distinction between primary and secondary qualities. For Descartes (and Locke) the only physically real properties are the mathematically describable ones. Sensible qualities are only "in the mind," and there is no way for one person to known what is in the mind of another. Hence, I cannot know that another person experiences the same color of green that I experience. Though the vibratory frequency is measurable, the reaction of individual minds to the frequency is unknowable.

62. Meditation II. Strictly speaking the inconsistency is performative rather than logical. Anytime Descartes is able to doubt the truth of the proposition "Descartes exists," the performance of doubting the proposition is inconsistent with the falsehood of the proposition. This was noticed by Jaakko Hintikka, the Finish philosopher, some decades ago.

63. Descartes, *Meditations*.

64. According to another account, the episode with vivisection was a mistake. He started to dissect a woman, only to find that she was still alive.

65. Descartes speculated in his *Replies to Objections*, that the mind might be located at the pineal gland, since there was only one pineal gland, and it was small and centrally located.

66. Meditation VI develops the distinction between mind and body and argues for the separability of the two kinds of substance.

67. This picture of the body as a machine is implicit rather than explicit in Descartes' *Meditations*. The philosopher who is most explicit on this point is Thomas Hobbes, the English contemporary of Descartes. However, the essence of corporeal substance as described by Descartes in Meditation V leaves little doubt but that he is in agreement with Thomas Hobbes. Where Descartes disagrees with Hobbes is in placing a mind within the mechanical body. For Hobbes, the person as a whole is a machine. The emotions and thought processes are mechanical phenomena. Cf. Thomas Hobbes, *Leviathan*.

68. Meditation II.

69. In the Introduction to his *Meditations* Descartes petitioned the Sorbonne to certify his proof of the immortality of the soul.

70. David Hume is famous for his rejection of metaphysics. All knowledge and reasonable belief (probability) must be based on experience (Hume 1978, p. 180ff.).

71. For an excellent summary of Hume's arguments for skepticism, see his *Treatise of Human Nature*, The Abstract (Hume 1978, pp. 645–62).

72. They fall under probability rather than knowledge.

73. With the possible addition of immediate sense experience and memory.

74. This paragraph summarizes part 1 of Hume's *Treatise* (Hume 1978).

75. *Webster's Third International Dictionary*, unabridged. Encyclopaedia Britannica, 1993, p. 743.

76. The language, "reasonable belief," is ours. Hume wrote about "probability."

77. The theory that the only universals are words is called nominalism. It was heatedly debated in the Middle Ages.

CHAPTER 4. UNIVERSALITY AND SINGULARITY IN NURSING PRACTICE AS ILLUMINATED BY IMAGINARY DISCUSSIONS WITH MODERN AND CONTEMPORARY PHILOSOPHERS

1. Hillary Putnam, a contemporary American philosopher, is stressing the importance of nonscientific knowledge in his courses and lectures in the late 1990s. Putnam has made a transition from being sympathetic with logical positivism to being a staunch defender of pragmatism. Part of this transition has consisted in a shift of emphasis from scientific to nonscientific knowledge. He does not reject science, but sees it as dependent on a nonscientific basis.

The best general source for Kant's thinking on this subject is his *Prolegomena to Any Future Metaphysics* (Kant 1950).

2. There are many tales about Kant. Most are apocryphal, impossible to either confirm or disconfirm. For example, the housewives of Konigsberg were said to have set their clocks by Kant's afternoon constitutional walk.

3. In the Transcendental Deduction of the Categories, a connection is made by Kant between development of the concept of the empirical ego and the ability to successfully reidentify empirical objects using the categories, with all of this presupposing the unity of the space-time manifold.

4. Refutation of Idealism.

5. First Analogy. Principle of Permanence of Substance.

6. Second Analogy. Principle of Succession in Time, in accordance with the Law of Causality.

7. Refutation of Idealism.

8. See Kant's Refutation of Idealism in the First Critique. It is essential to his transcendental deduction of the categories (Kant 1965).

9. The idea of the manifold is introduced early in the material leading up to the transcendental deduction of the categories in Kant's First Critique (Kant 1965).

10. The Schematism of the Pure Concepts of the Understanding.

11. The problem of the development of self consciousness is addressed much more fully by G. W. F. Hegel in his *Phenomenology* (Hegel 1966). This solution is implicit in Kant's Refutation of Idealism (Kant 1965, p. 244ff.) and in the larger argument that surrounds his Transcendental Deduction of the Categories (Kant 1965, pp. 120–75).

12. Kant posits three egos or concepts of self: (1) the empirical ego; (2) the noumenal ego; and (3) the transcendental unity of pure apperception (the "I think"). In any account of the emergence of self-consciousness, the empirical ego is very important for Kant. It is the concept of self that would first emerge (though Kant does not himself address the problem of the emergence of consciousness and self consciousness in children). See the Refutation of Idealism (Kant 1965, p. 244ff.).

13. All ideas are copies of antecedent impressions, with sense impressions being the original impressions.

14. The phrase "natural belief" is only occasionally used by David Hume. But his notion that these beliefs arise "naturally" and are "common to all humanity" is significant. It is safe to speculate that he might have done much more with these notions if the insights of evolution had been available to him.

15. See John Locke's *An Essay Concerning Human Understanding*, especially the opening sections of book I (Locke 1959). Descartes in his *Meditations on First Philosophy* argued that he had such innate ideas as the idea of God.

16. Kant called this his Copernican revolution in philosophy—that is, that the object of knowledge conforms to the knower rather than the knower to the object (Kant 1965, p. 22).

17. Transcendental Deduction of the Categories.

18. First Analogy. Principle of the Permanence of Substance.

19. First Analogy. Principle of the Permanence of Substance.

20. First Analogy. Principle of the Permanence of Substance.

21. Kant's actual example was the behavior of a barge in a canal in Konigsberg.

22. Kant called himself an "empirical realist" and a "transcendental idealist." Since all persons imposed the same universal and necessary structures on experience in the constitution of empirical or physical reality, the physical world is empirically real. But since the physical world was *constituted* by structures imposed by the subjects, the physical world is *transcendentally ideal*.

23. The distinction between the one world of objective experience and the many worlds of subjective experience should be credited to Heraclitus of Ephesus, 500 BCE. But the distinction is central to Kant's Transcendental Deduction of the Categories in his First Critique (Kant 1965, pp. 129–75). Without the categories, Kant argues that there would not be one world of objective experience. But the world of physical or empirical reality is one world, therefore we must be imposing the categories (and forms of intuition) on experience in order to constitute the world of empirical reality. For subjective experience gives us as many different worlds as there are subjects.

24. *The Original Mother Goose* (Philadelphia: Running Press, 1992). (Book lacks pagination.) The later stanzas include the earlier stanzas in a cumulative fashion. The sequences are chosen by the poet because they are unusual,

not at all like the constant conjunctions that David Hume associated with the causal relationship.

25. Kant in his First Critique is much more tentative than in his Second Critique on these issues. But it is correct to say that he argues for the legitimacy of faith or hope and is not making a knowledge claim about the self (the noumenal ego) being an unconditioned condition of its actions in his First Critique. Nor is he making such a claim in his Second Critique, because there he is concerned with the reasonableness of action rather than with evidence for knowledge claims.

26. The Ground of the Distinction of all Objects in general into Phenomena and Noumena.

27. Jürgen Habermas, *Communicative Action*, has somwhat influenced this interpretation of Kant. But it is difficult to read either Kant's Second Critique (Kant 1956), or his *Foundations of the Metaphysics of Morals*, without coming to view persons as unconditioned conditions of their actions. See Kant's Third Antimony (Kant 1965, pp. 409–14).

28. The Third Antinomy. But also see The Architectonic of Pure Reason (Kant 1965, pp. 653–65).

29. This remains a problem in the twentieth century. We believe that the one philosopher who may have a solution to this problem is A. N. Whitehead, examined later in this chapter.

30. *God, freedom, and immortality* are the three presuppositions of morality mentioned by Kant in a number of passages (e.g., Kant 1965, pp. 29, 325n).

31. A controversial but important point. Kant struggled with the relationship between theoretical and practical reason. If theoretical reason is superior, then the presuppositions of morality, especially freedom in the sense presupposed by the self as an unconditioned condition of action, remain merely "justified" tenets of hope or faith.

32. See the preceding note. Practical knowledge requires an inversion of Kant's hierarchy of theoretical and practical reason. In addition, it would require a new vision of nature inconsistent with the Newtonian vision of Kant's First Critique.

33. Heidegger, *Introduction to Metaphysics*. Aristotle, *Physics*, book 1, chapters 1 and 2.

34. Here we are forcing Kant beyond the insights of his own work, but in a direction that his works foreshadowed.

35. This statement about freedom being terrible, because controllable only by itself, is made by Kant in one of his lesser works on ethics.

36. This is the empirical ego (Kant 1965, pp. 28, 89, 167–69, 381–82, 408–9, 440).

37. We notice that this may be one of the grounds of singularity—decision making.

38. The will is *heteronomously* determined when a person acts from desire. The will is autonomous when a person acts from reason (Kant 1956).

39. For Hegel, freedom, spirit or mind, and consciousness, are aspects of the same reality, and have developed historically. In his *Philosophy of History*, history is the story of the development of freedom (Hegel 1900).

40. This combines insights from Hegel's *Phenomenology* (Hegel 1966) with insights from his *Philosophy of History* (Hegel 1900). The interpretation makes use of insights from Whitehead (1978).

41. This is a summation of the main argument of the *Phenomenology of Mind* (Hegel 1966). Martin Heidegger emphasizes this interpretation of Hegel in Heidegger's *Basic Problems of Phenomenology* (Heidegger 1982).

42. Here we are pushing Hegel a bit from his original emphasis on universality. In Hegel's Philosophy of Mind in his *Encyclopaedia of the Philosophical Sciences*, Hegel went so far as to argue that the "this" and the "here" were universals (Hegel 1971, part 1). In one sense they are universals. Hegel can be interpreted as denying singularity. We are giving him more credit than many of his critics. We do not think he meant to deny the uniqueness of individuals. Even if he did so intend in some of his works, this is an error he would have corrected by the time of the imaginary discussions in St. Francelyn's.

43. Again this material is from Hegel's *Phenomenology of Mind*, the opening one hundred pages after his very lengthy introduction (Hegel 1966, pp. 1–99). The reference to the development of concepts in children is our own, but it follows the general outline of the emergence of consciousness and self-consciousness provided by Hegel in his *Phenomenology*.

44. This example with the dog is discussed earlier in this chapter. In that passage it is Baby Kant who is in the high chair.

45. The example is ours. The philosophical insights are Hegel's.

46. The language "auto pilot" is ours, the notion of unconscious experience is Hegel's (and Leibniz's, among others).

47. This notion of operating on "autopilot" becomes important in Chapter 5 in the discussion of the relationship between the skills of caring and the sentiments of caring.

48. This tradition is traceable back to at least Leibniz—that consciousness is the result of perception of perception, apperception. Kant continues this tradition, and Hegel and his followers elaborate it. In this tradition most of the objects of experience are experienced without consciousness. Consciousness is the result of experience of experience because of novelty or interest.

49. See the sections in Hegel's *Phenomenology* immediately preceding and including the section on Master and Slave (Hegel 1966). Self-consciousness requires another self who is aware of oneself, and it is accomplished through experience of the experience of the other self's experience of oneself.

50. For Hegel, human history is not just the self-development of freedom, but the self-development of God.

51. Whitehead, *Adventures of Ideas*, Subject and Objects (Whitehead 1967).

52. This is a creative interpretation of key passages in *Process and Reality* (Whitehead 1978, especially part 2). In Whitehead's own words, *a person is a structured society of actual occasions, with a regnant society* that focuses the experience of the other subsocieties within the person. The regnant society is the soul, mind, or enduring personality. All of the subsocieties are experiencing entities down to atoms and elementary particles. Actual occasions are quantum events, the droplets of experience that are the parts of all of the more complex experiencing societies.

53. *Societies* are entities with sufficient internal unity to be single experiencing entities. A *nexus* lacks sufficient unity to be a single subject of experient. Living organisms are generally societies, and a rock is a mere nexus. We agree with Whitehead in regarding atoms and molecules as societies of experiencing entities.

54. Actual occasions are the quantum events of twentieth-century physics viewed as experient occasions.

55. The three major works from which these insights are taken are *Science and the Modern World* (Whitehead 1967a), *Process and Reality* (Whitehead 1978), and *Adventures of Ideas* (Whitehead 1967). Whitehead began the development of this revolutionary reconciliation of experience and physical reality in a technical paper he wrote in 1905, "On a Mathematically Possible Concept of a Physical Object." It was in this paper that it became apparent that the structure of experience and of the basic constituents of physical reality must be the same. All actuality is prehensive.

56. The Parkinson's disease example is ours, not Whitehead's. We are applying Whitehead's insights to what we have learned in caring for the nurse co-author's father, who has Parkinson's disease.

57. Actually, Whitehead on occasion accused his opponents of committing *"the fallacy of misplaced concreteness"* in trying to view actuality as constituted by mathematical relations rather than experience with its constituent feelings (Whitehead 1978, part 1). However, his little book *Symbolism* as well as his comments on *contrasts* in *Process and Reality* make it possible to interpret him as we have done in this paragraph. There is truth and error in both characterizations, though we share with Whitehead a preference for explanation in terms of experience.

58. The language is ours. We are reinterpreting Whiteheadian insights.

59. *Adventures of Ideas*, part 4 (Whitehead 1967) is useful.

60. See Whitehead's theory of symbolism (Whitehead 1978, part 2, Symbolism).

61. This important theory is developed in several different places in Whitehead's works. We have already cited the important passages in *Process and Reality*, part 2, Symbolism. Prehensions are vectorial internal relations; that is, prehensions are essential to the existence and nature of the prehending subjects, but they do not affect their objects. One is changed by looking at one's watch, but the watch in most respects is unchanged by being looked at.

62. Pragmatism emphasizes the tentativity and fallability of knowledge. Truth is not final. It is relative to the progress that has been made in an inquiry. The true is that which allows the inquiry to proceed. Hence, the true is the cognitively useful, and what is cognitively useful at one stage of an inquiry may be no longer be useful at a later stage in the same inquiry. John Dewey is probably the greatest of the American Pragmatists.

63. Note the preceding comment on the pragmatic theory of truth—truth is relative to the stage an inquiry has reached.

64. Hillary Putnam, as noticed in a preceding footnote, emphasized this notion of *nonscientific knowledge* in a fall 1996 unpublished lecture at the University of Colorado at Denver. In this he is continuing the tradition of the American Pragmatists, especially John Dewey, and he credits Dewey for this insight.

Scientific inquiry is supported and made possible by nonscientific knowledge. For this reason, though Dewey placed high value on science, Dewey emphasized both scientific and nonscientific knowledge.

65. The reference to nursing is added by ourselves. The rest of the insights are Whitehead's. The presence of the objectively immortal past in our present experience amounts to vague, visceral, unconscious "knowledge" or intuition, of vastly more than we consciously know. Hence, we "know" far more than we know that we know. (Whitehead 1978, part 3).

66. Though we are putting these words in Whitehead's mouth in the imaginary discussion, because we believe that he would have said them if he had lived longer and pursued aesthetics further than in such of his works as *Modes of Thought* and *Adventures of Ideas*, part 4, credit needs to be given to Benedetto Croce and R. G. Collingwood for the notion of a "concrete universal"—a universal so complex that it is unlikely to have ever occurred before or to be repeated in the future. Colingwood's *Principles of Art* contains the most accessible presentation of the "expressionist" theory of art (Collingwood 1938). That Whitehead should also be credited with this insight is supported by the chapter titled "Abstraction" in his *Science and the Modern World* (Whitehead 1967a) as well as by his comments on beauty (Whitehead 1967, part 4).

67. Here Whitehead is being viewed through the lens of R. G. Collingwood's philosophy of art, which we find very compatible with Whitehead's own ideas. See Collingwood's *Speculum Mentis* (Collingwood 1924).

68. R. S. Downey and B. Charlton, *The Making of a Doctor* (Oxford: Oxford University Press, 1992), p. 101.

69. Persons, like civilizations, are either advancing or are in decline. This is because of the presence of the past in the present. Whitehead shares with Bergson (see Bergson's *Creative Evolution*) the insight that repetition of past experiences, just as they originally occurred, is impossible. This is because the later experience contains the earlier experience, which makes it markedly different from that which is attempting to copy. Aesthetics and religious experience help channel the inexorable change in a positive or upward direction. If the change is not channeled, it is apt to be destructive. See Whitehead's *Adventures of Ideas*, part 1 (Whitehead 1967). Permanence and change need to be continually adjusted so that the mix is constructive rather than destructive.

70. Whitehead's Category of the Ultimate in *Process and Reality*, part 1, ch. 2, is creativity: "the many become one and are increased by one." When aesthetics is added to metaphysics, as in *Adventures of Ideas*, part 4, increasing richness of diversity while strengthening organic unity results in increased beauty (and reality or intensity of experience). (Whitehead 1978, part 1; Whitehead 1967, part 4).

71. Plato in the *Phaedo* refers to this notion of the Pythagoreans (Plato 1967).

72. This insight is not restricted to the Pythagoreans, but is central to their philosophy: *theoria, cosmos, catharsis*—the soul is purified by contemplation of the order within the universe. Whitehead's insight goes much further.

73. This is constructive channelization of the inexorable flux so that it is creative rather than destructive. Whether to credit these insights to Whitehead is

an unsolvable problem because of the poetic and epigrammatic nature of many of his statements on these subjects. Hence, we have deliberately not italicized much of this paragraph, for it goes beyond the rubric of Whitehead's works. Yet Whitehead deserves credit for having occasioned these insights whether or not they are his.

74. "Ghoti" was a joke used by Glenn's maternal grandfather, Albert Spaulding, in the 1940s. He, in turn, probably obtained the joke from George Bernard Shaw.

75. Most of these insights follow rather directly from Whitehead's Category of the Ultimate and his notion of the person as a structured society of experiencing entities. But the language departs sufficiently from Whitehead's original language so that we have not italicized this paragraph. For example, what we call cosmic significance Whitehead calls "importance" in the early chapters of his *Modes of Thought*.

76. Most of this paragraph is close to the language used by Whitehead in *Science and the Modern World* and in *Process and Reality*. He prefers the phrase "eternal object" rather than the word "universal." I have avoided the phrase "eternal object" because it is unnecessarily confusing to those lacking extensive background in Whitehead's philosophy. For example, by "object" Whitehead doesn't mean something fully actual, like a rock, but merely an object of experience. Since time is essential for actuality, eternal objects are "deficiently real." But because they are eternal, they cannot change. "Possibilities for definiteness" is a phrase often used by Whitehead, as is the phrase "possibilities for determinateness" or "pure possibilities" (Whitehead 1967a, 1978, 1967).

The notion that actuality is confined to the causal past focused in the causal present is fundamental to Whitehead's philosophy. Actuality is always relative to the here and now of the causal present. Hence the future and the causally contemporaneous contain no entities that are as yet actual (from the standpoint of the present) (Whitehead 1967a, Relativity).

77. There is one very important difference between Whitehead and Kant. Kant believed in absolute temporal simultaneity. Kant believed in an unambiguous present that extended to the farthest star cluster. In contrast, Whitehead endorses the speed of light cones of twentieth-century relativity. It follows, for Whitehead, that it is now only here. For example, all events taking place in the Sun are causally independent of the events taking place on Earth now from about eight minutes ago until about eight minutes in the future.

78. This follows the distinction between part 4 of *Process and Reality*, The Theory of Extension (which views space and time as a mathematical continuum) and part 3 of *Process and Reality*, The Theory of Prehension (which views the actual world as a plenum of vectorially related droplets of experience—each a subject remembering its past and anticipating its future) (Whitehead 1978, parts 3 and 4).

79. This combines the extensive continuum with the prehensions of each unique actual occasion.

80. Chapter 8: Symbolic Reference.

81. William James, the American Pragmatist, is often credited with having said this. But we have failed to find an original text.

82. The phrase "lens of universals" is ours rather than Whitehead's. But the insight about symbols being either universals (eternal objects) or individuals (actual entities) is from Whitehead. For Whitehead 'anything can symbolize anything.' See Whitehead's small booklet, *Symbolism*, but also the chapter, Symbolism, in part 2 of *Process and Reality* (Whitehead 1978).

83. This is not a misspelling. The political active Deaf view themselves as having their own culture based on their own natural language, American Sign Language. As a consequence, they capitalize the word "Deaf" when referring to themselves.

84. These insights are initially introduced in *Science and the Modern World* (Whitehead 1967a). They are developed in depth in *Process and Reality*, especially parts 2 and 3 (Whitehead 1978).

85. See the preceding sources.

86. This insight is emphasized by Heidegger: truth always contains untruth. But it is much clearer and less one sided in Whitehead's theory of symbolic reference. For Whitehead we become consciously aware of unique individuals through high abstractions that leave out almost all of the detail, and that emphasize a stereotype that is potentially misleading. Whitehead leaves us with more hope—that we can be wise enough to use symbols so as to avoid being mislead by them. Here, the chapter on Symbolism in part 2 of *Process and Reality* is the most accessible source (Whitehead 1978).

87. Whitehead does not directly address these subjects in his works. This is a creative interpretation based in his Category of the Ultimate, his concept of persons as structured societies of experiencing entities, and his notion that unity comes in varying degrees.

88. But in *Symbolism*, and in the chapter by the same title in *Process and Reality*, part 2, Whitehead, as previously noted, says that 'anything can symbolize anything.' It does not require much imagination to understand that hormones and other chemical tracers can function as symbols, focusing the experience of subordinate experiencing entities within a person.

89. Language enables experiencing entities to act rather than just behave, as this distinction is developed later in this work. Language empowers; it increases positive freedom—the degree to which a person is the unconditioned condition of her actions. Hence, if neurochemistry in the brain is a kind of language, rather than an instrument of efficient causation, we need to view what is happening in neurochemistry from the new perspective of experiencing entities.

90. This is the point on which Whitehead differs from Hegel. Hegel continued to view the body as merely natural in the seventeenth-century sense, that is, as something appropriately described by mechanistic atomism. Whitehead rejects the seventeenth-century view of nature in favor of what he calls "process organism." The result is a body that is a society of experiencing entities rather than a complex machine (Whitehead 1967a, pp. 75–112).

91. This is a summation of passages already referenced.

92. We are unaware of any passages where Whitehead draws these connections between his philosophy and Aristotle's philosophy. For the sake of the imaginary discussion we are assuming that Whitehead is aware of Aristotle's views, though Whitehead did not profess any knowledge of them during his lifetime.

93. References for persons as structured societies have already been provided. A nexus is defined in *Process and Reality* (Whitehead 1978, pp. 20, 22, 24, 194).

94. Whitehead embraces the primacy of teleology over efficient causation. Goal seeking is primary; efficient causation is metaphorical. In this he fundamentally disagrees with the seventeenth-century worldview, the Cartesian or Renaissance worldview (Whitehead 1968, final two chapters).

95. They are lured to action rather than compelled to behave.

96. The language, "cascading of experience," is ours rather than Whitehead's. But the insights are his.

97. In *Adventures of Ideas* Whitehead accounts for the conformity of present to past experience in terms of *concern* as that notion is understood by the Quakers (Whitehead 1967).

98. For the new insight in this paragraph about the passage of time depending on transition from occasion to newer occasion, see chapter 10, of part 3, *Process and Reality* (Whitehead 1978).

99. N. Park (Director), *Wallace & Gromit: The Wrong Trousers*. Ardman Animations. Beverley Hills, CA: Fox Video, 1993.

100. These works are *Science and the Modern World, Process and Reality, Adventures of Ideas, Modes of Thought,* and *Religion in the Making.*

101. Prehensions are the foundation for the prehensive aspect of space-time. That is, space-time holds events together in one world; it does not merely separate them.

102. These are pseudonyms that Søren Kierkegaard adopted for the authorship of his various books.

103. The famous mid-nineteenth-century Danish existentialist who, among other things, held that "truth is subjectivity." *The Concluding Unscientific Postscript* is his major work. This 600-page book is a "postscript" to a 35-page booklet.

104. Given the epigrammatic nature of his writing and his disparagement of systematic philosophy, Kierkegaard is very difficult to interpret.

105. It seems to make more sense of the passages toward the end of *The Concluding Unscientific Postscript* to interpret *recollection* as presence of the past in the present than to interpret it as Platonic *anamnesis* (recollection of the Forms). Our struggle with these concepts was initiated by a reading of John Caputo's *Radical Hermeneutics* (Caputo 1987).

106. Existentialists emphasize the nonbeing of the future as the ground of their freedom, of their ability to exist authentically. Whitehead puts equal emphasis on the presence of the past in the present and on the anticipation of the future. Also, contrary to the existentialists, Whitehead finds universals important as a ground for creativity and novelty.

107. We are blameworthy for most of this paragraph. It is an imaginative construction of the manner in which Kierkegaard might have reacted to the American health care system of the late twentieth century. Kierkegaard's attacks on Hegel provide evidence that he is apt to have reacted in the manner we have constructed.

108. An "ecstasis" is something that stands under or supports. The three temporal ecstases stand under or support the actuality of the present.

CHAPTER 5. FROM JEAN WATSON'S
THEORY OF CARING TO A PHILOSOPHY OF CARING

1. We have chosen a dance metaphor, the adagio, to convey the nature of the balance between subjectivity and objectivity in the nursing occasion. This metaphor is described in, detail in the next chapter.

2. Grimal 1990, pp. 403–4. The story,of the Sirens is rich with potential insights concerning the dangers of turning away from love that aptly symbolizes the sentiments of caring. The Sirens' skill at music and song, symbolizing the skills of caring, not only destroyed those who heard the Sirens' songs, but eventually even the Sirens themselves. The danger is not just to individual nurses but to the profession of nursing. Too narrow a focus on the skills of caring at the expense of the sentiments of caring creates the danger that the profession will not be able to survive when the skills are no longer needed.

3. In Greek mythology, having offended the gods, Tantalus was condemned for all eternity to stand in water up to his neck, but without being able to drink from it. Thus Tantalus could never satisfy his thirst. In like manner, though Tantalus could see fruit on the branches of a tree overhanging the water, the fruit was always just beyond his grasp. Hence Tantalus was also never able to satisfy his hunger. The term "tantalizing" is rooted in this mythological figure (Grimal 1990, p. 414).

4. Interestingly Kant's concern with the synthetic *a priori* addressed a problem similar to the one we are touching on here. The synthetic *a priori* was significant (not trivial) knowledge about (what is in) the world. But since caring is concerned with both what is and what ought to be, in nontrivial senses, caring may be seen as straddling the concern of theoretical (what is, science) and practical reason (what ought to be, morality, the categorical imperative), of Kant's First and Second Critiques. Caring would also require consideration of Third Critique material, in that caring is concerned with teleology in nature. Kant might say that health cannot be understood and promoted except in terms of goals, on nature's part, on the part of the persons providing care, and of course, on the part of the patient. Health is the goal of patient, nature, and care provider, and thus the final cause, the lure, of caring.

5. The reader is referred chapter 4 for expositions of the analytic *a priori* of David Hume and the synthetic *a priori* of Immanuel Kant.

6. Although Kant does not address this problem explicitly, and the structure of his system forbids his making any knowledge claims in this area, the overall structure of the three critiques allow for speculation that the ground of the pure forms of intuition and the categories of the understanding is God. Hence, the givenness of the synthetic *a priori* may come from God. Kant would prefer that we rest the givenness on pure reason. But only the eccentricities of the architechtonic (Kant's term for the overall structure) of his system prevents his explicitly identifying Reason and God.

7. Theoretical reason gives us science. Practical reason gives us technology and morality, as well as prudence. Hence when nursing observes caring in order to increase knowledge, this inquiry is theoretical and one may speak of nursing science. But when nurses are caring for patients, the activity is practical. The rel-

evance of nursing science for the practice of nursing is that nursing science, and other sciences, are useful for increasing the repertory of hypothetical imperatives.

8. This distinction between the *true* and the *right* is often ignored or misunderstood. It is very important to Kant, as well as for understanding the distinction between science and technology, and to the study-of caring and the practice of caring. The study of caring is theoretical, it is concerned with determining what is true. It is the science of caring. But the practice of caring is practical, it is concerned with what ought to be done. The practice of caring makes use of all three of Kant's imperatives. More will be done with this insight in the next chapter.

9. But of course it much more pleasant to take care of someone you like. It does not hurt to want to do what you are morally obligated to do.

10. The Five Rights are: (1) the right patient; (2) the right medication, (3) the right time; (4) the right dosage; and (5) the right route of administration.

11. It is motivated by enlightened egoism.

12. Heidegger and Whitehead also notice the same phenomenon. "The past though gone is yet still present" (Whitehead 1967).

13. Although Hume and Husserl both wrestle with the problem of universals, they begin from two different perspectives. For Hume, immediate experience is of the individual object, but in a sense that downplays the element of universality in the individual object. For Hume, one gets to universals only inductively if at all. Thus awareness of chairness is the result of experience of a number of individual chairs. One has the word "chair' and the individual chairs. One senses some sort of resemblance between the chairs that makes the use of the same word seem appropriate. Thus chairness is the meaning of a word rather than a universal present in individual chairs. Chairness is an idea in the mind of humans, not a way in which things in the world are definite. Hume draws the conclusion of nominalism that only words are universals.

Husserl begins from another perspective. For Husserl the essence of chairness is already an element in the immediate experience of the person observing a chair and in the chair itself as an object of experience. Husserl's critique of Hume involves the relationship, between subjects and objects within experience.

14. What "ought to be" was initially, encountered in the discussions with Plato, (chapter 3 of this book) especially his Form of the Good, which functions archetypically for things and activities in the visible world. The reader might remember Plato warning us about allowing things in the visible world to distract us from the Forms themselves. At the same time, what ought to be is central to ethics in both the modern and contemporary periods of philosophy.

15. This study was begun a few years ago at the University of Colorado Health Sciences Center, School of Nursing. It is ongoing at the time of this writing (1998).

16. The topic of human science needs at least a complete book for its development. For example, R. G. Collingwood and Wilhelm Dilthey both make a case for history as a human science. And for both of them it is necessary to argue that there can be a science of the individual, for history is concerned with individual events. But this is certainly not science in any traditional sense of the

word "science." Even if Collingwood and Dilthey can win their argument against the traditionalists, nothing would be altered concerning the givenness of caring.in the nursing sense. For history, like traditional science, would have to accept caring in the nursing sense as a given. All that would change would be the possibility,of a scientific study of past human actions exemplifying caring. But history is able, when done well, to be sufficiently plausible without the addition of the accolade "science." Hence, the argument over whether history is a human science is largely verbal, or "philosophical" in a negative sense.

17. This dualism continues to be present in Watson's work as late as 1995 (Watson 1995c, p. 64): "Indeed, the most valuable role of alternative medicine may not be its curative potential, but rather, its caring-healing potential."

CHAPTER 6. PHILOSOPHY OF NURSING

1. Though we acknowledge our debt to Whitehead for the metaphysics of process organism, his language, "societies of actual entities," was coined with atoms and molecules in mind. Our language, "communities of experiencing entities." represents a contribution of nursing to philosophy. Without Whitehead, our philosophy of human nature would not have gotten started, but it goes considerably beyond his work.

2. We have used several different expressions for the same insight: "one and One," "individual and Individual," "self and Self," "I to Thou," "finite individual to Infinite One," finite person and God," To decide which terminology is better would require a major work in philosophical theology. Interchanging the terms helps forestall answering unanswerable questions. Perhaps no human theology is adequate or could be adequate because of our limited capacity for understanding and the limitations of our natural languages.

3. Perhaps this is what Jean Watson means by the ontology of caring.

4. Resusci-Annie is the practice dummy used in training nurses and others in the techniques of cardiovascular resuscitation.

5. The insight concerning deformations and periodicities can be traced from Heraclitus of Ephesus, 500 BCE, through Hegel and Whitehead in the nineteenth and twentieth centuries. Although these philosophers did not specifically mention systole and diastole, and only Heraclitus might be seen as worrying about the sleeping and waking cycle, they saw all of the processes in the universe as involving these factors. The fact that deformation and periodicity are fundamental to humans, both as a whole, and to their subordinate experiencing entities, shows the synchrony between persons and the universe.

6. To add to the weird and unsettling feeling of caring for a dead patient, the relaxing of the sphincters and the release of residual air and intestinal gases, creates sounds often associated with the living. Turning the body over to wrap it in the shroud can produce a sigh or moan as the residual air from the lungs is expelled over the vocal cords. The nurse may never have heard the comatose patient's voice while he was alive. But in death she hears his "voice" for the first time. Perhaps the eeriness comes from the nurse's sadness in realizing that the sound that would have been part of a greeting is an involuntary farewell.

7. "Full actuality" should not be confused with "self-actualization." What Whitehead had in mind when he used the phrase "full actuality" was the contrast between mere possibility, ideas or dreams, and concrete reality, everyday objects such as the telephone or the table.

8. Marcel Proust, *Remembrance of Things Past*, vol. 2: *The Past Recaptured* (New York: Random House, 1932), p. 873ff. This is an impressive passage on the nature of the fading of the past.

9. Whitehead discusses the distinction between *interest* (second phase) and *importance* (fourth phase) in *Modes of Thought*, chapters 1 and 2.

10. Kant's metaphors of "measuring rod" and "mainspring" can be useful for understanding the different roles of the first and fourth phases of the universe as they relate to caring. The first phase, the primordial nature of God, provides the measuring rod for determining what ought to be done. The fourth phase, the return of heaven into earth, provides the flood of emotion, the mainspring, that makes one want to do what ought to be done. While the metaphor of the mainspring suggests a back-and-forth-ness, compatible with Whitehead's notion of the movement from earth to heaven and from heaven to earth, the metaphor fails to suggest the magnification that occurs in the cycle from earth to heaven and back again. Hence the smallest act of caring on earth is experienced as something of great and enduring satisfaction.

11. We have added the italics to highlight the special significance of this passage. This relates to the taking up into heaven of the simplest act of caring, so that it returns again greatly magnified in importance. It explains why a simple act of caring can yield deep and enduring satisfaction or happiness.

12. Stories of alien invaders are quite common in the substitution of myth for real history. Individual members are often asked to adopt new names to adapt to the common mythical history.

13. Suddenly we are in sympathy with Aristotle's attempt to use words to describe uniqueness. The best he could come up with was the phrase "this such," with the "this" referring to the unique individual and the "such" to shared forms (universals). See chapter 3.

14. The "nonrational" must not be confused with the "irrational."

15. The language is from Whitehead, *Process and Reality*, part 5.

CHAPTER 7. CONCLUSION

1. One notable exception among twentieth-century philosophers is Alfred North Whitehead. But we tended to view Whitehead's comments on Plato as one-sided and peculiar, until we saw the usefulness to nursing of a more realistic interpretation of the Forms and of their value-ranking. The result is the primordial nature of God.

2. Again, and this was surprising, the lens of nursing has prompted us to view Plato, Kant, and Whitehead, as providing a much more realistic ground for morality than the popular late-twentieth-century view of philosophy that has tended to be relativistic and nonrealistic with respect to the ground of morality.

3. When T. S. Kuhn defended himself against the charge that the term

"paradigm" had many different senses or meanings, he did admit that there were at least two senses of the word in his *Structure of Scientific Revolutions*: (1) a methodology and worldview shared by the members of a group of scientists; or (2) a key historical example of success in the discipline that provides guidance to later practitioners (Kuhn 1970, introduction). The narrative in this book functions as a Kuhnian paradigm in sense 2.

4. The most important of these terms and concepts are "universal" and "individual."

5. While science, with technology, provides excellent measuring tools for both space and time, and the identification of the exact coordinates in space and time of an event or an enduring individual is very helpful in distinguishing the unique individual from other unique individuals, science focuses on the universals and not on the uniqueness of the individuals.

6. From the perspective of philosophy, especially the philosophy of logic and mathematics, this use of the term "algorithm" is very grating. For the algorithms in logic and mathematics provide us with yes-or-no answers in a finite number of steps with *certainty*. In the context of nursing and health care, certainty is impossible, because health care is concerned with the empirical and not the *a priori*, with individuals and not just universals. The answers provided by the use of tree protocols must always be adjusted to the uniqueness of the individual and the circumstances. The present popular use of the word "algorithm" in health-care contexts, though initially humorous, is frightening in its potential effect on the health-care system and on patients. How many of us want to be treated by machines incapable of making adjustments for our individuality, because they are incapable of being aware of our individuality? This is reminiscent of Dr. Strangelove and the machine that could not be turned off once it was started.

7. The danger is that the new technology may become more important for the caregivers than the persons it and they are supposed to serve.

8. But in contrast to some mystics, specifically Plotinus, the body encapsulates nature, which in turn encapsulates the One in the sense of the consequent nature of God. The return of heaven into earth effects not just the regnant experiencing entities within persons, but all of the actual entities which constitute the physical world.

BIBLIOGRAPHY

Aquinas, St. Thomas (1952). *The Summa Theologica*. Trans. by Fathers of the English Dominican Provence. Revised by Daniel J. Sullivan. In Britannica Great Books, vols. 19 and 20. Chicago: Encyclopaedia Britannica.

Aristotle (1941). *The Basic Works of Aristotle*. Edited by R. McKeon. New York: Random House. [Written in the fourth century BCE]

Beck, Lewis White (1960). *A Commentary on Kant's Critique of Practical Reason*. Chicago: University of Chicago Press.

Brencick, Janice M., & Webster, Glenn A. (1994). "The Primacy of Nursing Practice." In Joan C. McCloskey & Helen K. Grace (Editors), *Current Issues in Nursing*, 4th ed., pp. 87–91. St. Louis: The C. V. Mosby Company.

Brough, J. B. (1972). "The Emergence of an Absolute Consciousness in Husserl's Early Writings on Time-Consciousness." *Man and World* 5.3: 298–326.

Brunn, E. Z., & Epiney-Burgard, G. (1989). *Women Mystics in Medieval Europe*. New York: Paragon House.

Buber, Martin (1965). *Between Man and Man*. New York: Collier Books, Macmillan Publishing Company.

——— (1966). *The Knowledge of Man: A Philosophy of the Interhuman*. New York: Harper & Row (Torchbooks).

Caputo, John D. (1982). *Heidegger and Aquinas: An Essay on Overcoming Metaphysics*. New York: Fordham University Press.

——— (1987). *Radical Hermeneutics: Repetition, Deconstruction, and the Hermeneutic Project*. Bloomington: Indiana University Press.

——— (1993). *Demythologizing Heidegger*. Bloomington: Indiana University Press.

Chinn, P. L. & Kramer, M. K. (1991). *Theory and Nursing: A Systematic Approach*. St. Louis: Moby Year Book.

Chinn, Peggy & Watson, Jean (1994). *Art and Aesthetics in Nursing*, NY: National League for Nursing.

Collingwood. Robin George (1924). *Speculum Mentis*. Oxford: Clarendon Press.

——— (1933). *Essay on Philosophical Method. Oxford: Clarendon Press.*

——— (1938). *The Principles of Art*. Oxford: Clarendon Press,

——— (1940). *An Essay on Metaphysics*. Oxford: Clarendon Press.

——— (1942). *The New Leviathan*. Oxford Clarendon Press.

——— (1946). *The Idea of History*. Oxford: Clarendon Press.

Derrida, Jacques. 1981. *Dissemination*. Trans. by B. Johnson. Chicago: University of Chicago Press.

——— 1973. *Speech and Phenomena: And Other Essays on Husserl's Theory of Signs*. Evanston, Ill.: Northwestern University Press.

—— 1981. *Positions*. Trans. by A. Bass. Chicago: University of Chicago Press.

—— 1987. *The Truth in Painting*.Trans. by G. Bennington and I. McCloud. Chicago: University of Chicago Press.

Descartes, René. (1931). *The Philosophical Works of Descartes*. Translated by E. S. Haldane & G. R. T. Ross. Cambridge: Cambridge University Press.

Dewey, John (1969). *The Quest for Certainty*. New York: Putnam.

Downie, R. S., & Charlton, B. (1992). *The Making of a Doctor: Medical Education in Theory and Practice*. Oxford: Oxford University Press.

Elliston, F., & McCormick, P. (Editors) (1977). *Husserl: Expositions and Appraisals*. Notre Dame, Ind.: University of Notre Dame Press.

Fawcett, J. (1989). "Analysis and Evaluation of the Neuman Systems Model." Ch. 2, in Neuman (1989).

Foucault, M. (1995). *Discipline and Punishment: The Birth of the Prison*. Trans. by A. Sheridan. Second Vintage Books edition. New York: Vintage Books.

Fox, M. (1985). *Illuminations of Hildegard of Bingen*. Santa Fe: Bear & Company.

Freud, Sigmund (1938). *Civilization and Its Discontents*. Trans. by J. Strachey. New York: W. W. Norton. [Republished in 1989]

—— (1960). *A General Introduction to Psychoanalysis*. New York: Washington Square Press. [Originally published in 1924]

Gale, R. M. (Editor) (1978). *The Philosophy of Time: A Collection of Essays*. Atlantic Highlands, N.J.: Humanities Press.

Grimal, P. (1990). *A Concise Dictionary of Classical Mythology*. Edited by S. Kersahw. Translated by A. R. Maxwell-Hyslop. Oxford: Basil Blackwell.

Grimm, J., & Grimm, W. (1812–22). *Kinder-und Hausmarchen*. [Translated into English as *Grimm's Fairy Tales*]

Harkness, G. (1973). *Mysticism: Its Meaning & Message*. Nashville, Tenn.: Abingdon Press.

Hegel, G. W. F. (1900). *Philosophy of History*. Translated by J. Sibree. New York: The Colonial Press. [Originally published in 1830]

—— (1966). *The Phenomenology of Mind*. Translated by J. Baillie. London: George Allen & Unwin. [Originally published in 1807]

—— (1971). *Hegel's Philosophy of Mind*. Translated by W. Wallace. Part Three of the *Encyclopaedia of the Philosophical Sciences*. Oxford: Clarendon Press.

Heidegger, Martin (1975). *Poetry, Language, Thought*. New York: Harper & Row.

—— (1977). *The Question Concerning Technology and Other Essays*. New York: Harper & Row

—— (1982). *The Basic Problems of Phenomenology* [Published in German as *Die Grundprobleme der Phenomenologie* by Vittorio Klostermann, 1975]. Translated by A. Hofstadter. Bloomington: Indiana University Press.

—— (1985). *Schelling's Treatise on the Essence of Human Freedom*. Translated by J. Stambaugh. Athens: Ohio University Press.

—— (1996). *Being and Time*. Trans. by J. Stambaugh. Albany: State University of New York Press.

Hildegard of Bingen (1986). *Scivias*. Translated by B. Hozeski. Sante Fe: Bear & Company.

Hume, David (1978). *A Treatise of Human Nature.* 2nd ed. Edited by L. A. Selby-Bigge. Revised by P. H. Nidditch. Oxford: Clarendon Press. [Originally published in 1839]

Husserl, Edmund (1964). *The Phenomenology of Internal Time Consciousness.* Translated by J. S. Churchill. Bloomington: Indiana University Press.

—— (1965). *Phenomenology and the Crisis of Philosophy.* Translated by Q. Lauer. New York: Harper & Row.

—— (1970). *The Crisis of European Sciences and Transcendental Phenomenology: An Introduction to Phenomenological Philosophy.* Translated by D. Carr. Evanston, Ill.: Northwestern University Press.

—— (1973). *Cartesian Meditations.* Translated by D. Cairns. The Hague: Nijhoff.

James, William (1958). *The Varieties of Religious Experience.* New York: The New American Library.

Kant, Immanuel (1950). *Prolegomena to Any Future Metaphysics.* Indianapolis: Bobbs-Merrill.

—— (1951). *Critique of Judgement.* New York: Hafner.

—— (1956). *Critique of Practical Reason* [1788]. Translated by Lewis White Beck. Indianapolis: Bobbs-Merrill.

—— (1959). *Foundations of the Metaphysics of Morals.* Translated by Lewis White Beck. Indianapolis: Bobbs-Merrill.

—— (1963). *Lectures on Ethics* [Originally given between 1775 and 1780]. Translated by Louis Infield. New York: Harper Torchbooks.

—— (1965). *Critique of Pure Reason.* Trans. by Norman Kemp Smith. Unabridged ed. New York: St. Martin's Press. [Originally published in 1781]

—— (1980). *Foundations of the Metaphysics of Morals* [1785]. Translated by Lewis White Beck. Indianapolis: Bobbs-Merrill.

Kuhn, Thomas S. (1970). *The Structure of Scientific Revolutions.* 2nd ed., enlarged. Chicago: University of Chicago Press.

Kierkegaard, Søren (1964). *Concluding Unscientific Postscript.* Translated by D. F. Swenson and W. Lowrie. Princeton: Princeton University Press, for the American Scandinavian Foundation.

Krysl, M. (1988). "Existential Moments of Caring: Facets of Nursing Social Support." *Advances in Nursing Science* 10.2: 12–17

Linsky, L. (1977). *Names and Descriptions.* Chicago: University of Chicago Press.

Locke, John (1959). *An Essay Concerning Human Understanding.* New York: Dover Publications.

Loux, M. J. (Editor) (1970). *Universals and Particulars: Readings in Ontology.* Rev. ed. Notre Dame, Ind.: University of Notre Dame Press.

Martinez, Ruby (1993). "Meaning of Illness." Unpublished paper submitted at UCHSC, School of Nursing.

Meleis, A. I. (1986). "Theory Development and Domain Concepts." In Moccia (1986), pp. 3–21.

Moccia, P. (Editor) (1986). *New Approaches to Theory Development.* New York: National League for Nursing.

Neuman, B. (1989). *The Neuman Systems Model.* 2nd ed. Norwalk, Conn.: Appleton & Lange.

O'Brien, E. (1964). *The Essential Plotinus*. New York: Mentor Books (New American Library).

Phillips, S., & Watson, J. (1993). Letter to the editor. *Nursing Outlook* 41.4: 188–89.

Plato (1963). *The Collected Dialogues of Plato*. Edited by E. Hamilton and H. Cairns. Princeton: Princeton University Press. [Written in the fourth century BCE]

Plotinus (1952). *The Six Enneads*. Translated by Stephen MacKenna & B. S. Page. In Britannica Great Books, vol. 17. Chicago: Encyclopaedia Britannic.

Rogers, Martha (1970). *Introduction to the Theoretical Basis of Nursing*. Philadelphia: F. A. Davis Co.

Rosenthal, K. A. (1992, Nov./Dec.). "Coronary Care Patients' and Nurses' Perceptions of Important Nurse Caring Behaviors." *Heart & Lung* 21.6: 536–39.

Sacks, Oliver (1992). *Migraine*. Revised and expanded. Berkeley: University of California Press.

Sallis, J. (Editor) (1987). *Deconstruction and Philosophy: The Texts of Jacques Derrida*. Chicago: The University of Chicago Press.

Sartre, Jean Paul (1964). *Being and Nothingness: An Essay in Phenomenological Ontology*, special abridged edition. Translated by Hazel E. Barnes. New York: The Citadel Press.

Silverman, H. J. (Editor) (1989). *Continental Philosophy II: Derrida and Deconstruction*. New York: Routledge.

Singer, C. (1958). *From Magic to Science: Essays on the Scientific Twilight*. New York: Dover Publications.

Strehlow, W., & Hertzka, G. (1988). *Hildegard of Bingen's Medicine*. Folk Wisdom Series. Sante Fe: Bear & Company.

Teilhard de Chardin, Pierre (1957). *The Divine Milieu*. New York: Harper Torchbooks.

——— (1959). *The Phenomenon of Man*. New York: Harper Torchbooks.

Underhill, Evelyn (1967). *Mysticism: A Study in the Nature of Development of Man's Spiritual Consciousness*. 12th ed. rev. London: Lowe & Brydone.

Varcolis, E. M. (1994). *Foundations of Psychiatric Mental Health Nursing*. Philadelphia: W. B. Saunders Co.

Walker, L. O., & Avant, K. C. (1988). *Strategies for Theory Construction in Nursing*. 2nd ed. Norwalk, Conn.: Appleton & Lange.

Watson, Jean (1979). *Nursing: The Philosophy and Science of Caring*. Boulder, Colorado: Colorado Associated University Press.

——— (1985). *Nursing: Human Science and Human Care: A Theory of Nursing*. Norwalk, Conn.: Appleton-Century-Crofts.

——— (1987). "Nursing on the Caring Edge: Metaphorical Vignettes." *Advances in Nursing Science* 10.1: 10–18.

——— (1988, October). "Human Caring as Moral Context for Nursing Education." *Nursing & Health Care* 9.8: 423–25.

——— (1988a). "Introduction." In Krysl (1988).

——— (1990). "Caring Knowledge and Informed Moral Passion." *Advances in Nursing Science* 13.1: 15–24.

———— (1990a). "The Moral Failure of the Patriarchy." *Nursing Outlook* 38.2: 62–66.

———— (1994). "Poeticizing as Truth through Language." In Chinn & Watson (1994), pp. 3–17.

———— (1995). "Postmodernism and Knowledge Development in Nursing." *Nursing Science Quarterly* 8.2: 60–64.

———— (1995a). "Advanced Nursing Practice . . . and What Might Be." *Nursing & Health Care: Perspectives on Community* 16.2: 78–83.

———— (1995b). "The Wait, the Wonder, the Watch: Caring in a Transplant Unit." *Journal of Clinical Nursing* 4: 1–2.

———— (1995c). "Nursing's Caring–Healing Paradigm as Exemplar for Alternative Medicine? *Alternative Therapies in Health and Medicine* 1.3: 64–69.

———— (1996). "Poeticizing as Truth in Nursing Inquiry." In J. F. Kikuch et al., *Truth in Nursing Inquiry,* pp. 125–39. Thousand Oaks, Calif.: Sage.

Watson, Jean, & Phillips, Sally (1992, January/February). "A Call for Educational Reform: Colorado Nursing Doctorate Model as Exemplar." *Nursing Outlook* 40.1: 20–26.

Wheelright, Philip (1966). *The Presocratics.* New York: Odyssey Books.

Whitehead, Alfred North (1958). *The Function of Reason.* Boston: Beacon Press. [Originally published in 1929]

———— (1960). *Religion in the Making.* New York: Meridian Books.

———— (1967). *Adventures of Ideas.* New York: Free Press. [Originally published in 1933]

———— (1967a). *Science and the Modern World.* New York: Free Press. [Originally published in 1925]

———— (1968). *Modes of Thought.* New York: Free Press. [Originally published in 1938]

———— (1978). *Process and Reality.* Corrected edition. Edited by David R. Griffin and Donald. W. Sherburne. New York: The Free Press.

Wright, Blanche Fisher (1992). *The Original Mother Goose.* Philadelphia: Running Press. [Based on the 1916 Edition]

INDEX